C000178467

# The Tide Turns

*Another Fishy Tale*

## Dedication

This book is dedicated to the skippers, shipmates, fishermen, crew and shore-men with whom I was fortunate to spend my fishing career. These unique years were unforgettable and are now consigned to history.

# The Tide Turns

*Another Fishy Tale*

Fred Normandale

Also by the same author
First of the Flood
Slack Water

Bottom End Publishing
Scarborough
PO Box 318



First published November 2006



ISBN-13: 978 0 9543686 2 3
ISBN-10: 0 9543686 2 2

Cover design by Barry Perks Design

Cover photographs (left to right): Barry Bryan, Sean Crowe, Mick Bayes, Gordon 'Gogga' Mann, Sid Withers, Fred Normandale and Tom 'Bluey' Sheader.

Prepared and printed by:
York Publishing Services Ltd
64 Hallfield Road
Layerthorpe
York YO31 7ZQ
Tel: 01904 431213; Website: www.yps-publishing.co.uk

# Contents

## Thanks

First and foremost, to my wife Dorothy and parents Doris and Fred for their unstinting support. Special thanks to my sister Jan Palmer, Jilly Manser and Jilly Swales for their dedicated proof reading. To my sister Sue Wood, Arthur Godfrey, Ian Forbes, Val Winterbottom, Dave Bevan and Colin Jenkinson for their reading, helpful comments and reminders of stories. Grateful thanks to John Hobson, Ian Robinson, Dave Bevan and Ann Bevan for the loan of photographs and to Barry Perks for his magnificent cover design. As ever, I'm indebted to Dave Mercer and all at YPS for their professional attititude and helpful, friendly assistance in the production of this book.

# About This Book

In writing this book, the author intended to give his readers an insight into the way of life in the late 1970s and early 1980s around Scarborough Harbour through his eyes. Some events depicted may not be in chronological order. No offence is intended to anyone named. Some characters are fictional.

The 'Bottom End' of Scarborough was a thriving, insular community in the mid 1950s and early 60s in the author's formative years. The harbour, boats and piers of the historic old port were the playgrounds for young boys. In their early teens most lads were competent at rope-work, could bait the winter long-lines and construct and net crab pots in preparation for spring. These young men mostly followed in their fathers' footsteps, joining the fishing industry where, though the work was hard, the challenge of the sea brought fulfilment and rewards greater than any to be found on shore.

It was in this environment young Fred grew up and after a short spell in the Merchant Navy joined the crew of the *Whitby Rose*, a fifty-foot trawling vessel. At the age of twenty he married Dorothy and after working on other vessels, at twenty-three and with two young children, hired the fifty-four foot *Pioneer* from Grimsby. This venture proved successful and two years later he bought the *Courage* from her Scarborough owners. Though quite an old boat, she was in good condition and in 1977 this craft became the deposit for a new, purpose built fifty-nine foot trawler *Independence* from the Fraserburgh yard of James Noble.

This book, the third in the series, tells of storms, wrecks and salvage, strange catches and life both at sea and ashore in the late 1970s and early 80s with an emphasis on humour.

## Chapter 1

# An Early Start

We walked hand in hand down the steep, cobblestone street under a spectacular show of stars. Only an occasional streetlight remained lit now the clock had turned midnight. In my other hand was a clean pillowcase containing a couple of books and a change of clothes. Danny carried a rolled up sleeping bag stuffed with sweets, a drawing book and crayons. My parents' house to our left was in darkness, as expected at this early hour.

My Mother had been quite vocal and strongly against the idea when I said I was taking my son to sea on his first trip. "That bairn's far too young t' go t' sea yet."

My wife, Dotty had remained tight lipped and non-committal on the subject. I'd waited weeks, throughout the summer holidays for the finest of forecasts before telling Danny he was sailing at midnight. There wasn't an isobar to be seen on the television weather chart the previous evening. He hadn't slept and was out of bed and dressing as soon as I pushed his bedroom door ajar. Danny was six now and had been asking to go to sea with me for as long as he'd been able to talk. When he was younger it broke my heart every Saturday night when he asked if he could sail with me and I had to refuse him. I was happy to take him tonight. I'd had an early introduction to the sea myself, sailing with my Dad in the coble *Rosemary,* potting for crab and lobster and with my uncles, Johnny and Robbie, trawling on the keelboat, *Floreat*.

There wasn't a breath of wind as we walked along the fish market towards the *Independence,* berthed near the harbour entrance. We passed at least half a dozen boats in various states of readiness, their crews assembling on the quay near their vessels. The navigation lights of an early leaver could be seen passing at speed between the piers. Arriving at the boat we paused momentarily to look down around her deck. She was a superb vessel of wooden construction, a few inches under sixty feet in length, which I'd brought home only six weeks earlier from her Scottish builders. With amazing good fortune I'd acquired this wonderful craft with a government grant and loan scheme, plus the proceeds from the sale of the *Courage,* my lovely, twenty-five year old craft and the faith of a friendly bank manager. He offered me the bridging loan plus additional funds if required, enabling me to continue working the old boat for the ten-month building period while my new baby developed, even though his bank couldn't take a legal charge over either vessel. Noel White had been my Godfather when he put his trust in me.

My crew of four, Rusty, Bluey, Sid and Barry were already on board and called out to Danny, Sid enquiring what he was doing out at this time of night, asking if he'd wet the bed.

Rusty shouted, "I 'ope yer lucky." Danny enjoyed the attention immensely.

Once on board, I dropped down the ladder to the engine room where the olive green machine with eight, polished cylinder head covers reflected the deck-head lights. This Kelvin engine was 375 horsepower and every one of them could pull. Following a quick check on water and oil levels, I pressed the starter button. The lights dimmed as the starter motor drained energy from the batteries, then, with a clatter the machine fired up. Easing back the throttle to slow, she idled at four hundred revolutions per minute. The lights now burned brighter than before as power surged back into the batteries from the dynamos. Before leaving the engine space I turned the twenty or more electrical circuit breaker switches on the mains panel to 'on'.

Exiting the engine room, a small flight of stairs took me to the wheelhouse where an array of the latest electronic equipment was installed for best access on all sides. To the front, close to hand was the automatic pilot, two of the latest 'Decca' navigators separated by a mechanical plotter, a radar and two paper-recording sounders. A scanning sonar was located on the deck-head to starboard. All this gear could be monitored from the comfortable wheelhouse chair, which hydraulically absorbed the worst of any swell. This was a far cry from the *Courage's* sparse electronic gear and the polished plank that spanned her wheelhouse.

The mooring ropes were stowed as I set up the navigators, then the *Independence* was easily manoeuvred from her berth. We sailed from the harbour, giving Richard Oakes the lighthouse watch-keeper a friendly wave. Rich had been a fisherman, working with drift nets, lines and trawls during his career before coming ashore. At six feet plus, he was bigger than most around the harbour. Richard Hoax would have been a more fitting name, such were his tall stories, which he delivered with deadpan conviction. My Dad was also one of the watch-keepers manning the lighthouse on eight hourly shifts, since selling his coble.

Rounding the outer pier we headed northeast on a sea so smooth it appeared to be glass. Danny was sitting on the chart table, legs dangling, watching my every movement. I suggested to him that he might want to turn in and get some sleep. It would be four hours before we reached the fishing grounds, some thirty miles distant. He wouldn't hear of it and said he was going to stay in the wheelhouse to keep me company. Ten minutes later he was curled up asleep. I tucked him under the chart table, covering him with his sleeping bag. He didn't stir when we shot the trawl, though there was plenty of noise from the deck. It was eight o'clock in the morning and hauling time when the sound of trawl boards banging on the boat's side woke him.

Sleepily, Danny looked out of the wheelhouse window then at me, perplexed. Instead of the bright summer day and miles of sea in all directions he'd expected, he saw only fog. It was a thick 'pea-souper' and we'd been enveloped in it since daylight. The trawl was hauled up and the bag of fish lifted inboard. Danny was amazed as the wriggling mass dropped onto the deck; half a ton of fish, tails kicking and flapping. The net was quickly lowered to the seabed again, a process which continued relentlessly every four hours until late evening.

My little lad spent the entire day running back and forth from the deck to the wheelhouse, getting in everyone's way and when not eating, asking unanswerable questions or wanting to play games, as six year olds do. He'd attempted to gut some small fish but had soon got bored with the process. Now early evening, Danny was exhausted and didn't complain too much when I took him below, pulled off his wellington boots and tucked him into the back of my bunk. "That's t' last we'll see of 'im 'til tomorrow" I thought, somewhat relieved.

We continued fishing and the radar worked well, marking all vessels within the twelve-mile range setting. The fog got even thicker and the atmosphere heavier, becoming more oppressive. Something was going to happen and it did, just before midnight. The heavens opened and rain of monsoon proportions fell from the sky. Huge forks of lightning pierced the night, lighting the sky as though daylight. Thunder rolled overhead. This was indeed a storm to remember. With no wind to move the cloud, nature's spectacular firework display continued for hours. We were all more than a little apprehensive. Lightning was stabbing the sea all around us and the *Independence* was the only object above sea level. A little voice behind me said, "what's 'appening Dad?"

My first thought was to say, "go back below Danny it's scary up 'ere," but an inner voice said, "he'll be even more frightened down in the cabin on his own," and I heard myself saying, "come up 'ere and watch this Danny, it's really excitin'. Every time t' lightnin' flashes, it lights up the whole sky."

For the next two hours my little lad, eyes like saucers shouted things like, "wow!" or, "that was a good one, Dad." I enthused as best I could.

Eventually the storm abated leaving the air clear and fresh. We'd caught a reasonable amount of fish during the twenty-four hours and weren't far from port so I decided to take the catch back to Monday's market, which could be lucrative. I'd also take Danny home.

Arriving in port at 0800 hours, we tied up astern of the *Valiant*. Her skipper, Bill Pashby Jnr. must also have come in early for the good prices offered. Bill's father had been the Scarborough

Fishermen's leader and spokesman for many years and an inspiration for a generation of youngsters.

Climbing the ladder to the pier, we left the crew and our shore helpers to unload the fish. In passing I took note of the other boat's catch. Her crew were weighing the few remaining oddments and part boxes. The quantity of fish under the market seemed similar to our own. The vessel's cook/deck hand was manning the scales and every box was weighed with precision and labelled. If the boat hadn't been sailing again, her other crew members would have long since gone home, leaving the boat's lumpers to drag away the tallied boxes. They were impatient with his accuracy. The deck hand/cook had a reputation for frugality.

My pal Dave 'Bev' Bevan, when younger had sailed on this vessel before becoming a skipper and took extra food to sea with him, considering the cook's portions insufficient for his appetite.

Danny and I walked back up the hill together but unfortunately, we had to pass my parents' house again. I held my breath and tried to hurry past but it was a futile attempt. My Mother saw us passing and was out in an instant. "You should 'ave more sense than t' take that poor bairn t' sea in weather like that," she called out. "You 'aven't got the sense you were born with."

I attempted to explain that the extreme weather wasn't forecast and it was fine when we sailed, but the words fell on deaf ears. There was no point in arguing with Mum.

Feeling a tug at her skirt, my Mother looked down to see two eyes like saucers looking up at her and Danny said, "but Grandma, it was brilliant. Every time t' lightnin' flashed, it lit up the whole sky."

It wasn't often Mother was lost for words but little Danny's expression of wonderment left her speechless. Delivering him home, I had time for a quick cup of coffee and to hear the latest news from Dotty, then left as Danny was describing his adventures in garbled confusion to his Mum and sister, Paula.

Returning back down the hill I looked across to the harbour where the *Independence* lay alongside the fish market. She looked superb with the morning sun on her blue sides and grained wheelhouse, though her starboard side looked a little scuffed. Not surprising as the heavy, iron trawl doors had been hauled up her side more than a hundred times since she'd arrived at her home port. This part of the vessel had been double planked and coated in protective steel, so the damage was only to her paintwork. There was also a trace of green weed along the waterline near her bows. I made a mental note to finish fishing early in the near future to paint her bottom and adjoining white line. The varnished landing pole, though still topped, wasn't moving so I surmised that the catch must now be ashore.

As I crossed the road, I could see Rusty and Sid on the quayside with our net mender/lumper, George 'Joxy' Scales. Rusty, named for his hair colour, was my uncle and had been with me as my right hand man since I'd first become a skipper, more than five years ago. Sid had been a deck hand on the deep-sea trawlers from Hull for many years and had made the transition to the inshore vessels successfully. The two jobs were very different and though the huge Arctic vessels saw much worse weather and dreadful conditions, crewmen on our smaller boats had to be more versatile. Our men had to be able to take a watch and to mend nets but more importantly, be available to sail at a few hours notice by phone if we were in port during the week. The culture of employment was different too. We were totally 'share fishermen', paid only with a percentage of profits from the sale of fish caught. There was no weekly wage. We were self-employed, so no fish, for whatever reason, bad weather or mechanical breakdown, meant no pay. This wasn't a concept the deep-sea men were familiar with. They were used to a basic wage plus a small percentage of their catch's value.

Sid was a good hand and an excellent cook, having been an officers' cook during his period in the Army. He hardly seemed to sleep and was always pottering in the galley either cooking or cleaning. His food was superb and plentiful and Sid would cook in any weather. "If it's good enough t' fish in, it's good enough t' cook in," he'd say. Sid's own design frying pan, which filled the stove, had baffles to return any splashing oil. Our cook's steaks were excellent and cooked to perfection but his fried fish, which we often had for breakfast, was the best I'd ever tasted.

*Gutting lessons for Danny alongside Bluey.*

*Sid dispensing dinner ready for his shipmates coming from the deck.*
*Photo by John Hobson*

*Monitoring the Decca Navigators, plotter and sounder.*
*Photo Ian Robinson*

*Net mending both wings of the trawl. The after door is hanging from the gallow.*
*Photo by John Hobson*

The catch was ashore and mostly weighed when I approached the group. Only a few part boxes of differing species remained to be weighed and these were quickly dealt with. The merchants were gathering round the show of fish spread under the market, and were talking animatedly. The men were delighted to have a good selection of fish so early in the week. The day boats' catches were mostly of smaller fish and these vessels didn't take ice, so I hoped we'd get a premium price for our good-sized, quality, chilled fish.

Bluey and Barry, having despatched the catch from below to the market had scrubbed and hosed the empty hold and were ready to receive a fresh batch of clean containers. Sid and Joxy had stacked the light, dry, wooden cases on the quay edge in columns of ten and had the first pile hooked on. Rusty, now back at the winch, was taking the strain to lift the first batch. The team had the job in hand so I wandered under the market to watch the auction, though watching the proceedings usually made me angry.

At least twenty men were gathered round our fish, some at the edges but mostly standing on the boxes, their hobnail boots chipping splinters from the wood. There were fishmongers, fish and chip shop proprietors and wholesale merchants. All carried distinct books of coloured tallies with their name or business logo. On successfully bidding for items, they'd tear leaves from the wad and liberally spread these on the fish. Following the sale, their porters would know which boxes to collect and stack on their wheelbarrows. It wasn't uncommon for the occasional box of fish to go missing, misappropriated by some of the more unscrupulous labourers. The buyer of the missing items usually refused to pay for his lost purchase, so the boat would take the loss at the end of the week.

In the centre of the gathering was my pal Barry, the auctioneer, who'd been my Best Man when Dotty and I were married. Among those on the edge, notebook and pencil poised, was his boss Charlie Simmons, ready for the action.

I looked round at this disparate bunch with mixed feelings. Some were honest, friendly traders, who would genuinely bid for their requirements and pay top prices. High among this section was Dennis Cappleman, a jovial red-faced man with short, straight black hair and a droopy moustache. Dennis was a fish fryer, whose reputation for quality fish and chips was the best in town. To this end, Dennis bought nothing but the finest cod, haddock and plaice, of a size that cut to give generous portions. He would outbid anyone for his choice of the catch and the other merchants knew this, so didn't put up too much opposition, though I found it almost impossible to tell who was bidding at the sale. The auctioneer, aware of interested parties for the various species, would act on a nod, a wink or slight finger movement.

Ronnie Manning, a tall, wavy-haired man with a distinct Hartlepool accent was another fryer with a good reputation. Ron specialised in haddock and though his shop was on the road out of town, 'Mannings' was always busy. Like most people from Hartlepool, Ron disliked anyone mentioning 'hanging the monkey'. Folklore has it that during the Napoleonic War, a monkey was washed ashore from a shipwreck near the town. The locals thought this creature was a French spy and hung the poor animal. Now, when anyone said they were from Hartlepool, the derogatory response was always, "isn't that where they hung the monkey?"

At the other end of the fish and chip spectrum was a man called Wood, owner of the 'Green Star Fisheries', in nearby St Sepulchre Street. A small, narrow-nosed, thin little man with shifty eyes, he was permanently clad in a khaki overall. He bought the inferior parts of catches, damaged fish and species of little value, which he would sell as haddock when skinned. He never bought haddock. This was well known among the fishing fraternity, none of whom used his shop. There were at least four other establishments within a quarter of a mile of the harbour, though none on the sea front. All the amusements, cafés and shops along the foreshore closed down at the end of September until Easter. There was a stark contrast between summer and winter.

Les Dowkes was new to the fish trade and was treated with suspicion by some of the other dealers. He'd recently acquired a wet fish shop in town and a merchant's license from the Council to buy fish on the market. Les, with blond wavy hair, a handlebar moustache and horn-rimmed glasses, dressed in the manner of a country squire. He soon became a friend of the fishermen when they realised he wasn't intimidated by the big players at the auction.

Les bought small lots of several species to give a range of choice on his counter.

There were other small buyers, each acquiring fresh stock for their trade. Old Bob Wheeler supplied some of the top hotels in town with quality fish such as lemon sole, plaice and turbot. If Bob was around when we were landing he'd identify choice pieces and sidle up saying, "can ah draw these bits afore t' sale starts. Ah'll pay yer cash at t' weekend. Ah'm on'y a poor pensioner yer know."

Bob was reputed to be rich as Croesus and was one of the shareholders and directors of Scarborough Football Club. On Saturday morning I'd visit him on his stand at the far end of the market for an amount of cash that bore little relation to the quality and quantity of fish drawn and again he'd say, "ah'm on'y a poor pensioner yer know."

His only member of staff, Chris Louth, a giant of a man with a round, sallow face and bushy greying beard, would roll his eyes and look skywards when he heard the same old story over and over again. This money, known locally as 'stocker' or 'wrangam' was divided among the crew and also anything received for the odd lobster, queenies, squid or bait, saved for the potting vessels.

Most of the fish auctioned on the market was purchased by the half-dozen main merchants, each employing numerous staff to process the produce. When separated from the head and bones, the resulting fillets were dispatched overnight to inland markets throughout the country. Their premises, in a large block at the back of the West Pier behind the market area were new and purpose built. Before this construction their men would get to work under the fish market immediately following the sales. Their large, wooden tanks, overflowing from constant, hose-fed tap water, brimmed with fish. These skilled men with razor sharp, long bladed knives, quickly and cleanly separated flesh from bone, their knives flashing deftly.

Derek Watson, also a director of the football club, was one of the main buyers. He occasionally employed some of the semi-professional players from the team during the week and the main topic of conversation at the auction was the success or otherwise of Scarborough FC. One or two of these players had become fish merchants in their own right. Dad said there had always been good footballers on the fish market, villains who could kick a cod or haddock into a corner or hiding place with skill.

Alf Goacher, another of the major buyers, small and stocky with straight hair was also a racehorse owner and bet heavily on the horses. It was the talk of the harbour when Alf had a big win, though he probably lost large amounts too.

The sale began and there was competition for the limited supply. It made me cross when fish was plentiful on the market. The auctioneer would take bids for the majority of catches but when the bidding stopped, half a dozen different tallies would be spread across the catch. "I'll have six at that price," one would say. "I'll have a few," from another and the catch would be divided up, allowing them all to have a share without paying too much. This wasn't strictly legal practice but there was nothing the fishermen could do. The merchants could just as easily share out the fish at their premises after the sale with just one or two buying.

Some days the buyers would say, "there's no demand for fish," but there was never any left unsold on the market. Another ruse these wholesalers used, would be to say there was short weight in the boxes that were supposed to contain six stones. Due to the huge variation between wet and dry boxes, anywhere between twelve and twenty-three pounds, it was impossible to get the weights exact but we allowed twenty-one pounds for each, plus two or three pounds for ice. This allowance almost always worked in the favour of the merchants but it didn't stop them arbitrarily deducting an amount from their weekly account, stating 'short weight'. This was another loss to the boats and one which skippers were getting increasingly angry about. One day we'd do something about these injustices.

The busiest days on the quay were Thursday and Friday, when there would be thirty or more boats landing. The market would be full from end to end with shots of fish. The late arrivals stacked their catches in front of the building, impeding access along the pier. It wasn't unusual to see the auction still in progress after noon with ice long melted and fish drying in the sun.

Today was different. It was a quiet day on the market and I was confident of a good price for our quick return. The bidding was brisk and the sales were almost completed as I returned to the boat, where the landing gear was stowed and hatches battened ready for sea. I'd contact the agent's office by radio later in the morning to discover what price our shot of fish had made. Back in the wheelhouse there was a comforting hum from the electronic equipment and an occasional crackle from the VHF radio. At a wave, Joxy released the ropes. "Thanks Jox. I 'ope yer lucky," I called to our net mender and lumper. It was a superstition that only people considered to be lucky were asked to let boats' ropes go. My call was only in jest.

"You'll be alright", he shouted back cheerfully. Joxy had been in steam trawlers when he was younger, then had graduated to smaller inshore trawlers. His last vessel, before he came ashore was the *Brilliant Star*. Now he was an invaluable shore-man for us. His knowledge of net construction surpassed my modest skills and he kept our nets in top condition. We always carried two spare trawls on board and a further two on shore, either under repair or mended and ready to be exchanged for damaged nets from the boat.

When homeward bound, I'd contact the lighthouse by radio, an hour from port, requesting the watch-keeper to telephone Joxy and Dad, when they weren't on watch. They'd be waiting on the quayside with a supply of empty boxes, ready to assist with lumping the catch when we arrived. Today Dad was on the 0800 to 1600 hours watch so hadn't been available to us. He was standing on the edge of the lighthouse pier as we drew near.

"Did you 'ave owt?' he yelled.

"About thirty kit," I called back, leaning out of the open window. "It was good stuff. Switch to channel fourteen." With that we were rounding the pier end and Dad entered the cosy little office to contact me by radio.

Heading into the bay I observed two motorboats, known locally as wops, with half a dozen people on each. Apart from these little vessels, Scarborough Bay was empty. Not many years ago this area would have had maybe fifteen to twenty wops and rowing boats with seven or eight passengers in each. At anchor, they were fishing for whiting, dab and the occasional codling. Now these craft were almost history.

When I was a little boy my Dad owned one of these rowing boats, a seventeen-foot craft named after my sister, *Christine*. I spent many days during the summer holidays fishing in the bay, and could remember seeing the keelboats returning home from daily trawling trips each evening. When not being seasick I'd try to guess the names of the boats as they hove into view. Dad would know each one long before it came close. The crews, still gutting fish would wave as they passed. The wash from their wake rolled our little cockleshell severely.

On making contact with Dad on the radio, I told him how Danny had fared, about the storm and how Mum had told me off as we'd walked up the hill.

I heard Dad's laugh through the receiver. He knew Mum was like a lioness, so protective was she of her grandkids, just as she'd been when my sisters and I were small. "Yer know what yer mother's like. She's never bin any different," he said, then changed the subject, asking where we were bound for the remainder of our week and if anyone else was catching anything.

I set the autopilot to east, scanning the radar for traffic as I replied, locating a plastic plotter roll for the area we were heading to. I signed off from our conversation, saying, "see you on Thursday, sometime."

He replied, "Aye OK, good fishin'."

There was nothing at all within six miles on the radar. The two wops were now lost in the centre screen clutter. I looked from the starboard window to see 'Blondie' Wood sitting at the back of his square stern, red-painted, *Adventure,* his usual flat cap and cigarette in place. As we passed he stood, shrugged his shoulders and raised his palms as if to say, "what else can I do?" He then held up a string of little fish to show his catch.

Unable to contact him, as his boat had no electronic gear of any sort, not even lights, I gave him a 'thumbs up'.

Seeing Blondie with the fish reminded me that I had to save some fish when we landed next time. Dotty had bought me a guitar for Christmas and after racking my brains to find a tutor, I'd remembered my old school pal Mel, who owned a guesthouse in town. For a few weeks during early summer, Mel turned up in the evening to give me a lesson. Dotty would immediately head for the bathroom where she would spend an hour soaking till Mel departed with his bag of haddock fillets. Sadly my musical aspirations came to nothing, though through no fault of my tutor, who was an excellent musician. After teaching me a few chords he said, "what do you want to play?"

I replied, "Streets of London." This lovely, slow ballad, a favourite of mine by Ralph McTell, turned out to be a difficult tune to learn, but after a few lessons I could get through most of the work. We'd sit face to face, instruments in hand, he being right handed and me using my left, his clever strumming and fretwork disguising my clumsiness. After several sessions we tried other tunes but now, whatever I played always seemed to sound like, 'Streets of London'. When Mel suggested I sing along to the music, I realised my talents didn't extend further than being good at catching fish.

* * * * * *

Sid turned up in the wheelhouse with pot of tea in hand. I glanced into the mug. The contents were dark brown with the tea bag floating in the pot. He laughed when I cringed at the potent brew. As cook, Sid took most steaming watches while we other four took trawling watches in rotation. This worked out at approximately one watch a day. Sid would maintain this easterly course for about two hours then call me. I'd steer her to the 'Decca' position where we'd shoot the trawl. Closing the wheelhouse door I went down the steps to the alleyway. Looking into the dimly lit mess-deck below the wheelhouse, I was faced with three pairs of eyes, briefly averting their gaze from the television. All three men were smoking and in this confined space the galley had the appearance of how I imagined an opium den. My old skipper, Tom Pashby would have felt at home in this smog. Tom smoked eighty, 'Capstan Full

Strength' cigarettes daily until he began hand-rolling his own. Then he was making cigs so thick, he occasionally needed more than one paper to contain the tobacco. I opted for my bunk and a chapter of the latest 'Wilbur Smith' instead.

When we stopped to shoot the net there were seven or eight small targets on the radar screen within a six-mile radius, denoting other craft. None were close. The boats were scattered not congregating, so no one had detected any of the vast shoals of herring that were sure to be somewhere in the area. According to Sid, the catch reports on the VHF radio were only moderate and even those skippers using 'private' frequencies, which our scanner picked up, were having no more success.

The sea was flat calm and it was impossible to detect a breeze when the way was off the vessel. The strip of ribbon on the foremast stay hung limp. We'd have to be careful when dropping the net or we could foul the propeller. Even a light air would blow the boat away from the net. The trawl was soon in the water and Sid, boat hook in hand, encouraged the headline, with its many plastic floats attached, away from the boat's side. He gave a nod, signalling the gear was clear of the boat and I gave the engine a quick burst astern. The wash from the screw pushed the net clear and I was able to go ahead, allowing the trawl to stream astern to starboard.

Suddenly, two large fish broke the surface close to our net, thin dorsal and tail fins making erratic wakes on an oily sea. These creatures were unlike anything I'd ever seen before. They were not porpoise or dolphins as these mammals broke the surface in an arced movement, taking air or jumping from the water. I'd seen plenty of sharks and the fins on the fish I was now viewing bore no resemblance to any sharks I'd seen. It suddenly dawned on me these must be 'tunny'. The blue fin tuna had been a common visitor to our coast in the past, feeding on the mass of migrating herring, spawning by the billion in August and September. No one had seen a 'tunny fish' in these waters for more than twenty years.

Excitedly, I shouted to the lads on deck, busy paying out the wires. I pointed in the direction of the rare sighting but before they could get a glimpse of these strangers, the pair had disappeared. The looks directed to the wheelhouse were of disbelief but I was sure I had indeed seen 'tunnies'. There were plenty of photos on the wall of the Leeds Arms from the days in the 1930s and 40s when these huge fish were caught for sport with rod and line. I'd compare my sighting with these old pictures. I'd also ask Ernie 'Soapy' Williamson when I saw him next. Ernie's Dad, 'Old Ern', had been a successful skipper, chartering his little keelboat, *Shirley Williamson* to the gentry in pursuit of this big game. His two sons had sailed with him on these expeditions.

We were unable to locate the elusive shoals during the remainder of the voyage, though the herring couldn't be far away. The 'tunny' would be feeding on the 'silver darlings'. Average fishing for the remainder of the trip meant we still ended our week with a good pay packet. As we discharged our second catch, Melvyn, one of the wholesale merchants, who also owned a fish and chip shop, asked if I'd consider letting him have a few boxes of cod each landing, prior to the sale. He would pay cash at ten percent less than market price. This seemed a good idea. The thought of cash was tempting. Little did I know what repercussions this arrangement would have.

* * * * * *

"Testin', testin', is anyone listenin' on 'ere?" I was calling on the working frequency of the fleet. The airwaves were unusually quiet on this mid-week morning. Normally the ether was buzzing as the day boats, either newly fishing or en route to their chosen grounds, talked incessantly.

"I'm gettin' yer. Yer transmittin' alright. It's quiet. Where is everybody?" came a reply with confirmation of my message and sentiments. This was Colin 'Dilt' Jenkinson in the *Our Heritage*.

"That's what ah was wonderin'. There's nobody at sea at all."

Col was a top fisherman and seaman who'd fished all his life. His first vessel in the early 60s was an old forty-five footer, *Margaret and William,* which he'd renamed after his children. Subsequently he'd built the new vessels, *Our Margaret, Our Rachel* and his latest, *Our Heritage*. In his first new vessel, Colin lost a man overboard while trawling in poor weather. Turning hard to port in a full circle, putting a turn in his trawl warps, Col was able to retrieve his elderly Uncle Matt, shaken and waterlogged but otherwise unhurt.

We fished through the day, several miles apart, comparing catches but there was no one else at sea. The weather was fine and unable to understand the lack of vessels, about mid afternoon I called the agent's office on their private channel. There was no answer. The mystery deepened.

Soon after, Col, equally perplexed spoke to the lighthouse watch-keeper, who'd just arrived on duty. I listened in. "It's t' Queen's Silver Jubilee. There's parties goin' on all over town," Joxy said. "Ah've jus' come past City Square an' it's full o' people. Old Tom an' Wally set off wi' one table, two chairs, a bottle o' whisky an' a few beers an' now it's buzzin'."

No one would find City Square on a map. This was the local name for what is Princess Square, formerly Low Conduit Street. Tom Rowley and Wally Johnson fished from the *Rosemary*, a large blue coble, which my Dad had formerly fished on. Tom, a widower and Wally, who'd never married, were larger than life characters, well known to everyone and it was easy to see how they'd started this impromptu party.

I was aware that it was the Queen's Jubilee Day. Dotty had made fancy dress costumes for Paula and Danny and there was a party on Princess Street for all the youngsters but I hadn't expected the boats to stay in port. "We're in bother, aren't we?" I said to Col.

He confirmed my thoughts. We were labelled as greedy and party-poopers when our crews discovered they were the only ones at sea, yet we were guilty of nothing other than ignorance. Things grew worse next day when the airwaves were full of tales of revelry and hi-jinx. A promise to stay in harbour when any other national celebration took place was no consolation. Even back on shore I was made to feel guilty listening to Dotty's lovely stories of the day's events.

## Chapter 2

# The Paint Up

It was late August and my *Independence* was now definitely in need of a coat of paint. There'd been no reports of large herring shoals yet, though the multitude would be sure to turn up soon. As planned, we finished fishing a day early, removing the trawling gear with a big, harbour crane. This was one of two vehicles normally used to discharge cargo from the various commercial ships bringing trade to the harbour. Manoeuvring close past the two white-hulled, passenger carrying vessels tied to the Vincent Pier, we anchored the *Independence* at the top end of the harbour, putting a head rope ashore on each bow to keep her in position during the brief time she'd be afloat overnight.

The two pleasure cruisers, *Regal Lady* and *Yorkshire Lady* were large vessels with an upper deck, wheelhouse and funnel. Capable of carrying in excess of a hundred passengers each, these two ladies were almost fifty years old and well past their prime. *Regal Lady* had seen service at Dunkirk. Their heyday was post war, when people again flocked to the seaside following years of austerity. The vessels had, over the years, taken tens of thousands of trippers to sea and were still operating. They'd seen several skippers, including Donny Dalton, a local councillor, nicknamed 'Dewdrop' from the constant wet globe on his nose.

An earlier skipper, 'Dickie' Blogg, was a 'real ladies' man' and would be drawn to any attractive member of the opposite sex who boarded his vessel. If they showed any interest at all in his advances his favourite line was, "me name's Dick. I hope you like it."

Leaving the *Independence* moored in position, we scrounged a lift ashore from Blondie. He accepted the five-pound note offered but also suggested we keep him a box of bait next time we landed. He'd probably get a 'fry' of fish too. It was difficult to refuse Blondie Wood. He was almost the last of these small boat men, making a living by whatever means were available, depending on season and weather.

As the tide ebbed, my lovely vessel gently grounded then leaned to starboard, as planned. On the next morning's tide we'd list her to port with the half dozen fifty-gallon metal drums, filled with seawater from the deck hose. I'd have to shut off the stops on the fuel lines to the engine, preventing diesel oil flowing from the high side and overflowing through the tank ventilator on the low side. Even a small spillage of fuel could cover most of the harbour.

A couple of hours later, with the water surrounding the vessel ebbed down to thigh-boot level, we waded out armed with long handled brushes and began scrubbing the green weed and slime from her bottom. Those with undiscovered holes in the tops of their boots quickly found the offending gaps as cold water seeped in. This scrubbing was warm work and our time was limited as the tide receded quickly. Soon the *Independence* was left high and dry on the hard sand but we'd managed to achieve our goal. She was scrubbed clean. A stiff breeze, blowing from the east was already drying the forward section where we'd begun our labour.

We had time for a pot of tea from the nearby 'Teapot' kiosk on the East Pier then collected paint and brushes from the chandlers while the wind completed its work. The four crewmen began painting the boat's bottom with maroon, anti-fouling paint while I removed the lid from a two-pint tin of white gloss. I climbed a ten-foot ladder and began to paint the six-inch band above the water line, where the plum red joined the dark blue of the hull. Below me, a shipwright was replacing a small section of caulking that had worked loose from between two planks.

Above the harbour on the promenade, holidaymakers strolled leisurely along the harbourside, many stopping to watch our activities. I slowly scaled the ladder, full tin of paint sat in the palm of one hand, brush in the other, holding on to the ladder tenuously with the brush hand. I began to paint, carefully cutting in the straight lines and avoiding streaks of white running into the maroon. I'd only applied a few strokes when a gust of wind swirled into the harbour from around the Castle Headland and I felt the ladder begin to move. I had a split second in which to make one of two choices, to drop the paint and attempt to hold on to the boat or try to run down the ladder very quickly, before it fell over. Unfortunately I opted for the latter. The ladder slid sideways, picking up speed and the tin of paint went up in the air as I fell to the ground, landing heavily on the hard sand. A moment later, most of the contents of the inverted paint tin covered my head.

The shipwright, working close to where I'd been painting heard the ladder fall and received splashes of white on his navy blue boiler suit. Swearing loudly, he turned but immediately burst out laughing. My crew also heard the ladder fall and as one, looked in my direction. They too began to laugh, as did the dozens of spectators watching my plight from the pavement. I sat stunned for a moment on the wet sand, coated in white gloss, then carefully opened my eyes. At least I could see. Aching and bruised but with nothing broken, I slowly stood. The four other painters were now on their knees in a huddle, holding each other, crying with laughter and I couldn't appreciate the humorous side of the situation at all.

I was in a dilemma. Paint isn't an easy substance to remove from hands so how was I to get this quantity from my head. I couldn't let the stuff dry, that would only add to my problems but decisive action was required. My only option was to quickly make for the Marine Engineers workshop along the road, mingling en route with several hundred holidaymakers. Walking swiftly, ignoring the giggles, pointing fingers and some wit commenting, "the seagulls must be huge round here," I arrived at the safe haven. Gingerly, I stripped to the waist with assistance from Jack Redman, the firm's resident joker, who at a glance realised my predicament. Jack, thin, alert, red-faced with black, curly, unkempt hair, poured a quantity of paraffin in the workshop sink and I liberally swilled my head and shoulders. This dowsing eventually removed the offending gloss. Until now I'd used a minimum of words, not wanting the dreadful stuff in my mouth but now I was able to swear profusely, then thank Jack for his help. He'd have great fun relating the story to his pals.

Though the worst of the ordeal was over, I was still obliged to coat my upper body with a strong detergent to remove the oil. Subsequently, my saviour poured large quantities of warm, fresh water over my head to eliminate the liquid soap. Looking in the mirror, I wasn't surprised to find my skin glowing and even the whites of my eyes were red. I looked like a character from a horror movie. I gratefully accepted a cup of tea and an old shirt from the now smirking Jack. He'd earlier retrieved this top from the many bags of rags the company supplied to the boats for engine-room use. My own discarded shirt was a white, sticky mess on the floor and would never be worn again. Most of Jack's working clothes came from this endless source.

Vowing never to paint my boat again and to leave the work to professionals, an hour later I returned to the *Independence,* sore-faced and subdued, only to find my tear-streaked crew still grinning.

The wind had fallen away at high water on Thursday morning when we rowed out in a little workboat to empty, relocate and fill the drums on the other side of the boat. I was praying the little craft wouldn't capsize and insisted everyone sat down. I didn't need any further upsetting incidents. Word had gone round the 'Bottom End' by jungle telegraph and wherever I went, some wag would have a witty comment. My emotions were still raw from the experience, so I didn't complain at all when Sid offered to paint the white line when the boat dried. It was Sid who'd finished the job on the previous day, following my mishap. He made a show of securing the top of the ladder to the boat with a short end of rope, making his shipmates chuckle.

I felt quite vulnerable throughout the remainder of the work and still thought my crew were laughing at me. I wasn't sorry when the work was completed and was pleased to tie the *Independence* up alongside the North Wharf on the next tide. The harbour crane was standing by to lift our fishing gear back in place. Ken Roberts, the crane driver was sitting in his cab and we were waiting for him to lower the trawl doors on board. We'd put a rope strop on the first board and were waiting for Ken to take the weight when the driver spotted an elderly, moustached gentleman wearing a kilt and beret, passing his vehicle. He turned off the engine, jumped from his cab and to our amazement the crane driver stood before the old Scotsman and saluted very smartly. "Sergeant Roberts, Sir. I was with you at Arnhem, Sir."

The elderly gentleman was quite moved and his eyes filled. "Thank you Roberts. It's good to see you. Carry on." He continued his amble along the quay, drawing a handkerchief from his pocket.

Ken, a Mancunian who'd married a fisherman's daughter while stationed in Scarborough, wasn't big in stature but was wiry and must have been a formidable soldier. Ken returned to our group saying, "he was my Commanding Officer during the war when we were parachuted into Holland and he was bloody fearless." The driver climbed back into his cab and restarted the engine as if a meeting like this happened every day.

Our usual Thursday evening in the Leeds Arms was fairly predictable. The topic of conversation and butt of the jokes was going to be me and my painting incident. I entered the pub slightly ahead of Dotty to receive a barrage of comments.

"You're cleaned up well Nommy, yer face is glowing. Yer won't need t' wash for a week."

"Wer' yer off colour yesterd'y. Somebody said yer wer' looking pale."

"Aren't yer supposed to put the paint on yer boat."

There were many other witticisms directed my way. Les, the landlord just grinned at my discomfort. The comments were drying up but I was pleased when the focus of attention shifted from me briefly, as four casually dressed young men entered the little pub. They were laughing at a shared joke and seemed totally inoffensive.

Les held up his hand as they approached the bar and said loudly, "sorry, no gangs."

The room fell silent and the youngsters looked dumbfounded. They'd done nothing wrong and were obviously not unpleasant or looking for trouble. That didn't matter to Les. They were strangers, not welcome in his pub and wouldn't get served. Looking at each other in consternation they shrugged and crestfallen, left the building.

For a while the silence remained unbroken. No one spoke to the barman in defence of the youngsters, though there was much sympathy for the lads. It didn't pay to upset the landlord. I'd only recently begun frequenting the Leeds Arms again following an extended, self-imposed exile after being told to leave. I'd stayed away from this lovely pub with its low ceiling, nautical memorabilia and excellent beers and wines, having fallen foul of the landlord's temper. I was pleased to be using the place again.

Les wasn't usually unpleasant and frequently did favours for people. He was a talented sign-writer and could also turn his hand to building and renovating property but he could also be quite perverse and ran his pub as if it was a private club for his friends.

Every year in summer, a small group of visitors from Belgium would turn up at the pub and he'd greet them warmly, as if they'd travelled to the town just to see him, though on one occasion, how the tourists got from their hotel to the pub was quite miraculous. Their spokesman asked the taxi driver in broken English, to take them to the 'Legs of Les'.

Scratching his head in confusion, the driver said, "do you mean the Leeds Arms?"

The little pub had quite a diverse clientelé and was busy most evenings. There was always a pleasant atmosphere with jokes, banter and friendly insults flying to and fro. Old Bob Kitto and his boozing partner, George 'Pudding' Appleby were sitting in a corner by the window, yarning and occasionally joining in the conversation with our party, gathered near the bar. Both men were in their mid-seventies but were quick witted and had a lovely, easy presence. These men didn't take life too seriously.

Bill Sheader, the lifeboat coxswain and his circle of friends were seated at the other window table of the bar and it was pleasing to hear his loud, guffawing laughter, usually at his own jokes. There were other customers in the larger, back room though this was less inviting.

Weekends were fun and landing on Thursday mornings meant almost three days at home each week. We'd sail again around midnight on Saturday, so I didn't spend a whole weekend ashore but always had an extended break from sea.

The pub door opened again and instinctively heads turned to see who was entering. Two attractive, leggy young ladies entered, gaining approval from all the men in the pub and getting me a kick on the shin from Dotty. The pair were quickly attended to by the hovering Les, who ignored the queue of waiting customers to give the girls priority treatment. "Hellooo and what can I do for you?" he growled in a soft, husky voice, reaching for and kissing the nearest one's hand. He was a pushover for a pretty girl and had a real fetish for coloured ladies, or as he called them, 'sooty birds'.

As he delivered their drinks, the two fluttered their eyes and instantly won his heart, though he was quickly disappointed when the pair picked up their glasses and left the vicinity of the bar. Looking round for a seat, their eyes alighted on two vacant places next to George and Bob.

"Come an' sit down 'ere you lasses, you'll be alright wi' us," called Bob in encouragement as the pair hovered indecisively.

"Aye you'll be safe wi' us, we're queer," said George, touching the peak of his cap and grinning in support of his pal.

The girls laughed and moved in the direction of the window to the two, mischievous old men. All eyes were on the mini-skirted legs as they took the few strides to the proffered seats. The old boys couldn't believe their luck and shuffled along to make room for the ladies. I received another painful kick and turned to pay attention to our group's faltering conversation. Another loud burst of laughter from the other corner of the bar distracted me and to show I was paying attention, I called to the lifeboat coxswain, asking what the joke was.

Bill, who now had everyone's attention, told a tale he'd heard of four Scarborough lads who'd been fishing out of Peterhead, in northern Scotland. They'd been working hard for several days, were weary and had drunk too much beer on the train as they travelled home from Aberdeen. Stanley had fallen asleep and his pals thought it hugely funny to leave him unconscious when the train stopped in York, where they had to change trains. It was only when the guard shook Stan at Kings Cross Station that he finally woke up. Still disorientated, he moved along the station, getting on the next northbound train, where he promptly fell asleep again. It wasn't till the train had again passed York and was pulling into Darlington that he fully woke to look for another southbound train. Bill received another roar of laughter for his tale and laughed once more at his own story.

As ever, the evening was pleasant, though Les was clearly unhappy at losing the attention of the two, lovely ladies. This clearly showed when a man from a group of customers in the back room entered the bar and picked up a small stool with the intention of taking the seat back to his company.

"What do you think you're doing?" Les asked the perplexed customer. "You wouldn't like it if I came into your house and started moving your furniture about."

The poor man was lost for words and stood open mouthed, stool still in hand. Les wandered back to our end of the bar muttering something about bloody IFLs.

"IFLs? What d' yer mean, Les?" I ventured.

"That bloke there," he muttered. "He comes in here two or three times a year and says, 'pint of the usual, please Les'. I'm supposed to know what he wants."

"But what does IFL mean?" I pushed him, knowing he was cross. He'd already lost his posh accent, which was a dangerous sign.

"Instant fuckin' locals," he snapped and continuing to mutter, he shuffled back to the far end again.

George and Bob were thoroughly enjoying talking to the dolly birds and there were giggles coming from the nearby table as naughty jokes and innuendos flowed from the two pals. Eventually, on finishing their drinks, the girls decided it was time to leave.

"Where are yer goin' now?" Bob asked the nearest pair of legs, which were inches from his face.

'We're going dancing in town at the new nightclub that's just opened," she replied with a voice of pure velvet.

"Can we come wi' yer?" George chuckled at his own suggestion.

Bob, glass at his lips, coughed as the half swallowed beer caught in his throat.

"If you want," came the mischievous reply and another flutter of eyelashes.

"What d' yer think Bob?" he asked his pal, who was still spluttering. "Shall we go dancin'?"

"Ah suppose we could go," Bob eventually said, downing the dregs in his glass.

The pub was silent again as we all watched events unfold. Even Dotty was intrigued. Both men, grinning, looped an arm, inviting the girls to take hold and the beauties dutifully obliged. Winking in our direction, the old boys left the pub. The ladies blew a kiss to Les as they departed. The barman's bottom lip was on his chest.

"Bloody 'ell Les, what d' yer reckon to that?" I asked.

"It'll kill 'em," he replied, wishing he'd been given this death sentence.

"What a way t' go," I agreed and received another kick for my thoughts.

## Chapter 3

# A Close Shave

The long-awaited herring had finally turned up and there were massive shoals gathered between ten and twelve miles offshore, as the countless billions of silver fish spawned before migrating south. This annual fishing bonanza, first recorded in the middle ages, was the original 'Scarborough Fair'. Vessels from all the countries bordering the North Sea either caught or traded these fish. Wars were fought over herring and soldiers fed on them. For over five hundred years, these little fish had been a major trading commodity and they were still being pursued, though now with the assistance of the latest technology.

We were back at sea following the nightmare paint up, though Bluey was taking a trip off to go on holiday and had asked one of his mates to sail in his place. We were among the boats that had found the big marks early. There was good cod fishing to be had as these voracious feeders gorged on the fat, slow swimming herring, full of eggs and ready to spawn. The cods' stomachs were bloated too, their bellies stuffed full, some containing seven, eight or more, whole fish, which slid out as the lads on deck sliced the abdomens open to remove the guts. Many of these big, green fish also had herring stuck in their throats as if there was no more room within. What a massive feeding frenzy this must be on the seabed.

The airwaves were buzzing as skippers from the three Yorkshire ports reported marks as the shoals appeared on their sounders. Boats not in the swim were looking for these vessels and attempted to head in their direction. This caused occasional congestion and any attempts to follow the 'rule of the road at sea' went out of the window. It was a case of 'who dares wins', though there were 'fraps', when two sets of trawling gear became entangled. These incidents were usually sorted amicably, even if there was much bad language over the radio in the first instance.

There were some huge, Dutch trawlers to be avoided and a few of the latest Scottish vessels, using the new purse seine nets were also targeting the gigantic shoals. These pursers could locate shoals of fish almost a mile distant with their sophisticated sonars and drawing closer, encircle much of the multitude with nets which extended from the surface to the bottom, harvesting vast amounts of herring with ruthless efficiency. What a far cry this was from the days of my youth, when these two nations fished for herring with drift nets. In those days herring were only caught in the dark, with nets draped mid-water like curtains, waiting for the fish to swim in and be trapped by their gills. As a schoolboy, I'd spent many nights at sea with friendly Scotsmen in the drifter fleet, who landed their fish by the cran* daily. Now, instead of waiting to mesh them, these mid-water fishermen took their nets to the fish and landed catches by the hundreds of tons.

An older, green-coloured Scarborough boat, trying to get into the mark that most boats were trawling through, was towing northeast, across the tide. This was a radical and not very wise move. If his gear snagged on the bottom, there were craft heading towards him from both directions, though we were the nearest.

My fears were borne out when I heard a curt, "*Independence*, we're fast 'ere," over the radio.

Recognising the skipper's voice, I shouted loudly, "Bloody 'ell, I knew that would 'appen," though as I was on my own in the wheelhouse my frustrated yell went unheard. I had three options and had to decide quickly. I could stop my boat, which meant hauling our gear and missing the mark; I could go hard to starboard, not

---

* There are four baskets of herring in a cran. This is a measure of volume, not weight. The baskets, holding approximately seven stone of fish, must be officially branded with a crown.

our best turning direction, with the possibility of hitting the offending boat, or turn to port and hope to avoid his net. I chose the latter, putting a ninety-degree course alteration on the autopilot. The rudder went hard to port and I reached for the handset. "We're goin' 'ard over t' port. D' yer think we'll clear yer gear?"

"Ah think so. We're 'eavin' up already," came the reply.

A minute or so later I felt a slight nudge but *Independence* kept moving through the water so we hadn't tangled our fishing gear. I eased the autopilot gradually back to mid-ships to resume my original course, fearing the worst and waiting for the result of this close quarter encounter with the other vessel.

"Yer fore door's gone right through our lower bellies. Our codends are 'angin' off. We're gonna 'ave t' change trawls," came the glum report.

I'd feared this result when feeling the tug on our warps when we passed by the immobile vessel. It would take the crew about half an hour to change trawls and deploy a spare net onto the existing, heavy footrope. "Sorry about that," I replied, genuinely disappointed to have caused the damage. "Ah couldn't do owt about it. You were crossin' our 'ead from port t' starboard. It should 'ave been your give way."

My pointing out the regulations relating to safe navigation clearly didn't help the already angry skipper's temper and a few expletives were all I got in return.

Following three good hauls, the *Independence* was lined up at the pier that evening with many other vessels, landing a good catch and the market was soon full from end to end with boxed fish, mostly cod of varying sizes, some stacked four boxes high under the market. A few skippers were taking up more space than necessary, spreading their wares out, hoping the merchants would see what they wanted and pay more. We stacked our full boxes, only laying the part full cases of various species, singly. Some had already stacked their fish in front of the fish market, almost blocking the access along the quay. This was selfish and led to arguments but would ensure their catches sold early in the auction. When there was a mass of fish for sale from thirty or more boats, the bidding could often be still in progress long after noon from a 0700 start. The fish quickly deteriorated in quality when the ice melted. Some merchants left the auction to process their early purchases so the late-selling boats received less revenue for their fish.

Dad and Joxy had scoured the pier for empty boxes but had only managed to find a few dozen clean ones. This was another cause of squabbles and even fights when there were barrow loads of boxes, reserved by eager shore staff while the vessels they represented were still at sea.

When we'd landed our fish, shovelled extra ice across the boxes and sheeted them over, we rounded up another thirty or forty boxes, which were either still soiled from the morning market or were in need of minor repairs. I could hear my crew complaining that this wasn't their job. "We pay commission t' agents t' supply clean boxes. We shouldn't 'ave t' wash or mend 'em," I heard one say.

He was quite right. The lads should have been on their way home now but we needed boxes for the following day and if it meant washing some or hammering in a few nails, we had to do it. I'd complain to the agent tomorrow on the radio when asking for our grossing but it would do no good. All we ever got were excuses and platitudes. The service from our agent was not acceptable. To make matters worse, as I was finally leaving the pier, an angry voice called me from behind. "Oy Nommy, I want you."

Turning, I was confronted by the skipper whose net had been damaged earlier in the day.

"Are you gonna get Joxy t' mend our net or d' yer want t' pay our mender t' do it?"

I wasn't in the best of moods at this point either and wasn't going to enter into a debate. "Yer jokin' arn't yer? It was you that crossed my 'ead. I tried t' miss yer and you said yer thought we were goin' clear. I'm not payin' for yer mendin'" Not waiting for a reply or a thump, I turned and walked off.

Another shower of abuse followed, ringing in my ears. We never spoke again.

* * * * * *

The shoal of herring we'd targeted had gone when we returned the next day, as had their pursuers but the vast numbers had left a mass of white, sticky spawn, which boats were trawling up in clumps and the eggs coated everything. Much of this deposit would provide food for other, smaller fish and it was only a matter of time before the haddock and whiting congregated, but meanwhile we had a few days left to fill. I opted to travel further offshore and set a course northeast. It was a beautiful morning, with a magnificent display of stars in the sky. The sea was flat calm and there wasn't another vessel in sight or even visible on radar. The previous evening's unpleasantness was far from my mind. I had a pot of steaming coffee in my hand, the BBC World Service in the background and knowing we had a decent landing under our belts, I was totally relaxed. I watched the sky in the east begin to lighten and gradually turn from dark blue to red, then orange as the sun rose from the sea on our starboard bow. I was overwhelmed with a sense of wonderment and filled with a feeling of wellbeing. What a privilege it was to see nature in all her glory on a morning like this.

We stopped about fifty miles from home and shot the trawl at the western edge of a fishing area known for more than a century as 'Bruce's Gardens'. Bruce's origins have sadly, been lost in the mists of time but his name is still marked on the fishing charts. The lads retreated to their bunks and I was again on my own in the wheelhouse. The ground we were to trawl was a narrow piece of hard ground about three miles long, running west-northwest to east-southeast. At the eastern end, on the edge of the ground an old wreck made working this strip difficult, requiring total concentration. Heading in this direction, my eyes were scanning from the sounder paper, marking the ground in forty-fathoms, to the navigator giving our position, to the compass to keep the course, then to the sonar in a vain attempt to locate the wreck. It was impossible to hear the sound of the fastener, hidden in the echoes from the hard ground.

Unable to detect the wreck as the *Independence* drew close to its site on the plotter, I erred on the side of caution, altering course a couple of compass points to the north, ensuring our trawl missed the obstruction. Still watching the 'Decca' clocks, I gradually relaxed when I was confident that our net, dragging the bottom an eighth of a mile astern, was past the wreck. The water was deepening, the ground below was now soft and the sonar detecting nothing of substance. Now was the time to turn through one hundred and eighty degrees and reverse our heading. Turning hard to port, in seconds the sonar speaker began to bang loudly, echoing something very hard ahead of us. "Bloody 'ell, it's that wreck," I thought, "I've set the plotter wrong," but knew I couldn't have. All the information I'd been reading and working to, added up. The plotter was correct.

For the first time in ages, I looked up from the instruments. Charging towards us at a rate of knots was a giant oil tanker, her white bow wave looming large. It was the steel hull of this monster that the sonar beam was bouncing off. Without looking, I'd turned to cross this huge ship's head. The range of the sonar was set on nine hundred metres but this leviathan was closer than that. I turned hard back to starboard and fortunately *Independence* quickly resumed her original course, thanks to the drag of the trawl. I stared at her name, picked out in large, stark, white letters against the black hull. FANNY. Her alert watch-keeper was already turning the great craft hard to starboard in an effort to avoid the stupid fisherman turning into his path. The mammoth, which must have displaced at least eighty thousand tons, passed really close down our port side. As she passed, her bow wave caused us to roll heavily. At the same time, her siren boomed loudly.

Leaving the wheelhouse, I went to the stern of *Independence* to look at the retreating vessel. I was joined there seconds later by my crew who, much to my embarrassment had been awakened by the swell and noise and had leapt from their beds. They looked towards me, then followed my gaze to the name on the transom of the departing, Spanish-registered ship. Rusty again looked in my direction and said loudly, "me mother said fanny would be t' death of me. She was nearly right."

Hauling for a few kit of good fish, we headed further to the northeast where the ground was patchy and where there was chance of a bag of cod.

"You'll 'ave t' take me in skipper. I've got a bit of a problem." Bluey's pal had come into the wheelhouse and having sent the recent catch below, he requested that I take him back to port.

"What's wrong with yer that's so serious, it won't keep till t' weekend?" I asked.

He told me he had a rash on his tummy and needed to see a doctor.

Curious, I said, "let's 'ave a look. It mus' be bad if yer need tekin' in."

Reddening, he said, "well it's not really on me tum, it's a bit further down."

Not particularly wanting to see the regions below his stomach, I asked if there was any other information he could give me to help with a diagnosis. Discovering the symptoms and hearing his story, I realised his problem and consulted the 'Ship's Medical Manual'. The comprehensive, graphic guide gave me the remedy, two tetracycline tablets, to be taken four times, daily. Unlocking the large, wooden medical chest below in the cabin, which contained a range of drugs including morphine, I sourced the required remedy and though not convinced, he took the first dose. I handed him the little brown bottle, so he could continue the treatment and he went off to the mess-deck muttering.

We shot the trawl again and it was my watch below. Late in the afternoon, the engine eased down. On arriving in the wheelhouse I noted the gear had come fast while trawling across soft ground and I knew we were in for trouble. It's only rock that normally stops a trawl, so this had to be an obstruction of some sort. The gear broke free from the fastener with a jerk and there was a large part of the forward section of the net missing. Several pieces of aluminium, from what appeared to be an aeroplane were littered in the remaining trawl, along with several large cod. If we'd managed to tow over the plane wreck, we could have taken a good haul. I reported this to Col in *Our Heritage,* who was fishing nearby.

The following morning he aimed his trawl at the position I'd given him and he towed clean over the obstruction, taking about six hundred stone of cod from the wreck for his efforts.

On our return to port on Thursday morning prior to the market, Bluey's pal was the first ashore, but not to help in landing. He was going home for a shower then to visit his doctor. I suggested he take the medication I'd prescribed for information to assist his GP.

When we'd finished landing our fish, the pieces of wreckage were given to the 'Fisheries Officer', more out of curiosity than for his benefit. It must have been a big plane to totally stop *Independence* and badly damage our trawl. Feedback weeks later, informed us that the wrecked plane was a huge, delta-winged, Vulcan Bomber, reported as crashed into the sea with her crew onboard, due east of the river Tyne, the approximate latitude we'd been fishing in.

In the 'Leeds' that night, I couldn't wait to ask the two old boys, George and Bob, how they'd got on in the nightclub with the two, leggy girls the previous week and asked the pair on their arrival.

The old boys looked at each other and grinned, not answering, while waiting for Les to pull the two pints. On arrival of the ale, deliberately prevaricating, they quaffed the brew, while I awaited an answer, as did the barman, who'd also drooled at the two lovelies.

"Shall we tell 'em?" Bob asked his partner in crime.

"Ah don't know, what d' yer think?" from his accomplice.

"One of you tell us," Les called out, frustrated. No one was going to get served till his curiosity had been satisfied.

"You tell 'em then," Bob said.

"Naw, you tell 'em."

When the pair couldn't string out their tale any longer without the landlord blowing a fuse, Bob said, "yer pair o' daft buggers, yer don't think we'd go nightclubbin'. We left 'em outside t' pub an' went t' Dolphin for a couple o' pints."

* * * * * *

The massive spread of herring spawn on the grounds had, by the following Sunday, attracted huge amounts of haddock, whiting and codlings and dozens of boats were again traversing back and forth across this ground, all taking huge hauls. Much of this mass was immature fish but with significant quantities of quality stuff. The sorting, handling and gutting of this bulk was labour intensive, especially for the smaller boats with only three hands on board. On taking big hauls, some were forced to return to harbour to sort their catch. The work was difficult for the bigger vessels too, even those carrying five crewmen, as they were taking more fish. We'd shipped up a young lad, Dougie, on a half share, to help with this bulk and were just managing to clear the decks each time before hauling. We were only doing short tows in case our net became damaged with the weight of fish and spawn so there was no time for any rest or even, on some hauls, a cup of tea. It was exhausting work.

I opened the wheelhouse window in the early afternoon of the second day and could see the exhausted faces staring back. I announced the news they were expecting but didn't want to hear. "We'll pull it up as soon as yer get cleared away. Ah've been over the ground a few times now."

Sid, who'd been unable to prepare a proper meal for the lads, vented his wrath shouting, "we'd get a cigarette and a cup o' tea even if we were in jail."

Equally tired and annoyed at the outburst I yelled back, "yea but t' difference is, you don't 'ave t' be 'ere."

We'd both forgotten the outburst by the time we'd hauled up the net but I took his point and as soon as we'd shot again, I asked him to go to the galley and start preparing a dinner for after the next haul.

Mid-afternoon, as always, the Whitby vessels began to radio ashore, notifying their agent of their various requirements for their return to port in the evening. The first skipper came over the airways saying, "can you ask John Oliver t' look at our hydraulics when we get in, we're losing pressure."

The next one, shortly after asked, "can John Oliver come an' fix our electrics, the dynamo isn't chargin'." John Oliver was this famous old port's mechanical troubleshooter and the requests for his services were endless and diverse. This procedure had long been a source of humour among the Scarborough skippers.

It was immensely funny when, during a break in the transmissions, an anonymous Scarborough voice broke the silence saying, "my Missus is about to 'ave a baby, can you ask John Oliver t' go round and deliver it."

Not to be outdone another said, "me granny needs some 'eart surgery. When can John Oliver operate?"

"It's time we switched to a private channel fo' reporting in," came a disgruntled Whitby voice. It wasn't long before this happened.

By the end of the week we'd had two landings with two hundred kit each time. This was a tremendous amount of fish, yielding a large wage packet but at a huge physical cost. I certainly wasn't in any state for a long night in the pub following our Thursday evening landing.

## Chapter 4

# An Anniversary to Remember

Gathered in the Leeds Arms one evening in October amongst a crowd from the Diving Club, three of us were relating and reliving a voyage we'd done together on board the *Independence* when she was almost new. The vessel had to return to her birthplace to be slipped and have a second sonar installed. This electronic equipment worked on a different frequency from the existing machine and had a greater range. Though part of her original specification, this kit hadn't been available when she was built. Rather than bother my crew with this twenty-four hour passage trip, Pete and Roger had volunteered to accompany me. Both were good sailors and able to keep watch.

We sailed late in the afternoon, when both men had finished work for the weekend. The weather was fine but we got off to an uncertain start. A few hours into the trip, as I lay in my bunk reading, my new crew plotting and charting our course north, an emergency alarm sounded. I thought I was familiar with all the electronic sounds my vessel could make, but this was a new alert and I flew from my berth in a panic. "What's wrong?" I asked Pete, who was standing at the top of the wheelhouse steps.

"Dunno," he said, shrugging his shoulders. "Rog' was cooking some stew in the galley and the gas bottle ran dry. He went onto the roof to change it."

I walked out onto the afterdeck to find an embarrassed Roger, spanner in hand, looking down at me. Instead of swapping the flow valve from the empty cylinder to its full neighbour, he'd opened the little cabinet door marked, 'Halon Gas'. This locker was alarmed and housed the valve and bottle intended to flood the engine space with inert gas in the event of fire. There was no harm done and the sound died with the closing of the door, but it was fun teasing Roger about this faux pas.

Roger laughed nervously when I repeated this tale to those present in the pub but then said, "ok smart arse, let me tell 'em about your dumplings." Without awaiting a response he described how, when his stew was almost ready, I'd suggested we have suet duffs to complement the meal. Roger didn't know how to make these delicious savouries so I'd volunteered, knowing the instructions were on the packet. I didn't tell him I'd never made dumplings before. Raiding Sid's baking cupboard, I found the required ingredients and mixed the full box of suet, together with proportionate flour and a pinch of salt into a bowl with water, making a thick, gooey, white texture ready for moulding. Rather than making the eight to twelve, small dumplings recommended on the box, I opted to make just one dough-ball for each of us. Shaping the entire mixture into three spheres, I attempted to space the balls equally in the bubbling pan of delicious, lean beef and vegetables. I wasn't sure if I'd achieved this aim, as my 'twenty-minute floaters' almost sunk without trace. I replaced the lid and went up to the wheelhouse to see how the enthusiastic navigators were doing and to report that the duffs would be ready soon.

Fifteen minutes later Roger went below to the galley to prepare the table and came back chuckling. "Come an' look at your puddings, Master Chef." Pete and I followed him, to find the galley full of steam. The pan lid was raised several inches from its other half and three huge dumplings, almost the size of footballs were supporting the dome and hanging over the edge of the pan. Tasty liquid was dribbling down between the duff and the steaming pot onto the stove, sizzling and turning the blue flame to flickering yellow.

The story of my culinary disaster brought more loud laughter and in a vain attempt to salvage some scrap of dignity I said, "yeh, but they tasted alright."

The tale of our exploits moved on to our arrival in Fraserburgh, the following day. After a brief meeting with the boat-builder and tradesmen to ascertain the work programme, we cleaned the boat and ourselves then went ashore. It was too late to catch the train south from Aberdeen, so we'd sleep aboard tonight and leave the following morning. I intended to return with my crew on completion of the work at the end of the week and fish our way home. Our plan now was to have a few beers then eat ashore, rather than mess up the galley again, and eventually we arrived at the Royal Hotel's restaurant, a little wobbly and giggling.

We enjoyed a good meal, washed down with beer and a bottle of wine then opted for cheese and biscuits. Within a minute of our dour, plump waitress placing the basket on our table, Roger, reaching across, knocked the full container of crisp crackers to the floor, scattering its contents. "Crumbs," I said. "Yer in bother now," and looked round for the lady in black. She was already on her way and before we'd any chance of retrieval, the fiery dragon was at our table, muttering in her broad, Scottish dialect.

The lady was not in the least mollified when Pete chipped in, "he was countin' 'em."

The remains of the disaster were efficiently recovered with dustpan and brush, quickly removed by the still clucking woman but the lady had the last laugh and won our hearts and a tip when, two minutes later, she returned with another basket of biscuits, which she firmly slapped on the table and said, "fifty."

The story told, Colin Lawson, the Diving Club's Chairman, arrived from a committee meeting in the clubhouse, next door. Colin was the unsung hero of this thriving club, who as well as being the figurehead, also kept the place going with the one thousand and one, day-to-day jobs behind the scenes. He loved the controversy and debate within the membership, reporting that at the meeting it had been announced that one of the more shady members of the club had been taken ill. Colin said, "the Committee decided, by a vote of four to three, to send him a get well soon card."

Minutes later I mentioned to our little gang that the following week would see Dotty's and my tenth wedding anniversary. The comment was overheard by Les, listening to our exploits from behind the bar, while pretending to polish glasses. He immediately leaned over, interrupting the conversation and chipped in, "I've beat that twice, with two different wives."

On receipt of various comments, mostly caustic, he retreated to the other end of the bar to serve some long waiting customers.

Also in the gathering was Alf, the Diving Club's 'Honorary Medical Officer'. Alf was an eminent, consultant radiologist at the local hospital who owned a yacht, a private plane and who seemed to have an amazing lifestyle. We'd often spoken in the club and pub and he was affable company. Alf expressed the hope that this significant occasion was to be celebrated and asked what we had planned.

I replied that we were doing nothing special and surprised, he immediately undertook to arrange a dinner for four at a prestigious hotel, overlooking the bay. He confirmed this to Dotty by phone during the week and said he'd also invited along a lovely, widowed lady friend Liz, to make up the quartet. Liz, a former Mayor of Scarborough was delightful company, though slightly eccentric. Her large collection of hats was regularly mentioned in the local press and these were the theme of her numerous talks to ladies guilds and various women's gatherings.

The next Friday evening quickly arrived following an uneventful fishing voyage and we made a special effort to dress for the occasion. Our host was exceedingly kind and courteous, making a point of putting us at ease. Our knowledge of wine was limited so Alf kindly selected appropriate bottles for each course to compliment the choice of food. This was certainly not a lifestyle we were accustomed to and Dotty and I were overwhelmed by the trouble and expense he'd gone to, making our occasion special. Following the meal we retired to the bar and were introduced to the owner of the hotel and also to his son, Anthony, who was busy making cocktails and various other exotic concoctions behind the bar.

The conversation moved to surgery and life at the hospital, where Liz's late husband had been a colleague of Alf. During a lull in the conversation I mentioned that I'd personally performed thousands of open-heart surgery operations. The total focus of attention was on me in an instant and the look of disbelief was obvious.

"Not one of my patients survived though," I said, pausing for effect. "But they were all cod," I added belatedly.

The evening was a memorable occasion for us, one we'd long remember. Anthony seemed very friendly in the intervals between serving and extremely interested in, what for him was a very different way of life, that of the fishing community. He asked lots of questions relating to my work, where I lived and what pubs I frequented. At the end of the evening, following profuse thanks, we took a taxi home, agreeing on our good fortune in having such a genial friend.

The following lunchtime I was in the Diving Club and recounting our special evening to Colin, the Chairman. I suggested that perhaps we should make a reservation for the following Friday, with our wives, to experience this unique hospitality. Colin, very impressed with my narrative, willingly agreed to the plan, so on arriving home I duly rang the establishment and made the booking.

Sailing as usual in the early hours of Sunday morning, we steamed off in a northeasterly direction for about seventy miles. The day was fine and with the barometer steady, there were no imminent weather changes to bother us. The first few hauls were uneventful but when the catch dropped from the net late that night, a nasty looking, porbeagle shark, about six-feet long with savage, jagged teeth dropped to the deck. Sadly, though fortunately for us, the creature was dead.

Leaving the lifeless catch in situ, the net was quickly shot back into the sea and the lads began picking up the haul of cod, haddock and flatfish into ten boxes from around the inert fish, leaving the detritus to be swilled back through the scuppers. A knock on the wheelhouse side caused me to open the window to discover Rusty, looking up. "What we gonna do wi' this?" he asked, looking at and pointing to the inert shark.

The girth on the animal meant it would be extremely heavy to lift and drop below to the fishroom, even if we managed to get the dead weight below without breaking any of the bottom boards. In the hold, the fish would be a major inconvenience to the men boxing and stowing fish. The hold contained five tons of ice in the sides, empty boxes forward and the catch to date stacked at the after end. There was no space to ice and keep this strange catch. The porbeagle was of little value and as we were to be at sea for a few days yet, there was no point in keeping the carcass on the exposed deck, where it would deteriorate quickly and soon begin to smell.

"Kick it through t' scuppers," I answered, eyeing the size of the fish and the hole in the boat's side. It looked a tight fit but I thought the shark would pass through the gap with some persuasion. We'd nearly lost Bluey through the scuppers one day in poor weather, when he'd lost his footing while kicking unwanted material back into the sea.

I watched through the window as the four positioned themselves around the unfortunate creature, two holding the pectoral fins, one pulling from the dorsal and one raising the tail and pushing. Using the rolling of the boat to the best advantage, they manoeuvred the fish's snout into the gaping scupper. The head of the animal entered the orifice but was soon touching the sides. There was little room to get close now to push or pull, so those closest began stomping and pushing with their heavy sea-boots each time the *Independence* rolled to port. Gradually, inch by inch, the miserable creature made its undignified exit from our vessel, back to the sea. Suddenly, as the widest part of the beast passed through the gap, gravity took control and the rear end of the fish vanished from the deck as the shark nosedived into the depths. Immediately the entire boat began to judder and vibrate, violently. Confused, I leapt for the throttle and eased back the handle to slow speed. My *Independence*, still shaking, though not as severely, was now stationary in the water, restrained by her trawl. The vibrations stopped and I realised we were surrounded by white particles, floating on the surface in the gentle swell. It was a great relief to realise we were not experiencing a major engine failure but that the shark's corpse had been drawn into the nozzle surrounding the propeller and had been minced into morsels. The fulmars following our vessel and feeding on discarded offal, were now gorging on the mass of chopped, buoyant, sharks liver.

With trepidation, I eased the gear lever forward and was delighted when the gauges monitoring the engine were reading normal as the revolutions increased, though there did seem to be some additional vibration. With the stress the machinery had taken, we could have suffered a problem with the gearbox and this was still a possibility. The *Independence* would have to be grounded on our return home so we could inspect her stern gear. The nozzle, about three feet in length, was tapered to draw water in at the forward part, giving more thrust at the narrower, output end. There was less than a half-inch gap between the tip of the sixty-inch diameter propeller blades and the internal tube of the nozzle. The shark must have been well and truly chopped to pieces and it must have been the fish's skeletal bones that caused the boat to vibrate so intensely. This theory was proved when a mangled tail was discovered among the catch when we hauled the trawl.

The engine continued to perform faultlessly for the remainder of the trip, despite the massive trauma the shark had caused, though I remained anxious till we were safely back in port. We arrived home at high water, late on Wednesday night, so had time to land our fish then berth the vessel at the top end of the harbour. Here, I was able to visually inspect the propulsion unit next morning before breakfast, to discover the tips of all four propeller blades were distorted. This damage explained the vibration but was only superficial and if the distortion was the only problem, it would be easily rectified.

Crossing the road to the engineers' workshop, I asked for our spare propeller to be fitted and the damaged unit sent for refurbishment. This would be a task for Jack Redman with some assistance. His prowess with big spanners and sledgehammers was well known. Jack wasn't a man for anything technical or intricate but he'd relish attacking and replacing our damaged screw. There was just room to ease the propeller from the nozzle without removing the rudder, which would disappoint him.

It was easy work taking the *Independence* astern again from the dry berth after noon, when the work was completed and the water returned. A quick run around the bay proved the vibration to have gone.

That same evening, once more in the Leeds Arms with our regular, Thursday evening company, I was surprised to see Anthony, the barman from the prestigious hotel walk into the bar. I welcomed him to our little alehouse and introduced him to the members of our group. Thursday nights were always a lot of fun and this one was particularly enjoyable, though the ladies cringed when Paul, a diver who lived close by, mentioned his recent operation. He'd undergone a hip replacement, following a motorcycle accident and had been given the damaged bone as a keepsake.

"What did you do with it?" Dotty asked.

"Well," he said, "I gave it to my dog Sally and when I came out of the house, she was chewing on it by the fire."

When Les called time and rang the bell, Anthony expressed disappointment at the early closure, though out of earshot of the landlord. He'd been engrossed in the banter and was reluctant to see the revelry end. "Why don't you all come up to the hotel?" He suggested. "We've no one in residence until tomorrow. I'll open the bar and we can continue the party."

This seemed a good idea to all present and Colin from the Diving Club ordered two taxis, which arrived within minutes. Dotty and I were given a lift by Anthony, in his souped-up, Mini. This ride was a scary experience. Our driver, wearing driving gloves, charged through town like a bat out of hell. Dotty gripped my hand tightly and we were both pleased to get out of the car, rolling our eyes and wondering if we'd done the right thing. The cabs followed soon after and we entered the imposing building, with its baronial stone hall and fireplace. We followed Anthony through a labyrinth of passages to the basement bar. The place seemed spooky with no staff or clientele around but brightened up when the bar lights and music were switched on.

To our astonishment our host began opening bottles of champagne, mixing the bubbling liquid with Guinness. "You'll like this" he said, "it's 'black velvet'." This was a new concept to all present and quite acceptable, except to Dotty, who wasn't keen on the drink and surreptitiously consigned the contents of her glass to the nearest flowerpot. With more joke telling and silly antics, the time passed really quickly. Most of those present had to be at work the next morning, so in the early hours, cabs were again called for. Anthony was reluctant to drive and we were pleased to hear him say this. He must have been well over the legal limit when he'd brought us to the hotel.

Colin, who still had an almost full glass when the taxis arrived, opted to wait awhile to finish his drink and get a later cab, so we all bade him goodnight, thanking our host for his generous hospitality.

It was the same Colin who rang next morning in a state of extreme agitation. "I'm not going t' that bloody place again. You can cancel the meal. If you go, you're on your own."

"What's the problem?" I asked. "Why the change o' mind?"

"I'm just not going, that's all there is to it."

It was a while before I was able to draw out of him the reason for his sudden cancellation. "It was a bloody nightmare," he said. "When you left, your friend locked the door then dropped his trousers. He told me he loved me. I tried telling him there was some mistake, that this was a misunderstanding and I wasn't that way inclined, but he wouldn't listen. I told him I'd been waiting all my life to be seduced, but not by a bloody man. It wasn't till I threatened to thump him that he let me out and even then he asked me for a kiss. He didn't bloody get one. I'm not going back there, I'm telling you."

I couldn't help laughing, which made poor Colin even more irate. Eventually, when he'd stopped talking, I had to admit that if the same incident had happened to me, I wouldn't have told anyone.

"Well maybe I've saved you from the same fate," he said, matter of factly.

I cancelled the meal.

# Chapter 5
# Poor Weather

There was plenty of water in the harbour when I walked on the North Wharf to sail at midnight. It was a dark night, with no moon and hardly a breath of wind. The only light onshore was from a single lamp standard, set in a concrete block near the road but there was plenty of illumination from the *Cassamanda's* deck-lights. She was tied alongside the *Independence* and her crew were making ready to let go. I approached and spoke to her skipper, Bev on the quayside. He said he wasn't expecting to go far before shooting his trawl, having recently switched from bottom trawling for cod to mid-water fishing for sprats. These little fish were again abundant in their billions close inshore along the coast, all the way from the Tyne to Flamborough Head. Even the harbour was full of the small, herring-like creatures, their ripples like rain on the water as they broke the surface.

I realised Barry was already on board our vessel when *Independence's* engine fired up in a cloud of white smoke. He'd been looking after the engine-room for a few weeks now. "Yer engine seems OK again," he commented, reminding me of an incident a few weeks earlier, when a huge bang, then a dreadful clattering sound from below had summoned me to the engine-room in double quick time. I was horrified to see a cylinder block at the side of the engine smashed and a con-rod, which was normally attached to one of the eight powerful pistons, protruding through the gap, thrusting back and forth as the engine rotated. Avoiding this danger, I'd reached across, stopping the engine before the machine damaged itself further.

We were stuck thirty-five miles offshore with no motive power so I'd been grateful to Bev for recovering our fishing gear and to Colin in the *Our Heritage* for towing us back home. Luckily, it was towards the end of the week and they wouldn't lose too much fishing time. I told Bev how efficient the Kelvin engine company had been. I'd contacted the factory via a ship to shore link call and the firm immediately dispatched one of their team of 'troubleshooters', who arrived in Scarborough from Glasgow not long after we were secured alongside the pier. Laughing, I told Bev of one of these mechanics, Alan Duff, who was a legend, even among these tough, Glaswegian engineers. His workmates joked that he was kept in a cage and only allowed out when there was an engine to be repaired. Alan was a hard drinking, hard living man, known to take whisky even with his breakfast.

I quickly told Bev the tale of Alan Duff, who, while staying in a hotel in a large, Scottish fishing port, was drinking his way along the top shelf of the establishment's bar one evening, following a day in a boat's engine-room. Ordering a VAT 69 whisky, he'd downed the drink in one gulp, only to spew the spirit immediately onto the bar, to the disgust of the barman and customers. Unperturbed he'd growled, "thaats twa peppery, gimme a 'Bells'."

Bev crossed the *Independence's* deck and made his way to his own wheelhouse. At his nod I threw off his ropes, allowing the crew to haul them aboard. Two minutes later, deck-lights extinguished, with only her stern light and the loom from her galley door visible, *Cassamanda* crossed the harbour towards the entrance. It took only a few brief preparations before *Independence* too, was heading seaward. With the usual wave to the watch-keeper on the lighthouse, as he identified our vessel, logging us out, I took a wide berth of the outer pier and set the autopilot on northeast by north. Close ahead, *Cassamanda's* deck-lights were again shining brightly. Wondering what was occurring, I reached for the handset but as if reading my mind, Bev's voice came over loudly on the radio. "Mind my bloody codends as yer come past, Nommy."

Our mooring ropes were hardly coiled and he was already shooting his trawl. "T' water's black from top t' bottom 'ere," he reported. I turned on the nearest sounder and he was right. In the space between the surface and the bottom of the screen, normally white, the recording paper was showing continuous black.

"Yer'll be back in t' 'arbour an' tied up again before we get t' where we're goin'," I replied, altering to the east to avoid his stern, envious that he was on pay already. We'd be at least nine hours before arriving at the 'Potholes'. Sprats were back at fifty pounds a ton but I didn't really fancy this method of fishing. I'd tried the job in my old boat, *Courage* during the previous winter, when the glut of catches had reduced the value of sprats dramatically. Arranging to speak to Bev on the 'big set', the medium-range radio, following the 1400 shipping forecast if he was still at sea, I said, "I 'ope yer fill 'er up" and turned to see Sid hovering in the doorway, pot of tea in hand. I was pleased to let our cook take the first watch and retired to my bunk. Rusty and Bluey would also take three-hour spells before we stopped to shoot our trawl.

With three miles to go, Bluey switched on the cabin light and called all hands. There was tea and coffee on the mess-deck table but I took mine to the wheelhouse, taking over the watch. I was able to wake up and orientate myself, check shipping movements and position the boat where we were to start fishing. There was only one target on the radar, a large vessel, four miles ahead.

These grounds, at a depth of about forty fathoms, were patchy, with sand and hard rock and also what was thought to be a series of holes, nearly sixty fathoms deep, hence the name, 'Potholes'. As I and other skippers built up more information on subsequent visits to this area, these holes proved to be one long, narrow trench stretching for miles in an easterly direction. Weeks earlier there'd been good fishing here and I was hoping for more of the same. I picked up the binoculars and it was with disappointment that I realised the ship on the radar was a huge, modern, green, stern trawler. As we narrowed the distance, I made out the registration numbers, NS 138 on her flared bow. Checking the numbers and letters in 'Olsens Fishermen's Almanac', I was further dismayed to discover she was the 370 gross tons and 1800 horse-powered, *Ben Edra*. This was massive catching power but we were here now and they certainly wouldn't be here for nothing. Our net was soon on the bottom and I marked our every movement on the plotter, shading the plastic paper with permanent marker, orange for soft and brown for hard ground and marking the edges and depth of the holes.

"Hulloo, the bonnie, blue Scots boat on me portside. This is the *Ben Edra*. Are yer listenin' on this channel?" I looked to the ten-channel, VHF scanner above my head. The skipper, with a broad Tyneside accent, confirming my information, was transmitting on channel 13, the frequency of our local boats. He'd seen the FR registration on the side of my vessel and thought we were from north of the border.

Tuning to this number on the dial, I lifted the handset to reply. "Yea, *Ben Edra,* this is t' Scarborough boat, *Independence*. I'm receivin' you, over."

He wouldn't have been able to find our registration number or name, as we were not yet listed in 'Olsens'. The skipper was my instant friend when he said what a lovely looking vessel she was, expressing surprise that she was less than sixty feet in length, as we exchanged dialogue. He'd only been fishing in the area for a few hours I was pleased to hear and hadn't hauled his gear yet. We agreed to stay on this frequency and to keep in touch.

The Geordie reported a good catch when he hauled up his gear, so I was optimistic that we'd get something proportionate. I wasn't disappointed. The codend rushed to the surface as the mouth of the net came alongside and it looked a good haul. The floating bag was immediately engulfed by hundreds of fulmars, pecking at the fish heads protruding from the mesh. These seabirds, like mini albatross in appearance, were encountered only occasionally inshore. Fulmars were hardy seabirds, spending most of the year at sea, only returning to shore in the spring to breed. Locally known as 'mollies', they were the most stupid of birds and would cackle loudly and fight each other furiously, while the food they fought over sank beyond reach.

There was too much fish in the net to take onboard in one lift and we left half the haul trapped in the sleeve of the overboard net, but it wasn't long before this too was bagged and emptied into the fish pound on deck. The catch consisted of quality mixed fish, though predominantly haddock. My new friend on the big trawler was impressed with our catch report. He hadn't caught much more than us, though our engine power was about one-quarter of his. I was pleased too, as this clearly showed our fishing gear was working well.

The trawl was soon on the bottom again and the crew began processing the catch. It was obvious, even above the noise of the engine, radios and sounders when a box of guts was being swilled away. The loud cackling and flapping of wings from the hundreds of fulmars, as they half paddled and half flew to keep up with the moving boat grew to a crescendo. It was strange seeing these birds, splashing alongside, not airborne but keeping up with the boat, in contrast to the seabirds closer to home that followed the boats on the wing, diving into the sea for the scraps.

We fished on through the night and into the next day, hauling every five hours. The results were fairly consistent. We had the makings of a really good trip, but as always, something comes along to mar the expectations. The shipping forecast was predicting northwest gales, increasing to severe gale nine and perhaps storm force ten. I called my Geordie pal to inform him of the weather prospects but he'd also been tuned to the BBC. I was reluctant to leave this lucrative fishing, so decided to play the situation as circumstances dictated. I'd been in this fine vessel long enough to know that she could cope with anything the weather could throw at us, so wasn't unduly concerned for our welfare.

It was later in the day when the wind veered and strengthened and it happened quickly. In turn the sea state changed from a slight, rolling swell to large frothing waves in a few short minutes. We continued to tow the trawl but my little craft felt smaller as the seas grew and we were rolling quite heavily. I could hear unsecured cups and pans smashing and banging on the galley floor but knew Sid would soon sort those out. I looked at the tide tables for Scarborough and calculated we could be back in port in time for the morning's market. We had enough fish on board to make the run worthwhile so I called the lads from their beds, though I doubted they were sleeping. In bad weather we had to wedge ourselves in our bunks diagonally, using our feet to prevent plummeting from our 'holes in the wall', to the cabin floor. Dispensing with the usual hot beverage, we scrambled the net on board and in less than fifteen minutes we were homeward bound.

The meagre catch greatly reduced by the appauling weather affirmed my decision. Contacting the trawler, I was answered by the Mate, the skipper being turned in, and told him we were beating a retreat for home.

We were broadside to the waves, so I headed the *Independence* on a more southerly course, putting the swell on her quarter till the lads had cleared the fish from the deck. It wasn't long before they were beating a path to the galley. We headed southwest again. Following the next forecast, which predicted more of the same, I switched to the inter-ship Medium Frequency waveband making contact with Bev. We'd had several conversations since sailing together. The *Cassamanda* had been in to land once and was on her way back in again, though this time due to the poor weather.

Bev said, "Bobby's filled 'er up."

This was no surprise to me and I replied, "what's 'e got this time?" Bobby Mainprize, skipper of the *Pathfinder,* was a good fisherman and his boat was fitted with a very powerful sonar. This gear could detect dense shoals of sprats at a range of more than a mile. He'd had landings of eighty tons and more. His boat looked like a sand barge some days coming into port, she was so deep in the water.

"No, I mean 'e's really filled 'er up. She sank this afternoon, somewhere north o' Whitby. T' weather freshened when she was full o' sprats, an' 'e 'ad a deckload as well. 'E couldn't keep t' fishroom 'atches on. Nobody was lost but they all 'ad t' get into t' liferaft."

This was bad news. She was a big, fine sixty-eight foot boat with twin, 'Gardner' engines and had a fantastic catching record. Bobby must have been mortified when his vessel's fishroom had flooded but at least no one had been lost, which was a blessing. Boats can be replaced. I informed Bev that we were also on our way home but had about sixty miles yet to travel and we were rolling our sides under. I told him that despite the weather, Sid was in the galley, attempting to cook our dinner, something we both found incredible. I ended the conversation saying I'd see him on the fish market in the morning, then cradled the handset as a particularly large swell heeled the *Independence* massively to starboard, then back to port. I clung on to the arms of the chair and was almost catapulted out by the force. Water washed up the starboard side windows. For a second I thought she wasn't going to come back up, but she did. My faith in this lovely boat was instantly restored and I chided myself for doubting her. A loud curse came from below as she steadied down again. I looked through the toughened glass and was amazed to see the lifebuoy was missing from its bracket on the port side of the wheelhouse. The cork ring had been washed from its holder. How far over had she gone to do this?

Leaving the wheelhouse briefly, I made my way to the galley to see how Sid was faring. His face was like thunder. He'd been attempting to fry fish in the giant pan, designed to his own specifications. This rectangular vessel, fitting exactly on two rings of the stove within the fiddle, had been proved in poor weather on several occasions since we'd taken delivery of the boat, but to even attempt to fry anything in this weather was almost beyond comprehension. Strangely, there was virtually no spillage from the fish pan as he only used the smallest amount of oil, allowing the motion of the boat to move the cooking fluid around the fryer. The focus of Sid's annoyance was the pan of peas that had escaped from the retaining fiddle and spilled its contents, not only on the adjacent bulkhead but also across part of the deckhead.

Quickly regaining his composure, he wiped up the mess and grinned, pleased his construction had passed the ultimate test and said, "peas are off." Bracing himself like an acrobat, he cleverly handled the steaming kettle and a mug, brewing himself a pot of strong tea before setting off for the wheelhouse, shouting, "grub up," down the cabin stairwell, en route. Sid took control of the boat while I struggled to eat this tasty meal, which he'd miraculously produced. Minutes later three figures appeared in the galley to join me.

The table was covered with wet cloths and all the condiments were stowed in the rack in the centre. We sat at the table hardly speaking, concentrating on eating, apart from the occasional, "yer rollin' bastard," from Rusty, as a larger than average lurch occurred. Only a fork could be used. Our plates were kept horizontal with the other hand, tilting the platter to counter the roll of the boat. Any deviation from this movement resulted in spillage. It was quite surreal being part of a synchronized eating team.

When Sid returned to the galley, substituted by Bluey, he took his meal from the oven, where it had been wedged, joining us at the table. In this weather the conversation was of the *Gaul*, the large trawler, which had been lost at the North Cape of Norway a few years earlier. Sid was sure she'd been lost due to the stress of weather, despite the talk of Russian involvement. He'd been on board the *Arctic Galliard,* a ship bigger than the *Gaul,* for a couple of years and had experienced flooding of the factory deck from a huge sea, crashing up the stern ramp. He said a subsequent wave following up, could have had catastrophic results.

He was sceptical of the theory that the *Gaul* was spying, though confirmed that our government did indeed sponsor voyages by trawlers to the Barents Sea and White Sea on espionage missions. He'd served on such vessels and it was impossible to keep the trips secret. He said, "I was in Raynor's pub near the Hull Fish Dock one day an' the barmaid told me my ship was going spying next time out. She was right."

It was an uncomfortable passage home but we arrived unscathed to discharge our catch for the Tuesday morning market. We were greeted by Dad and Joxy, waiting to take our ropes. Both had cryptic comments as we berthed alongside the fish pier. "Yer must 'ave 'ad a pasting," Dad said, pointing to the empty lifebuoy bracket.

"Where've yer been, yer stormy bastards? Most o' t' boats were in last night," added Joxy.

The prices were excellent and we were delighted with the result of our broken trip. We'd done well for less than thirty-six hours fishing. If we could add to this, we were in for a bumper week. The weather was still poor but it was only Tuesday. The forecast was now promising an easing of the wind within the next twenty-four hours, so asking my crew to turn up again at 1800, I made my way back to see a surprised Dotty and family. It was unusual for me to be home midweek since I'd been in the *Independence*.

The television news headlines of the day were fears for the crew of a merchant ship, missing on her way from Hartlepool to Denmark, carrying a cargo of sprats to a fishmeal factory. The newsreader spoke of a 'Mayday' call and exceptional weather, hampering the search. This was bad news and I could vouch for the weather.

The wind had fallen away by 1800 and the forecast at that time predicted light to moderate winds. We sailed, along with three or four other boats whose skippers were also keen to add to their earnings for the week. The remaining vessels would leave on the next tide and the harbour would be empty before breakfast.

There was still a northwest swell in the water, which grew as we cleared the land but though dark, it was obvious the waves had lost their force and would fall away quickly with no wind for support. The inevitable inter-ship chatter on the radio came rapidly as the usual questions were asked across the airwaves. "Where are yer bound?"

"Where wer' yer fishin' last trip?"

"Did you 'ave owt?"

"What did it consist of?"

Though most skippers were in touch with each other regularly and exchanged catch information every haul, there were occasional tall stories told. Everyone could read between the lines and gained some insight from the information transmitted. I laughed as Bill Pashby, skipper of the *Valiant*, who'd landed another good catch, was telling Col most of his fish was caught in the last haul.

I said we were going back to the Potholes but it was a long way to go so late in the week, so no one expressed interest in accompanying us, despite our previous results. Maybe they were right. If the fish had taken off when we got there, there'd be no time left to try alternative grounds.

It was still dark when we arrived back on the grounds and the swell had reduced significantly, encouraged by a change of wind direction. A single target on the radar told me the big trawler was still in the area. It would be interesting to hear how they'd fared since our departure, so as soon as the gear was on the bottom I picked up the handset.

*"Ben Edra, Ben Edra, Independence* callin'. Are yer receivin' me Geordie, over?"

Seconds later, loud and clear, came the reply. "Why aye man, where've yer been these las' twa days. First sign of a bit o' weather an' you Yorkies run awa."

This wasn't meant maliciously. He was only joking but I was still defensive. In a ship of his size he was expected to ride out any weather and we could have coped too but I'd opted not to. I replied saying we'd gone for a quick landing while the weather was poor, to make the best of the markets.

"Ah dinna blame yer bonnie lad. Ah'd ha' done the same ma sel'." He went on to tell how only a few hours after we'd left the area, the Tyne Coastguard had relayed the Mayday message from the merchant vessel, carrying the sprats. The *Ben Edra* had been one of the vessels engaged in the search for the missing craft. The searching ships had little information to go on, as the position given by the casualty was imprecise. It was likely her cargo had shifted, causing her to list, then capsize. He said the weather had been horrendous and there would have been little chance of her crew getting in a liferaft. They'd have had no hope of survival at all in the water. The *Ben Edra* and a few other passing ships had searched all night and into the next day, covering a wide area but had found nothing. The skipper said they'd only been fishing again for about twelve hours. We'd missed very little and the fishing was only now picking up again, with the settling weather.

We fished away steadily for the next twenty-four hours then set off for home again on Thursday around midday, satisfied we'd enough fish to make a good wage and allow some time at home before sailing again early on Sunday.

Coincidently it was at the Potholes where we were to encounter our next spell of extreme weather, though we hadn't gone there through choice. On our way home, late on a cold, December afternoon with only a few miles to go, the bay and outer pier were clearly visible on the radar. The forecast was again bad and predicting northeasterly gales, possibly increasing to storm force 10 with poor visibility and snow showers. The wind and swell were already growing.

Mike 'Andy' Anderson, skipper of the *Nicola Suzanne*, nicknamed the 'yellow peril' due to her vivid hull colour, was already in the harbour and contacted me on the VHF. He'd been listening on the MF radio and heard Bev calling. The *Cassamanda,* now back trawling again, was ninety miles northeast by north of Scarborough with her net fouled in her propeller. Unable to free the obstruction, they were in need of assistance.

Andy said he'd leave port to tow Bev home but was concerned that if the forecasted weather came, his boat would struggle to make any speed, steaming head on into wind and sea. It had already strengthened to near gale force, so I said we'd go into the harbour to land our catch then I'd call him on the VHF to check his progress.

With our fish ashore and the wind still freshening, it had begun to snow. I contacted Andy and wasn't surprised to discover the 'yellow peril' was making hard work of the passage and had only travelled six miles since we'd last spoken, more than an hour previously. My *Independence* was slightly bigger, with a more powerful engine, so I offered to pick up the casualty, much to the disappointment of my crew, who were expecting to go home. I spoke to Bev, telling him we were on our way.

We passed the *Nicola Suzanne* about two miles out as she steamed down wind at full speed. We were punching the growing seas, throwing spray high in the air beyond the length of the boat, as we butted into the gale. It was a wild night and we were unable to make anywhere near our best speed as the *Independence* ploughed into the big seas. Her head was dipping deep then lifting, the buoyancy and height of her whaleback preventing most of the green lumps from engulfing the deck. The windows were occasionally obliterated by snow but the spray from each big wave quickly swilled them clear again. The radar screen was a mass of clutter from snow and sea, only clearing occasionally between showers. We were mostly steaming blind.

It was the following day, more than eighteen hours after setting out when we arrived at the approximate position of the *Cassamanda*. We'd kept in radio contact throughout the night and had been in VHF range for the past few hours, frequently updating her position on the chart as she blew downwind. It was still snowing heavily and we were closing on the location when I thought I could discern a target on the radar, among all the other clutter. Easing back the throttle to slow, we headed towards the constant blip as the lads made their way to the deck, wearing as many warm clothes as would fit underneath their oilskins. As we approached closer to the target, I opened a wheelhouse window, now completely opaque with snow. For a moment as the glass slid down, the layer of snow stayed in place, then a gust of wind suddenly breached the wall and a mass of snow shot into the wheelhouse, engulfing me and coating the floor.

A yell from for'ard informed me they could see the casualty, lying broadside to the swell. I notified Bev that we had visual contact and minutes later we passed slowly across his bows. Though rolling heavily, his crew, while holding tight to the whaleback railings, were able to grab our heaving line. Next they hauled the wire warp across, shackling the end to a chain bridle, which they'd prepared in advance. Bluey, at our winch, released the brake, allowing the wire to flow freely as I turned the *Independence* to starboard through a hundred and eighty degrees. The brake was screwed down with a hundred fathoms of wire between the boats and the cable quickly tightened, water flying in all directions as the wire stretched horizontally with a twang. The throttle was increased gradually and soon we were making good speed, downwind and downhill to enjoy an uneventful, relatively comfortable, passage home.

We slowed down and shortened the towline by fifty fathoms a few hours before dawn, knowing we'd have to wait till first light before attempting the entrance. I had grave concerns about our safe passage into port, until I spoke to Col, on the radio. He was calling from his boat in the harbour and offered to come out to assist with the difficult manoeuvre round the pier end. Signing off, he went ashore to ring his crew.

Daylight was slow in coming, held back by the heavy, snow-filled clouds. The weather remained poor and with the wind still from the northeast, big swells were breaking across the bay. Scarborough Lifeboat was poised at the water's edge on her carriage, the tractor belching exhaust smoke, which was carried horizontally in the wind. Her oilskin-clad crew were huddled in what little shelter was available on the thirty-seven foot 'Oakley' type boat, ready to deploy should we get into difficulty. She was no longer commanded by the legendary, Bill Sheader. He'd recently taken retirement from his voluntary position, due to age.

As the grey light strengthened, *Our Heritage* came steaming from the harbour at speed. Her head ploughed into a big sea rolling across the entrance, throwing white water skywards. She lifted her head, shaking off plumes of spray, only to plunge into the trough beyond the breaker. Her white masthead light, glowing brightly in the gloom, suddenly went out. The entire lantern, along with her fishing lights, had been unshipped from their mountings and were left swinging, uncontrolled, around the mast top, attached only by their wire flexes. Col wasn't aware of this minor mishap. He was steering his sturdy vessel into the next breaker, though now he'd gained deeper water, this sea didn't carry as much force.

Half a mile off, towing dead slow and head to wind, we waited for our pal to join us. On arrival, his crew passed a heavy rope from her whaleback to the stern of the *Cassamanda*. She was now our brake vessel and I felt we had a good chance of getting our charge into harbour safely.

Very slowly, the three boats in line turned towards the white, winking light, signalling the East Pier, still clear in the poor visibility. We hardly seemed to be moving but this was the best speed to approach, even when not towing other craft. Fifty yards from the harbour mouth, I engaged the hydraulics to power the winch and Bluey made his way forward. Our square stern was lifting and dropping in the surf and lumps of green sea were breaking over the transom, only to rapidly drain away though our gaping scuppers.

My heart was racing as very, very slowly, we hauled our wire back onto the winch, like an angler playing a giant fish. The distance between our vessels shortened as the *Cassamanda* was pushed towards us on the swell. "That'll do," I bawled to the winchman with about twenty fathoms remaining and he screwed the brake down hard. Taking up the slack, I nudged the throttle forward and we edged closer to the entrance. I had to take a wide sweep to starboard so as not to drag our charge into the Lighthouse Pier while the *Our Heritage* restraining her, took an even bigger curve, preventing the casualty from surging into our stern.

The *Cassamanda* missed the corner of the pier by inches and though going dead slow, we still seemed to be moving far too fast, but at least now I could disengage our engine periodically. The experience must have been even worse for Bev, as he had no control whatever of his vessel throughout the operation. The VHF airwaves crackled as we entered harbour and his distinct voice came over loudly. "Well yer got us 'ere ah suppose, but it took yer long enough."

I acknowledged his gratitude with a short profanity, then for the first time, took the opportunity to look to the West Pier, expecting to see the Pierman with a heaving line. The East Pier was crowded with onlookers watching the real life drama unfold and I could pick out many familiar faces. Ten minutes later we were tied up safely alongside the quay.

* * * * * *

Christmas was almost upon us. Cod had been plentiful the past few weeks on the hard ground between Flamborough Head and Filey Brigg, though the northern end of this ground was prohibited for trawling and policed by the Northeastern Sea Fisheries Committee. Offenders were prosecuted in the Magistrates Court and fined heavily if found guilty. The fast patrol boat frequently cruised the coast between the Tees and the Humber but concentrated on this area and a similar prohibited section to the north of Whitby. The Filey coblemen, or 'little Russians', as they were known, complained frequently and vociferously to the District Inspector about trawlers operating off their town, but when the fish were there, the trawlers would occasionally take a chance. These artificial zones, which had been closed to trawling for around a hundred years, served no useful purpose, apart from giving these coblemen an exclusive area for their own pots and lines. The Filey fishermen even resorted to dumping old washing machines, ovens and fridges on the grounds to damage the trawlers' nets.

We'd been fishing in and out of this forbidden territory for the past few days with several other boats but were keeping a close eye on the radar when transgressing, as the patrol boat sometimes steamed around in the dark without displaying navigation lights. It was now Thursday and six o'clock in the morning. We were on our finishing trawl before going to land a good catch. The last report from ashore said the bogeyman was in Scarborough harbour and had spent the night there. We could expect his appearance at any time and it was only six miles from the harbour to the edge of the zone. This was a very risky situation, but there were lots of fish marks on the sounder, so we were hopeful of a good haul. Dad had been on watch on the lighthouse since midnight and I'd asked him to let us know if the patrol vessel showed any signs of life. If the boat sailed unheralded, she could be among the transgressors before any of us could get our gear up and clear the area. It would be a close call, even with notice. We'd had a lucky escape two weeks earlier, when our trawl had caught a wreck inside the zone and we'd been stuck for hours, waiting for the tide to ease before we could pull the net free. We would have been a sitting duck, had the patrol boat appeared.

"The budgie has left its cage. Repeat, the budgie has left its cage." This was Dad's voice over the radio, warning us the enemy had sailed. The crafty devils must have made their preparations to depart under the cover of darkness so the watch-keepers had minimum notice of their leaving.

I dashed down the cabin ladder, turned on the light and called out, "come on lads, quick, t' patrol boat's on 'is way."

To their credit, my crew were out of their bunks in seconds, two of them heading for the deck to commence hauling in shirtsleeves, while the other two donned oilskins. The pairs exchanged places as the wires trickled in, so all would be prepared when the doors broke the surface. I noticed two of the other boats in the area were also lit up and hauling, but the fourth, which I thought was the *Cassamanda,* was in darkness, apart from navigation lights and was still fishing. I could see the blip which was the policeman on the radar and called out on the private channel, "get movin', t' bogeyman's comin'."

There was no answer or acknowledgement and it was several minutes before Bev's voice came over the airwaves. "T' bloody volume's been turned down on t' VHF while I was listenin' t' news on t' radio. 'Ave yer seen this boat on t' radar, t' nor'ard? It's comin' this way fast. It could be 'matey'."

"It is," I answered, "I've been callin' yer."

His deck lights came on immediately but they were going to be too late. Our net was alongside and the lads scrambled the sleeve of the trawl in quickly, finding a good bag of cod, which was hauled onto the deck. The catch was now ignored while the wing ends were lifted inboard, then with relief I headed east out of the area at speed with the lights off. The other two vessels, *Soolee* and *Our Heritage* were also making good speed, though the latter was a few minutes behind. The two blips astern were converging. Bev had been nicked.

The patrol boat skipper was heard on the radio as the two blips merged on the radar. "*Cassamanda*, *Cassamanda,* this is the Fisheries Patrol Vessel. According to my calculations, you are infringing the prohibited zone and I am obliged to caution you. I will be coming on board your vessel."

Bev replied, attempting to explain that he'd accidentally drifted into the zone while hauling his net, but he wasn't convincing.

"Take your punishment like a man, son," called out an anonymous voice over the airwaves, though the distinct, southern accent of Alan Jagger from *Soolee* was unmistakable. Alan, a tall, suave, Londoner was an ex deep-sea skipper who'd previously fished out of Hull. Now he commanded this smaller vessel working from Scarborough and fitted in well. His comment caused more amusing chatter on the radio from boats away from the area and a very ungentlemanly retort from Bev.

Col's voice came over the airwaves next. "We nearly came unstuck there ourselves. There was a bloody fridge stuck in t' bellies. Some bastard 'ad painted, 'From Russia with love', on it."

Knowing the bogeyman had apprehended Bev and we were out of the prohibited zone I altered course for home, arriving an hour later. There were still a few boxes of fish to gut and ice when we were alongside but these were soon cleared. Christmas was approaching far too quickly and now we were about to land our finishing catch before putting extra ropes and fenders out for the festive period. The day boats would fish for a few more days yet but by the weekend the fleet would be tied up. The crews, with time on their hands and plenty of money to spend, would be making mischief. As usual, it was the seafront pubs that would benefit most from this wealth.

"I've brought yer some o' Roy Nightingale's 'ome made wine, like you asked me to," Joxy said, as we chatted while weighing the fish. "You lads usually 'ave a few drinks aboard when yer clew up fo' Christmas, don't yer. I've got some apricot, raspberry and rhubarb. It looks good stuff."

He was right on both counts. When, by mid-morning, the boat was extra specially cleaned, scrubbed and secured and I'd been to the office for our settlings, we gathered round the cabin table with a pack of twenty-four 'Longlife' beers and Roy's wine. It was good stuff, though exceedingly strong. Roy was a driver and a useful, innovative mechanic, who'd married Betty Sheader, a fisherman's daughter. Roy didn't drink the wine himself but enjoyed making many varieties for others to try. He only asked for the cost of the ingredients and wasn't interested in making a profit.

We immediately emptied the first bottle into five mugs and relaxing, laughing and talking about our close call, began to celebrate the start of our Christmas holiday. An hour later we'd drunk the boat dry and were making our way unsteadily across the road to the nearest pub, the Newcastle Packet.

I could hear the noise before entering, so wasn't surprised to see the bar three or four deep with fishermen and all seemed to be talking at once. Rusty spotted some of his mates and with the others in tow, headed off to the end of the bar to join them. Spying Colin from the *Our Heritage,* accompanied by three of his shore helpers, I made my way in his direction. Col was very generous to these men, finding them work and paying them to help land his fish. The three also cleaned and maintained his boat, delivered messages and guarded his fish on the market from predators, both human and feathered.

Colin Jenkinson was one of the top skippers when I was still at school. Regularly breaking port records and fishing in appalling weather, he was an example to all young fishermen and was everything I aspired to be. On Saturdays in summer, when the ice factory couldn't cope with the demand, Col paid me to shovel ice, trucked from Hull, onto his *Our Margaret*. I also transferred ice from these lorries in five and ten ton loads into the icehouse and was paid a pound a ton for my efforts.

Two of the men present, Billy and George Haylett were twins, yet apart from the flat caps which both wore, it would be difficult to find two people more different. Billy, or 'Sausage' as he was known, was of medium height, thin, quick and energetic with twinkling eyes, while George, wearing bottle-bottomed glasses, was large, rotund, ponderous and made few unconsidered movements. When younger they'd worked as deck hands on various trawlers, George from Scarborough and Billy fishing distant waters from Grimsby. More recently, they'd found work wherever they could around the harbour. Billy cleaned and painted boats, helped unload catches or delivered boxes of ice by wheelbarrow from the icehouse for any merchant or fisherman requiring his services.

George had a certain dignity and enjoyed talking with all the port's users, though spent much of his time on 'Sandgate Corner', at the top of the harbour, where the critics and ne'er do wells gathered. Everything and everyone was debated, discredited and dismissed on this site. On landing days, George stood sentry on the rows of fish that *Our Heritage* offered for sale. During the summer, he was also the car park attendant on the pier, though chose not to work on Fridays. This was his day off and when he'd had a few beers in the 'Turks Head' with his pals, he'd sing in his deep, booming voice and would regularly entertain the customers with a stand up comedy act. George once won a hundred pounds in a talent contest at a local theatre but had asked all his fishermen pals and friends from the pubs to attend and cheer him on. The other contestants complained that this had intimidated the judges.

Billy spoke with a slight lisp but didn't say much and wasn't articulate. He could be found any day when not working, in any pub that would serve him. He consumed large amounts of beer, sometimes other peoples' drinks that had been left unattended and he took on a totally different guise when drunk. Billy became a romeo, though only in his own mind. To others, he was a pest. It wasn't uncommon for ladies to find Billy's wandering hands in places they shouldn't be and often a sudden squeal precipitated Billy's unceremonious dumping in the street.

Attending a dinner to celebrate the launching of *Our Heritage,* no one noticed him slip under the table and it wasn't until the ladies sitting at the long table began screaming and jumping up in sequence, that he was discovered, again to be escorted from the room.

Colin's wife Rachel, proprietor of 'Dilts' fish and chip shop was proud of her produce, mostly supplied from her husband's boat and had many, well-known customers. She was horrified to find Billy in the queue one evening, the worse for drink, standing next to a famous concert violinist and his soprano wife, who were appearing at the 'Spa Theatre'. The large-bosomed lady was clad in a full-length fur coat, open at the top. In an instant, before Rachel could say a word, Billy's head was inside the coat, resting on the heaving chest. His muffled voice could be heard from within saying, "be nice to Billy. Billy's a good boy." He was reluctant to move from the comfortable surroundings so was dislodged and forcibly ejected once again, leaving the woman gasping and speechless.

Billy's usual mode of transport to and from the harbour was his bike, which he rode while in some extremely inebriated conditions. His survival on the road was more by good luck than good riding. On more than one occasion he'd been summoned to court and fined for being drunk in charge of a bicycle. For all his failings Billy was never, ever aggressive, always mild of manner and willing. Even in his later years, when he found work, he'd work harder and longer than anyone else, particularly his brother George.

The third man present was Jackie Blades, universally know as 'Bludgie'. Jack was small, tanned, bright-eyed, wiry and full of nervous energy. He wore a single gold earring and was never seen without his little woolly cap, perched on the back of his head. Slightly bow-legged, in his younger days Jack had been a talented footballer and even now, approaching his late fifties, he was fitter than most youngsters and would be turning out again on Boxing Day for the manic, comic football match, played annually on the beach.

I elbowed my way to the bar, passing George 'Shaky' Cammish, who was downing most of his pint in one gulp. George, tussle-haired and red-faced, worked as a stevedore on the cargo boats but couldn't get through the day without a drink. His hands would shake early in the morning but as soon as the 'Packet' opened at

1030, he'd dash across the road and into the bar. Spilling beer whilst getting the glass to his mouth, he swallowed the majority of the contents in one long gulp, losing his shake instantly. Another quick pint would swiftly follow and he'd be back at work until lunchtime without a problem.

I attracted the barman's attention. "Who wants what?" I asked. The three shore-men requested rum, downing the remains of the tots they were holding in unison, as if rehearsed. Col took his usual lager and I added to my already semi-inebriated state with a pint of beer. We began joking about our close call at sea, earlier that morning and at some of the funny radio interaction, when a sudden commotion and a gobbling sound near the door turned everyone's heads. Loud laughter filled the room. A farmer from the Wolds had arrived with some huge turkeys, which Herby Nicholson and his mates had ordered for Christmas. One of the birds was not prepared and oven-ready but alive, with a piece of string round its neck and the doomed creature was being led into the room.

"That one's for Stan," Herby called out to all in earshot. "We didn't know when 'e was goin' to eat it, so we thought it best t' keep it alive."

"Yer rotten sod," said his pal Stanley, who'd been expecting an ovenready bird and was the butt of this practical joke. "What am I gonna do with that?" he asked his friend.

"Well, yer won't 'ave t' carry it like the rest of us," came the reply.

Several drinks later and in a brief moment of clarity, I thought it was time I went home. There'd be several days of drinking yet before Christmas Eve arrived and I'd been in trouble in the past for dallying too long in the pub. I staggered home to receive a lovely welcome from Dotty and news of her week and what Paula and Danny had been up to at home and school. I was finding it difficult to comprehend what my wife was saying but tried to concentrate.

"Oh! And a Mr Holmes rang," she suddenly remembered.

"I don't know any Mr Holmes," I replied, slightly confused. "Did 'e say what 'e wanted?"

"He just said he was a fishing inspector or something. He said he'd ring back later."

"Oh bugger," I blurted, sobering quickly. "I know who 'e is now. 'E's from t' Sea Fish Committee. What did 'e want?" I asked the rhetorical question. "Surely he can't nick me now I'm ashore. T' patrol boat would 'ave t' be alongside t' get our exact position."

Dotty hadn't a clue what I was mumbling about until I told her of the earlier excitement at sea with the inspectorate. I made her laugh with the story of Stanley's turkey but then she sympathised with the bird saying, "poor thing." Our conversation was interrupted by the telephone's ring. I took a deep breath before lifting the handset. "'Ello," I said curtly, then listened carefully.

"Mr Normandale. My name is Tony Holmes. I'm the local inspector for the North Eastern Sea Fish Committee," he said formally. "I'd like to come and talk to you."

"Well yer can't come now, I'm busy." I replied, not expecting that he would want to. "It'll 'ave t' be tomorra." He seemed pleased with such an early response and we agreed that he would come to our house at eleven o'clock the following morning. My fuddled mind began to race at the implications of this meeting.

It was mid-afternoon and Dotty suggested I had a bath and got a few hours sleep, as I'd been up half of the night and we'd be going out to meet friends in the Leeds Arms in the evening.

I retreated to the bathroom, my mind turning over the potential prosecution. Was he coming to give me a warning? I was sure he had insufficient evidence for any charge to stick, or had he? Even in bed, where I never had a problem sleeping, I was still thinking, "what does he want? What does he know?" The only answer I could come up with was that he had no concrete proof that would stand up in court and I was going to be very cautious and not admit to anything.

The next thing I knew, two little voices were saying, " wake up Dad, your tea's ready." It was Paula and Danny and it was past six o'clock. They'd been home from school for ages but I'd slept solidly for three hours.

The bairns were fun and it was lovely listening to their tales but my mind kept flitting to the looming visit by the bogeyman. I rang Colin to tell him of my earlier telephone call and to ask if he'd had a similar message but he just laughed and said, "why should I get a call? I 'aven't done anythin' wrong."

The arrival of Patsy, our babysitter brought my thoughts of the pending visit to an end. I'd worry about the matter tomorrow. Patsy Rowley was one of seven children and though only a young teenager, was a very competent girl. She was small for her age but amazingly strong and had little trouble carrying both Paula and Danny if necessary. Dotty felt totally confident leaving the bairns in her charge and she'd often sleep over rather than return home late.

We wandered to our rendezvous in the pub to find Les cheerful and friendly, though he was a Jekyll and Hyde character. His mood could change in an instant. There were several customers in the little pub, though not enough to create any problems for the host. As he served our drinks, he began telling us about a customer he'd had in earlier from Filey, who'd already had too much to drink and whom he'd asked to leave. This was nothing unusual. If Les didn't wish to serve someone, he'd either totally ignore them, ask them to leave or say, "sorry, the pub's full," even if there was no one in. He kept referring to the person he'd ejected as a 'bungalow' and I could tell he was baiting me; willing me to ask the question.

"Go on then Les," I eventually said, humouring him. "Tell me why you call him 'bungalow'."

Grinning, he tapped his head with his forefinger and said, "because he's got nothing upstairs." He went away happy, having told his new story and was pleased when we passed the tale on as our group gathered.

The appearance of Noel White, my bank manager enhanced an already good evening and he was in sparkling form. Noel, small, red-faced with wire-rimmed glasses and sporting a trilby hat, was a wonderful character and a true gentleman. He doffed his hat to Dotty and the other ladies, saying, "evening m' dears." A master of affectionate insult, he pointed his thumb in my direction asking of Dotty, "you're still married to this reprobate then? No one else would have him y' know. You deserve a medal as big as a dustbin lid."

"Yes I know Noel. He doesn't know how lucky he is," my wife said, smiling sweetly in my direction.

"Thanks very much for those kind words Mr White. I'd like to say it's a pleasure to see you," then pausing briefly, continued, "but I can't."

We frequently traded insults but he always won. Noel had a huge circle of friends and bank clients from all walks of life but was the same with everyone. He loved to hold court, centre stage and was known to all in the pub from his regular, Thursday appearances. Once comfortable, he took no persuading to talk of his exploits as a Captain in the Eighth Army during the North African Campaign. He began a lovely story about the supply of beer to the troops in the desert, where the bottled ale was always too warm and frequently exploded. "We learned that the stuff kept cooler if we buried it in the sand," he said. "Bladdy trouble was, we had to retreat sharpish when Rommell made a rapid push and we didn't have time to dig the beer up. We couldn't find the stuff when we advanced again. I bet our bladdy beer's still there to this day."

When he was a young man and had first started working at the bank, Noel had also played football for York City. Though he was supposed to be strictly amateur, the banker would find money in his shoe at the end of each game. "I got more money for playing football than I did from the bank in my early days," he'd once told us. "I wasn't a good player," he'd said, pausing for effect, "but I could stop those that were."

At the end of the evening there was an invitation to those who wished to join us back at home for a delicious chilli, which Dotty had made earlier, together with some of the wine, which I'd traded for a box of fish with a friendly hotelier. Godfather Noel would always decline our invitation, usually with some barbed comment, though apologised profusely to my wife.

Next morning and conscious of the pending visit by the inspector, I headed for an electrical shop not too far into town and bought a small, battery-powered cassette recorder. There was no way I was going to allow anything said in the forthcoming interview to go unrecorded. Back home again, I set the machine up on the dining room table and gave it a quick trial while awaiting his arrival.

The doorbell rang promptly at eleven and Tony Holmes introduced himself, though this really wasn't necessary. Every fisherman on the coast knew who he was and what he looked like. Tall, thin, with a sallow complexion and a large, hooked nose, Tony wasn't an unpleasant person, in fact he was always polite and friendly when encountered around the harbour. It was his occupation, not the man that was distasteful.

"Hello Tony, of course I know who you are, come in," I welcomed him, leading him into the dining room. Dotty was hovering close by and asked if he'd prefer tea or coffee. The inspector, somewhat taken aback by my gushing welcome, followed me, taking the proffered chair at the table.

"Now then, is this a social call or is it business?" I asked unnecessarily. There was no way he'd ever visit, other than officially.

"It's business I'm afraid," he replied, raising his eyebrows and totally missing my sarcasm.

"OK then, fire away," I said cheerily. "As it's business, yer won't mind if ah record this interview. On'y fo' me own record, in case ah forget anythin'."

He spotted the flat machine on the table for the first time and luckily he hadn't received his cup of tea at this point or he'd probably have choked on the liquid, such was his intake of breath. "I don't think there's any need to go that far," he said defensively when he'd recovered his composure. "I have my notepad for the record."

"Well, I've 'eard of people who've been set up in the past and who've been misreported. Not that I'd suspect you of such goin's on of course," I added hastily, but deliberately, "but I 'ave t' look after me own interests." Then I pressed the record button. The little red light gave an assuring glow and the spools began to turn. Dotty arrived in the room carrying a tray holding tea, milk, sugar and a plate of biscuits, which she put down quickly and departed, obviously sensing the atmosphere.

Clearly disappointed at the presence of my gadget, he cleared his throat and began to talk, not of his mission but of generalities and how I thought the winter fishing season was going, of market prices and the weather. It was as if he had some bad news but now didn't want to deliver it. The tape whirred softly, recording the trivia.

"So, t' what do I owe this unexpected pleasure?" I asked, as he paused for a drink of tea. I was itching to know his mission and yet at the same time was worried he was a harbinger of big trouble.

Suddenly official, he opened his notebook like a policeman, gave a little cough and began. "Two weeks ago, I was at the coastguard station in Filey." He went on to give the date and time but my mind had raced ahead of him.

So that's what this was about. He had seen us in the prohibited area when our gear was stuck in the wreck, after all. I tuned back in to his dialogue.

"I identified your vessel, FR 196, through my binoculars and took a bearing with a handheld compass. I then drove to Speeton Cliffs at the other side of Filey Bay and took another bearing. On putting these two cross bearings on the chart, I fixed your position as being a half-mile inside the protected zone. You are aware of course, that that is a forbidden area?" He'd regained his composure now and looked quite smug as he continued briskly, "you do not have to say anything at this point but anything you do say, will be taken down and could be used in evidence." He looked up from his pad to await my response and took another sip of tea.

My first response, which I thought but didn't utter was, "you crafty bugger." I took a breath and said, "well if yer don't mind me sayin', ah think you've been a bit over zealous in t' execution of yer duty in this matter." He didn't say anything, only smiled and sipped again from his cup, so I continued. "You can't prove we were fishin', even if we were in t' area and ah'm not sayin' we were."

Tea back on the table, his pencil scribbled swiftly as he recorded my response. When he'd finished writing he said, "I could see your trawl doors hanging overboard."

I knew that wasn't strictly true, because it was one of our boards that had been stuck in the wreck. We'd eventually parted a wire warp and chain at slack water and lost the for'ard board. I'd have to wait for late spring, when my pals at the Diving Club would recover this valuable piece of kit for me, but I couldn't tell him that either. Suddenly inspiration struck me and I blessed Mr Tribe, my old headmaster and navigation teacher from the Graham Sea Training School. The knowledge he'd imparted and which had been underlined when I'd gained my skipper's ticket was going to get me out of this situation. "Just a minute," I said, putting my response together in my head as I spoke. "It's miles from Filey to Speeton Cliffs." I wasn't sure how many miles but that wasn't too important. "Yer must 'ave taken ages t' get from one place t' t' other."

He'd begun writing again but raised his head briefly and nodded an assent cautiously, not knowing where the conversation was leading and said, "I'm not sure, probably about fifteen to twenty minutes."

"Well yer can't do that. The only way yer can get an accurate position, is t' tek simultaneous bearings. Any navigator will tell yer that." To add to my argument and create more confusion I said, "you were usin' a magnetic compass. Did you apply variation t' yer fixes?" I asked if he'd used the 'true compass rose' on the chart when he laid the plotted lines "You 'ave t' use t' magnetic part." To add further confusion and load my defence I changed the subject adding, "I know our doors were out. We were on our way 'ome from Flamborough an' we 'adn't lifted them in. We were 'avin' a bit of engine trouble an' I'd stopped t' change t' fuel filters."

His hand had stopped scribbling ages ago and he looked at me stunned. What I'd told him about simultaneous bearings and the corrections to magnetic bearings before plotting was true but he probably didn't know that. I knew he'd go away and check this information.

"I've made a note of what you've said," he commented, swiftly terminating the interview. Leaving his remaining tea, he stood. "I'll get back to you when I've reported to my boss and will let you know if further action is to be taken."

"Yes!" I mentally punched the air, knowing he couldn't prove his case conclusively. "Do call again if yer passin'," I said, opening the door for him. He left in silence. Returning to the machine, I stopped the recorder, removed the cassette and placed the recording in an envelope, licking and sealing the white folder. I wrote the date and contents then placed this safely in a drawer, though I was fairly confident I'd never have to refer to this information again.

Several weeks later, I would receive a letter from the Chief Executive of the Sea Fish Committee giving me a caution for a suspected infringement of the prohibited area but this would count for nothing. If that august body could have prosecuted me with confidence, they would have done so, but I'd avoid the wreck and be even more cautious in future.

Christmas Eve, with the usual boozy afternoon was followed by a lovely family day with excited kids on new bikes and a room full of wrapping paper from numerous other presents. Next came a wonderful dinner then a walk for Dotty and me and a bike ride for the bairns. All too soon it was Boxing Day again. Twenty-six potential gladiators were milling around on the beach, waiting for the kick off of what was supposed to be a football match and which required the permission of the district FA, the football associations' representative body. This match had however, over the years, evolved into a hybrid of soccer, rugby and wrestling. The players, of which I was a red-shirted participant, in various states of inebriation, were waiting for the referee to arrive. Though there were supposed to be eleven a side, no one was turned away. The crowd were just divided into equal teams.

The Mayor, waiting to officially kick off the carnage, was wearing a splendid, black top hat, grey suit, camel haired coat and in his chain of office, looked immaculate. Detracting from the civic dignitary's topper, everyone on the pitch was wearing battered headgear, painted red or white, mostly old bowlers or top hats. They were garbed in anything from Superman outfits to morning suits and though wearing red or white shirts, some of these were difficult to identify.

The rules of the game were simple. A lost hat meant a free kick, but there were no offsides', hand-balls or fouls. This traditional charity match had been played for more than eighty years and was born as a fund-raising scheme, following a disaster at sea. Now the Fishermen and Firemen's Charity funded Christmas vouchers for the old folks around the 'Bottom End' through collections and donations.

But who was the referee today and where was he? Rich Sheader had been in charge for the last few years since Harold Wharton had retired, but in his sixties, Rich hadn't been well recently. Harold had officiated this match for as long as anyone could remember until his retirement. Prior to closing his grocer's shop, Harold had provisioned the old steam trawlers in the port and was regularly seen crossing the road, a cane basket of supplies on his shoulder.

Time was marching on. "It doesn't look like we've got a referee. I'll ref if yer like," I volunteered to the milling group. "It'll get things goin'." My offer was accepted and from somewhere a whistle was found. In no time at all we'd tossed up, chosen ends and kicked off. The Mayor, surrendering dignity for speed, escaped the sandy arena and climbed through the railings to the promenade. It was totally confusing for the hundreds of spectators to have a referee in the same garb as some of the combatants; more so when I joined in the play, tending to side with the Firemen. I'd turned out for this team since I was fourteen. Originally, these were firemen from the stokeholds of the steam trawlers but this had long since changed.

The match was in full swing with much tripping, lunging and total miss-kicks when a lost hat deemed a free kick to the Firemen. About fifteen yards from the Fishermen's goal, this was in a dangerous position and a wall of white shirts lined up in their goalmouth. A small sandcastle was built and the ball mounted atop. On my whistle, one by one the red shirts ran over the ball, then, following up behind, I hit a scorching left foot shot over the heads of the defenders and under the crossbar. Delighted, I waved my arms in the air shouting, "goooaal," then blew the whistle, pointing to the centre, much to the annoyance of the Fishermen and amusement of the crowd.

As fate had it, this turned out to be the winning goal and dead on noon by the pier clock, I put the whistle to my mouth again, blowing for full time, but I'd forgotten Harold's golden rule. In his time as referee he must have had some previous nasty experiences, as he never blew the final whistle till he was off the sands. Someone shouted, "grab the bastard." I was instantly scragged by the entire team of white-shirted fishermen and carried by arms and legs to the waters edge. Wading knee deep, on a count of three, half a dozen of the losing team threw me, unceremoniously into the freezing North Sea.

I dashed home for a change of clothes then quickly returned to the seafront, where the Diving Club were holding their raft race around a marked course in the harbour. All funds collected were contributed to the Fishermen and Firemen's Charity. The piers were crowded with spectators watching the mayhem, which had already started. I squeezed through at a place where the crowd was thinner to watch the extremely amusing proceedings. There were paddles flying in all directions, wielded by wetsuited contestants, not trying to win, but to sabotage any other craft in proximity. Flour bombs were on sale to the public, who were encouraged to take pot shots at anyone on a raft within range. Some members of the club not on rafts, were swimming in the water, which I knew to my cost was icy, attempting to upturn some of the competitors. They in turn were being assaulted with paddle blades to discourage their efforts. The event was certainly a huge success and a big hit with the thousands watching.

## Chapter 6

# Les's Birthday

Early January found us out at the 'Bolders Bank' towards the southern end of the 'Dogger Bank', looking for cod. The only other Scarborough boat in the area was the *Our Heritage* and though we hadn't seen them, we'd heard a Grimsby pair team on the radio, proving they were working close by. This method of fishing, with two boats towing one large net had proved very efficient.

Cod congregated annually across these latitudes in January and February to breed and massive hauls could be caught, but this fishing was a real lottery. It was possible to spend days going around the region looking for a bonanza and catching virtually nothing. These big shoals of spawning fish could be found anywhere between our current position and the Dutch Coast.

The shipping forecast was predicting northerly gales and as yet we'd not found the elusive cod. We heard the 'Grimmys' talking on their 'private' frequency and realised they'd found fish. We were fairly close to their position so towed in their direction but the weather was deteriorating rapidly. The wind was freshening and the swell growing, so regardless of what we caught, this tow would be the finishing haul of our trip.

"We've a few marks ere," Col called over the airwaves.

A few moments later we too were seeing fish on our sounder.

The Grimsby boats hauled up and had a huge catch in their net but this proved so big they couldn't cope with the volume in the prevailing conditions, and the sheer weight of fish, hanging on a massive hawser, was damaging and threatening the safety of the vessel holding the net. I listened in dismay as the skipper of this boat took a single lift from the trawl, then slipped the remaining dead fish from the bumper bag. This catch would have filled our hold.

Col hauled and took about forty-five kit of big cod from his trawl. We took twenty-five kit of a similar size and as premature darkness fell on a storm-laden sky, we stowed our gear and set off for home in close company. The weather was now a full gale from the north and both boats were rolling heavily.

We were talking on the radio for a while in general terms without mentioning names but it was Les's birthday on the following Saturday. Unknown to him, we were part of a group of his customers who'd organised a special surprise. Our problem was, having arranged and paid for the visiting lady, we were now quite worried how he'd react to the 'present'.

To the north of us, visible on the radar, the blip of a large ship appeared, making its way down wind. At two miles distant we could see her port light and two white masthead lamps. It would be our give way, but with our crews still working on deck, it would be uncomfortable and very wet if we altered to starboard. Both our vessels were highly illuminated with deck lights blazing. "Put yer searchlight on an' shine it between us. I'll do t' same," I suggested. "'E'll think we're pair trawlin' an' alter course." A bright spotlight from *Our Heritage's* wheelhouse top stabbed the wild sea and ours bridged the gap from the other direction, though both beams pivoted wildly as we rolled. The effect was instantaneous. The cargo vessel turned to the east to pass across our sterns, lurching heavily in the big, beam seas and no doubt the officer on watch was cursing bloody fishermen.

Next morning, with dawn breaking and *Independence* drawing close to harbour, I glanced for'ard under the whaleback and could see daylight through her stem. This was most peculiar and I donned oilskins and sea-boots to explore. I discovered a full bulwark plank about ten-feet long was missing from her starboard bow above deck level. Thumping into the swells must have weakened and dislodged the six-inch wide piece. There was no danger to the vessel's integrity. As long as water didn't penetrate below, anything coming through this gap would flow out of the scuppers. Walking aft again I was amazed to see the missing plank wedged vertically between the after trawl door and the gallow. The odds of this happening must be millions to one. The lath must have soared high into the air and dropped like a javelin to slot into this position.

After landing our fish and settling the boat's account in the office, I notified the shipwright of the damage. Two hours later I stood toe to toe on the T of a squash court with Colin. He was teaching me the game, which was becoming popular and we'd been playing most Friday mornings in recent weeks. We didn't do much running about; just belted the ball as hard as we could against the wall, hoping it wouldn't be returned. It would be months before I played another partner, to discover the subtlety of lobs and drop shots.

At the end of the session, as always, we made our way to the bar of the Sports Centre, to replace some of the lost liquid and yarn about fishing. We usually discussed what we'd caught, where we'd fished and the next week's prospects. Today this topic was far from our minds. As co-conspirators in tomorrow's surprise we were both more than a little concerned. Col didn't know any details, having left me to make the arrangements, so wanted to know what was planned. We'd deliberately not mentioned the event on the radio while at sea, as the surprise could be lost if anyone was listening.

I'd obtained the phone number of a booking agent, based in the West Riding from a friend, who'd been to a similar birthday occasion and had no trouble making the contact. Agreeing the fee, I'd sent a cheque before sailing, the previous week. The visit was fixed for two o'clock in the Leeds Arms and we were to be near the door, ready to greet her. The lady would be quickly whisked out again to Bob Walker's adjacent house, where she could change into her outfit. Unfortunately I'd not been able to get Les a dusky maiden as planned. This was a setback as we were sure he'd have fallen in love instantly. Now we were both worried.

The following morning, though the matter was supposed to be secret, news of the surprise birthday treat had gone round the harbour like wildfire. Pandora's Box was open now, so I resigned myself to my fate.

Our usual group, all contributors to the afternoon's entertainment, met up in the pub not long after noon and I was the last to arrive. Sitting down with my mates, I suddenly jumped up again with a rush, attracting attention. "Sorry Benny," I said to the empty seat. The others laughed. Benny, the quiet old newspaper seller had suddenly died in this very place a few weeks ago. Benny, quite elderly, was a short, round, red-faced Irishman, softly spoken and well mannered. He'd never have dreamed of asking anyone for a drink but some of the regulars were pleased to leave a half of beer in the pump for him. The old boy would always acknowledge the gesture by raising his glass and saying, "God love yur sur."

"It's never convenient t' go," Bob observed, nodding to the place I again occupied, "but if you 'ave t' snuff it, where better than in yer favourite pub."

We all concurred.

"Especially if it's your round," Jack chipped in, bringing another chuckle from the gathering.

As well as Colin, Bob and me, there was George, Jack and Syd. None of these three men were involved in the fishing industry but all were familiar with our trade and way of life. We interacted wonderfully, enjoying these Saturday sessions immensely, each occasionally bringing food to this special, weekly gathering. There was dismay when I said our plan was no longer secret and that someone had let the cat out of the bag. The plan was irreversible now and no one was going to admit they'd blabbed. "There's safety in numbers," I said, then slid along the seat to hide behind Big George, for effect.

Big George was well named. He was a giant of a man who, prior to his retirement was the manager of a large, civil engineering company. George weighed in at over twenty-five stone and struggled to get up the steps into the pub. His upper thighs were the size of most people's waists. He was very keen on seafood and prepared and smoked many of his own favourites in a shed at the back of his house. He'd bring some wonderful samples of hot-smoked haddock, trout, mackerel and scotch eggs to the communal lunch, though he frequently had to be cajoled into buying his round at the bar.

Jack, a printer by trade, was also large and stocky, though proportionate, with long silvering hair and a large, broad nose. In his late forties, Jack thought himself an aging rocker, complete with motorbike, but he had the most conservative taste in food. He wasn't keen on George's fishy dishes and would bring pre-packed meat pies, sliced, processed ham and white bread buns to the party. Any mention of curries, pizzas or any type of foreign food would cause him to screw up his face. Jack's image was quite the macho man, so when Bob, Col or I pretended to stroke his leg, he'd get really irate, shouting, "ger off yer prats. Yer all queer, you lot."

We knew what his reaction would be.

Syd, another large man, was a precision engineer and ex Royal Navy. He still looked the part with his full beard and erect bearing. Syd usually called at the butcher's shop on his way to the pub and bought a large pork pie.

Bob, skipper of the *Jann Denise* would bring crab sandwiches and prawns from his wife Ann's seafood stall.

Col cooked whatever fish was in season on his boat. His gurnards, trays of baked, rolled herring, mackerel and scallops were terrific, though Jack wouldn't touch them. Jack did enjoy the milder of the variety of cheeses and biscuits I brought to the party.

This wasn't a private party. The food was shared with anyone who happened to be in the pub on the day. Marilyn, one of the attractive, part-time barmaids the landlord was now employing, looked forward to the Saturday lunchtime fest.

We were talking in hushed tones, conspiratorially, as questions were asked about the proceedings. I reiterated the plan to all hands, feeling much happier, having shared the burden.

Les, who'd just drawn up a notice for his pub window saying, 'no gangs, no coach parties and we don't serve tea or coffee', came over with sticky tape to position the document. "What are you lot cooking up?" he asked, more out of curiosity than suspicion.

"Nowt, just talking about women," I replied glibly, tucking into the food and quaffing the beer before me.

The door opened and we automatically turned to view the new arrival. It was Rob, a broad speaking Liverpudlian, with an accent so thick, most found him difficult to understand. Red faced, with thinning straight hair, he was limping heavily, wearing a shoe on his left foot and a soft slipper on his right. He hobbled to the bar, ordering a pint of beer as he perched his rear on a bar stool, breathing a huge sigh as he took the load off his painful foot.

"You're in a bad way today Rob," Marilyn observed, sympathetically. "Your gout must be playing up again."

"It's bloody merrder, I caan't bear anyt'ing to touch it," the Scouser said. "I caan't even 'ave a blanket on da bedt."

Marilyn listened to Rob's woes while we continued our collective meal, feeling braver having consumed a few beers. Our usual banter had returned, though all eyes were on the clock as the minute hand climbed to its zenith. There was still another hour to go yet. The pub was gradually filling up and already there were more people in than usual. Quite a number of trawlermen who usually drank in the pubs on the seafront were finding seats in the back room and Les was muttering under his breath about his pub being full of bloody strangers, though he knew them all by name.

Bob had just put his hand on Jack's knee again, causing him to start, then swear, when a really attractive woman walked through the door, turning everyone's head. Elegantly dressed, with a blond, pageboy hairstyle, this classy lady was clearly out of place.

"Bloody 'ell, she's 'ere already" spluttered Colin, who, facing the door, spied her first. He struggled to swallow a half eaten piece of herring, which was now sticking in his throat, causing him to cough.

Les wouldn't complain at this beauty. Half the room were staring at her with undisguised lechery and the lady, oblivious to this lust, was glancing round the bar, clearly looking for a contact. Luckily, Les, collecting glasses in the back room, hadn't spotted her. Both Bob and I jumped up and quickly walked over to this vision of loveliness. "Ah think yer lookin' for us love," I said, putting my hand on her waist, intending to guide her quickly back outside.

In a very cultured, soft-spoken voice she purred, "I don't think I am." With a look of total distain on her face, the lady took my hand between thumb and forefinger, dropping the paw from her side, as if contaminated.

"Trish," Marilyn called out from the bar. "How are you? It's been a long time. Thanks for coming to see me." A smile of recognition came to the lovely face and we were instantly forgotten as she turned to the bar.

Bob and I scurried back to our seats, heads down. Our company were laughing loudly at our discomfort. I wanted to crawl under the seat and daren't look in the direction of the visitor until I was sure Trish's back was turned and she was chatting to her friend at the bar. Her words and the look on her face were still haunting me.

Our pleasant conversation was renewed as the clock crawled and the pub continued to fill. One of the two cheeky kids who lived up the hill came in and as usual, rudely asked for a bag of crisps. Attempting in vain to draw some manners from the nasty little wretch, Les passed the packet to the youngster. As he turned to leave, one of the nearby deck hands, not realising the extent of his mischief, said to the boy, "I bet yer daren't jump on 'is toe," pointing to the slippered foot at his side.

Without a further word the horrible kid jumped, landing with both feet on the unprotected limb. The scream was ear piercing, bringing the crowded pub to standstill. The wail was followed by, "yer little bas—" but the words were lost as the grown man burst into tears at the unexpected agony inflicted upon him.

The young terror didn't wait to see the result of his assault. He realised in an instant he'd gone way too far and shot through the door like a bullet, before anyone could lay a hand on him. The fool who'd encouraged the boy slunk into the corner, unnoticed. It was several minutes and after much sympathy from Marilyn and her lovely friend that the poor chap could even lift his head. The tear-streaked face, with gritted teeth, broke into what was more a grimace than a smile, but the pain was easing and with it the atmosphere which had overtaken the little pub.

By two o'clock we were on tenterhooks, our eyes glued to the door with some of the fishermen throwing questioning glances in our direction. Our light-hearted banter had disappeared. There was no sign of our expected visitor and even the delightful Trish had gone, offering a sweet smile in our direction as she left. Thirty very long minutes later, when we'd given up hope and some of the customers were drifting away, a tall, not unattractive woman, around thirty, with long auburn hair, wearing a red vinyl raincoat and long red boots stepped through the door. She was accompanied by an elderly man and looked around the room uncertainly. This had to be our girl.

Despite wobbly legs, Bob quickly took the lady back outside and to his house, allowing her to change into her outfit. I bought the driver Bernie a beer and we sat him down, asking what the delay had been. It transpired that they'd struggled badly in the Saturday holiday traffic, then they'd been unable to find the location. The remaining onlookers had seen the arrival and now an air of expectancy filled the place. Ten minutes later Tina entered the bar again, still in the same red coat, though I suspected her garments beneath were somewhat different.

For the first time, Les spied his birthday surprise, though was still unsuspecting. As he came towards the door, it was Tina who spoke first. "You're Les, aren't you? I've heard a lot about you." The landlord was pleasantly surprised at this attention and my heart rose immediately. He was hooked and all was going to be well. Leading the landlord by hand, she led him into the back room, taking a small barstool from one of the nearby customers.

Bernie, who'd followed the pair into the back room, was carrying a portable cassette recorder, which he placed on a nearby table. As Tina sat her captivated, willing victim on the stool in the centre of the room, accompanied by suggestive calls from the men watching, Bernie pressed 'play' on the little machine.

To the evocative music of "The Stripper," this sexy lady slowly began to undo the buttons of her coat. Beneath the plastic mac, Tina wore a red and black basque with black suspenders. There were wolf whistles from the onlookers as the coat was dropped. Les was invited to undo the buttons on the long stockings as the lady tantalisingly strutted round him. Our party, with the exception of George, who would have blocked everyone's view, were gathered in the narrow entrance to the back room, now thoroughly enjoying the landlord's predicament and he seemed to be enjoying the situation too. Another slow, moody tune and the basque followed the coat to the floor. Next Tina, who had slowly and erotically removed a tiny bra, revealing an ample but well shaped bosom, was undressing Les and in contrast, this took no time at all. He was very quickly down to his briefs and spectacles.

Wearing only the smallest of frilly briefs, Tina began massaging the willing participant's back and chest with aromatic oil. The second tune had now ended and the only sounds to be heard were the groans from men who would have given much to exchange places with Les at that moment. For her finale, to another sensual number, the stripper, her back to the landlord, pulled away her remaining vestige of cover. Legs apart, the stripper bent over, showing him a beautiful, rounded bottom and more. Les couldn't resist and bent forward to kiss the exposed intimacy. Tina must have performed this act frequently for at the instant of contact, a large cloud of talcum powder rose from between her legs, released from a rubber bulb concealed in her hand. The landlord's desire turned to one of wanting to breathe and he sat up coughing and looking like a snowman as the talc stuck to the oil on his body. His glasses were opaque and he quickly took them off, though this didn't improve his sight much, as he squinted to focus.

A loud cheer and applause filled the room and the shrewd Tina, milking the moment, went round with a beer mug, taking a collection from the onlookers who, feasting their eyes, were pleased to contribute. Tina must have doubled her fee in those few minutes. We returned to our seats, while Les disappeared upstairs alone to shower. Our kudos in the pub soared when the entertainer, now dressed once more in her underwear, came to sit at our table for a drink and chat. Conversation was extremely difficult in this surreal atmosphere.

It had to be Jack who said, "d' yer come 'ere often?"

I was dreading Dotty walking through the door, as this situation would take a great deal of explaining. For the next few minutes we enjoyed an insight into the world of a stripper. She said how much she'd enjoyed coming to a really nice place, with people who could appreciate her performance without losing control. Tina told us of some of the horrendous situations she'd found herself in and how she'd had to escape quickly on the odd occasion.

*All hands hauling the trawl.*
*Photo by John Hobson*

*A huge haul of cod fills the fish ponds and deck on board Independence.*
*Photo FG Normandale*

*An early morning alfresco fish breakfast en route to Grimsby to land a catch.*
*Photo FG Normandale*

*Les's birthday present.*
*Photo FG Normandale*

Strangely, it didn't occur to her that coming to a fishing port might have been one of those times.

Les reappeared, freshly showered and changed. He took in the scene at a glance. "I knew you buggers were up to something. You were too quiet and secretive. Well I hope you enjoyed yourselves." Then he winked and in the direction of Tina said, "I did." He invited the entertainer to stay for tea but due to business commitments, this less than tempting offer was declined.

It was home time. Tomorrow we'd be back at sea and there was no doubt what the conversation would be on the North Sea radio frequencies for the next few days.

* * * * * *

It was turning out to be a harsh winter. On days when the weather was marginal and we were in port, I'd walk round to the lighthouse and give the watch-keeper a fiver, asking him to ring me if anyone went to sea. I could then ring my crew. I didn't want to be the first one to sail but wouldn't be left in the harbour.

Today we were at sea and the wind was blowing a severe gale, this time from the southeast. We were one of four boats caught out when it freshened and according to Denk, who was ashore, there wasn't a way in at home. "Seas are breakin' for 'alf a mile or more from t' piers. Yer'd be daft tryin' t' get in 'ere."

Col had called his father-in-law Denk for advice when we were considering our options. The prospect of the weather easing in the next twenty-four hours was negligible. The only choice, other than dodging head to wind for the foreseeable future, was to make for nearby Whitby. The scar of rock beyond the East Pier of the north-facing entrance protects the approach when the wind is southeasterly, but with this weight of wind it would still be a difficult entry, even in daylight.

Denk had phoned ahead and with plenty of water in the harbour mouth and the port's lifeboat standing close inside the whale jaw shaped piers, we drew closer. Col was manoeuvring the *Our Heritage* towards the narrows when one of the Whitby skippers came over the radio from his boat, safely berthed up river, above the swing bridge, linking the two parts of the picturesque town.

"If yer gettin' me Col, 'ead straight fo' t' East Pier on yer approach. Don't worry," he advised, "yer won't 'it it."

Colin acknowledged the call and thanked his friend for the information.

"That doesn't seem like a good idea t' me," I thought, as we grew closer. "There's no way I'm gonna steer my boat for t' pier end in these conditions. I'm gonna aim for t' middle, straight between two piers." We were only a few yards from the entrance, dead in line for a perfect run in, and I was hoping the lifeboat would move from our path, when the *Independence* was suddenly pushed bodily towards the West Pier by a tremendous tide surge. I pushed the throttle to full speed and the electric tiller hard to port to avoid hitting the sandstone construction. We passed into the harbour sideways, the starboard corner of the transom, missing the pier wall by inches. I was immediately forced to turn hard to starboard to avoid hitting the East Pier, narrowly missing the lifeboat. We were in the harbour and undamaged but we'd been so close to disaster. My legs felt like jelly. I should have listened to local knowledge.

Minutes later we were securely berthed in the harbour, our ropes willingly taken by our Whitby pals, who we spoke to on the radio regularly, but seldom met. Rusty came into the wheelhouse and said, "that was close, we nearly 'it that pier. You could 'ardly 'ave got a cig paper in the gap. Ah'm glad it was you in 'ere an' not me"

I mumbled my thanks, my legs still shaking and thought, "if on'y yer knew."

## Chapter 7

# The Presentation

Fresh offshore winds the following week found us working two to three miles from land, to the north of the Castle Headland. The conspicuous radar landmark was one of several prominent targets when navigating by radar. Variable range rings allowed the dozens of wrecks to be positioned accurately and though it took concentration and knowledge of the tides, we were managing to take reasonable hauls. To the south, in radio contact, the *Soolee* was fishing in the prohibited area. A fast moving blip on the radar, closing on our location turned out to be the patrol boat and I called a general warning to all interested parties listening. "There's a policeman 'ere an' 'e's eadin' south. I repeat, t' policeman's headin' south."

"We're clear," replied Col.

"We're up at t' Corner," said Bev, meaning he was at Flamborough Head.

"Oh shit Bev, we've just been nabbed by the bladdy bogeyman," came the distinctive voice of Alan Jagger, twenty minutes later.

"Freddy warned yer 'e was comin'," came the reply.

"My VHF was on the bladdy Coastguard frequency. I'd been asking for the weather forecast and I wasn't watching the radar either."

There was a pause, then a chuckle from Bev. "'E who laughs last, laughs loudest," he said. "Tek yer punishment like a man, Jagger."

"Law breakers should be punished," I chipped in.

There was another unsympathetic comment from Col but, "bastards," was the only reply.

Steaming into the harbour with the *Our Heritage* a few minutes astern of us, I glanced in the direction of the watch-keeper's hut, on the end of the West Pier, half expecting to see Charlie 'Dilt', Colin's Dad, looking out from the window. Charlie had died the previous year but almost up to his death in his eighties, the old man would be on the pier if he knew there were prospects of the *Our Heritage* coming in. Even if the boat wasn't due in until four or five o'clock in the morning, Charlie would still begin his vigil at midnight. Watery eyes, a large bulbous nose and lined face under his flat cap, spoke of a lifetime at sea.

In years past, Charlie had been a Trojan whenever his son's boat was alongside the quay. He'd carry fish, drag stacks of empty boxes back to the boat and shovel ice, but in his latter days, Charlie would write the weights on the tallies as boxes of fish came ashore and crossed the scales. He loved the feeling of being involved and being part of his son's success. This wasn't a job he needed to do and on days when the weather was poor, people misguidedly asked Colin why he allowed his Dad to come down to the pier, unnecessarily. The old man had collapsed more than once, having to be taken to his nearby home up the hill on a flat barrow, only to reappear for the next landing.

This troubled Col greatly. The skipper was also aware of his father's fragility but philosophically would say, "what can ah do? If ah stop 'im coming down, ah might as well shoot 'im. It's all 'e lives for."

Friday evening saw the annual dinner and presentation of the Fishermen and Firemen's awards. The Charity dating back to 1893, was formed for the dependants of the crew of the sailing smack, *Evelyn and Maud,* lost with all hands in November of that year. This low-key affair, organised by the fund-raising committee, was held in a small, local hotel and was a small appreciation to the invaluable people who shook collecting tins on the beach and round the pubs on Boxing Day. Now the money had been counted, these stalwarts were to be presented with certificates and trophies for their efforts. There were cups for the highest individual collector, the best group collection and a shield for the pub that raised the biggest sum during the year, plus runners up in each category. All the silverware had been donated over the years by willing townsfolk and companies.

Leaving Paula and Danny with Patsy, we'd decided to drive to the venue, as we'd arranged to collect Gladys Trotter, en route. Sadly, Gladys had recently been widowed. Her husband Jack had been the main organiser of the fund for many years and had been a master at persuading pubs, firms and traders to part with goods for raffle prizes. He fussed and worried over the smallest detail to ensure the match took place and was the one who ensured anyone in need received a voucher before Christmas. The value of this token had been increased to four pounds this year and more than a hundred elderly recipients exchanged these tickets for food in local shops or at the public market.

Gladys, despite her circumstances, wanted to attend the dinner. This remarkable woman, small, thin, with a sallow complexion and a narrow, sharp nose had severely bowed legs and for most of her life had suffered serious mobility problems, constantly relying on two walking sticks. This handicap, however serious, never prevented Gladys from making her way to the Leeds Arms, two hundred yards distant every night, even through hail, rain or gales for her two bottles of Jubilee Stout. She would have no more, no less and would refuse any offers of further drinks or assistance.

On the appointed evening, we collected Gladys, assisted her into the front seat for easier access then headed for the venue. Not wearing her usual headscarf, the lady had dressed in her best and was wearing a fine bonnet. From the back of the car Dotty said, "Gladys, we've got some news. We're going to have another baby."

"Oh never mind," she replied sympathetically, "these things 'appen." The dear old lady couldn't comprehend that we wanted and had planned another addition to our family and she continued, "I was the youngest o' twenty-two y' know, but then me Dad 'ad an accident."

I just couldn't resist the opportunity and said, "did 'e fall out o' bed?"

I almost crashed the car when Dotty hit me on the back of my head.

"Did they all survive?" she asked our passenger, who was unaware of my quip and subsequent hit.

"Oh yes, they all lived. We used to 'ave three sittings for meals and we only lived in a three bedroomed 'ouse, yer know."

This was food for thought and I was unsuccessfully trying to imagine where all these children would have slept or how their parents were able to keep control of them but there was no chance to dwell on this scenario, as we'd arrived at the hotel. Gladys allowed Sam Colling and Ronnie Bayes, two of the long-serving members of the committee to escort her inside and the sweet old lady was pleased to be seated and looked after by this pair. Both had participated in the Boxing Day mayhem in their younger days.

There was only a few minutes for a quick beer at the bar and then the group of about twenty, sat down to a traditional roast beef and Yorkshire pudding dinner. Prior to eating, a brief silence was held in memory of little Jacky Trotter, Gladys's late husband. The portion of meat was huge and the variety and quantity of vegetables meant everyone's plate was piled high, so I laughed when the waitress came round asking if anyone wanted more potato, cabbage, carrots or peas.

"Yes please," said Elizabeth, a plump, dowdily dressed lady, sitting further along the table. This elderly lady, a regular collector, had already cleared her plate. The waitress, surprised, plied more food in her direction then moved off. A minute later I received a gentle nudge in the ribs from Billy Blades, a long-haired, red-faced, cheerful young man who, with his wife Liz, was a recent member of the committee, willingly taking on some of the workload.

"Look over there," Billy whispered, surreptitiously pointing and nodding towards Elizabeth.

I cautiously looked in the direction indicated and burst out laughing. The old lady, her huge handbag on her knees, was scraping the second plate of food into various plastic bags contained within. Dotty, in conversation on her other side, turned to ask what I was laughing at and I pointed, none too tactfully, at the pensioner, still shovelling the vegetables into her copious valise. Others close by, also stared Elizabeth's way.

Not aware she was the focus of attention, the old woman completed her task and only when the bulging bag was snapped shut and she looked up, did Elizabeth realise she was under scrutiny. Unperturbed, she announced to all watching, "this is my dinner tomorrow. I'm a pensioner you know." Her husband was a retired sea captain and they were by no means poor but no one commented on her bad manners.

On arrival of the desserts, my loud comment of, "I wonder if she's got a thermos flask for 'er ice-cream," brought laughter from those close by, but a kick on the shin from my nearest and dearest.

Following coffee, it was time to present the trophies and Sam stood up to introduce someone who in Scarborough, needed no introduction, Councillor Peter Jaconelli. Peter, a former Mayor, was a descendant of the industrious, Italian ice-cream making family that had settled in the town via Glasgow early in the century. Only small in stature, Peter was hugely rotund with a large head, thinning, black, straight hair and small, bright, twinkling eyes. A local celebrity, who often appeared on regional television promoting the town, he was frequently to be found, front of house at his ice-cream parlour, across the road from the beach. As youngsters my friends and I would often ask him or the young men he employed, if they had any broken wafers. Sometimes we were lucky but occasionally were left scratching our heads when told, "we've lost the hammer."

Despite his shape, Peter was an expert in Judo, a trained, classical opera singer and talented piano-accordion player. His major claim to fame however and for which he held a place in the Guinness Book of Records, was for oyster eating. Peter had consumed more than five hundred of these shellfish in the unbelievable time of forty-eight minutes and seven seconds, in a highly publicised stunt. He'd attended a Civic Dinner soon after the event but declined the fish course. Speculation on his personal toiletry following this event was the talk of the harbour for weeks afterwards.

The Councillor made a little speech, thanking everyone for their efforts on the previous Boxing Day, then began his prize giving. Elizabeth Cowling won the cup for the top individual collector and her friend Alice, gained second place. For the first time, the landlord and landlady of the 'Durham' won the best pub shield. This trophy had been won consistently by Bob and Betty Swalwell over recent years until their retirement. This couple had been hosts in several alehouses during their career and had been tireless fund-raisers. They collected throughout the year with tins on the pub bar and not only for the Fishermen and Firemen. The Royal British Legion's Poppy Day appeal and RNLI's annual Flag Day also benefited from their efforts. This year, Durham Hotel would be engraved on the shield.

The 'Comic Band', who collectively couldn't hold a tune in a bucket, gained the prize for the biggest group collection. This bunch of misfits met up every Boxing Day and toured the pubs playing drums, kazoos, cymbals and any other gadget that would make a sound. What they lacked in talent, these so called musicians more that made up for in enthusiasm and collected a huge sum every year.

Finally Sam and Ronnie received a cup for taking control of the 'mile of pennies'. This was a great idea for raising cash. The public were encouraged to add their loose change to the line of coins, usually started with five pounds in fifty pence pieces, formerly in half-crowns, by Councillor Jaconelli. These stretched westwards along the kerb of the Foreshore Road, parallel with the beach. As the line grew, the two custodians almost ran up and down the road persuading contributors, but also trying to prevent predatory youngsters picking up the larger coins and running off. This was warm work and the 'Cass Mainprize Memorial Cup', which they were awarded, was well deserved. The late Cass Mainprize had played in every match between 1945 and 1971.

The evening wound up early as always and Gladys was safely delivered home. The committee wouldn't meet again until November, when the process would start again.

* * * * * *

On a Monday morning in May there was a strong wind blowing from the east. We'd been at sea for more than twenty-four hours and fish were scarce. Heartily sick of rolling around and not far from Scarborough, it seemed a good idea to return to port. The few other skippers still at sea were of the same mind and were also heading for home.

We had to wait for the tide to flow to give sufficient water for a safe passage in the swell, then followed each other into the harbour, according to our draft. We'd leave our meagre catches below to be landed before we sailed again. With fenders and ropes in place, the boats' crews were soon walking from the pier. "Are we gonna try one?" I suggested to Col, pointing to the Lord Nelson Hotel across the road. It was about noon and we weren't often in port on a Monday. It would be good to have a beer and a yarn.

The idea found favour and less than a minute later we were walking through the opaque, double glass doors with 'Bass Charrington' etched on each pane.

We realised a celebration must be taking place when we were greeted by Harry Sheader, who immediately thrust two large glasses of brandy in our direction. Harry, known to all as 'Baby' as he was the youngest of six children, was a large, powerful cobleman the total antithesis of his nickname. "It's Denk's birthday," he informed us. "'Ave a drink." There was no opportunity to say no, even if we'd wanted to. This wasn't an invitation, more of an instruction.

Denk was one of the older skippers, much liked and respected around the harbour. He and Harry had a tradition that on the occasion of their birthdays, one would buy the other a bottle of brandy. This bottle was at present being shared among most of the fishermen present.

The company was good and the beer flowing. The contents of the brandy bottle quickly disappeared. Colin bought a round of drinks and a replacement bottle and not long after, I did the same. Time passed quickly and the conversation grew louder. The stories of fish catches and bad weather became exaggerated and I retold a few of the recent jokes I'd heard.

The old skipper told us about one of his crew. "Yer know who ah mean lads, that one with t' squeaky voice. 'E came in t' wheelhouse an' burst out cryin' last week. Ah'd jus' told 'em we were stayin' at sea another night cos we 'adn't much fish aboard. Daft bugger said 'e was supposed t' be goin' out that night an' I was ruinin' 'is social life. 'E can 'ave all t' time off 'e wants now, cos ah've sacked 'im." Draining his glass, Denk thought maybe he should buy himself a bottle and no one challenged him, though I was finding it a little difficult to think and speak.

At about four o'clock, long after the official closing time, the landlord 'suggested' we should go home. No one was in a position to argue and we meekly made for the door. Staggering up the hill, my fuddled brain was saying, "Dotty'll be surprised t' see me. She won't be expectin' me in t' 'arbour on a Monday." Nothing could have been further from the truth, as I discovered when I fell through the open door.

My wife had seen the *Independence* entering the harbour before noon and had gone home to cook a dinner. She now sat glowering, knitting in hand, her needles clicking furiously. It didn't help matters that I was having difficulty standing and slumped into the armchair, attempting futile apologies.

Dotty got up, thrusting her knitting at Danny, who was sat playing on the rug. She said, "take this to Grandma's. Ask if it fits."

"But it's not finished yet," replied our eight year old.

"Take it anyway," she snapped, "while I get your Dad his dinner." Danny left the house with the knitting in hand, heading for my parents' house. I thought that under the circumstances it was pretty decent of Dotty to get my meal but I'd misread the signs. The steaming hot plate, held in oven gloved hands was brought from the kitchen to where I sat and was promptly dropped on my head, breaking on impact, covering me with what had once been a tasty meal.

If ever the expression, 'swearing like a fish wife' was apt, it was now and I received uncharacteristic, verbal abuse in no short supply. Sobering up very rapidly, I went to the telephone and called my crew members, informing them we were sailing in two hours time.

Their collective response was unanimous, "the weather out there's awful."

I was equally sure that it was more peaceful at sea than where I was at present.

There was much grumbling, muttering and glances in my direction as our ropes were cast off and without landing our few boxes of fish we sailed out through the harbour mouth and into the gale. Seven hours steaming southeast with the wind on our port bow didn't help to cheer the crew and I was feeling very lonely and hungover by the time we reached the fishing grounds, twenty miles off the River Humber.

The extraordinary thing was, that although it was still blowing hard, the swell had fallen away substantially and the weather wasn't too bad in our location. We shot the trawl and were into our fishing routine. We were taking good hauls and fished steadily until late on Wednesday night, by which time we had ninety kit of quality cod on board. I thought it was a good idea to take advantage of the short supply and get our catch back for an early market. I'd long since been forgiven by my crew for taking them out in the bad weather. We were on our way home with a trip on board, while the other boats in the fleet were just sailing.

Thursday morning found me walking from the pier, catch on the market, boxes stowed and the *Independence* washed down, ready for sea again. I was feeling rather pleased with myself. I spied Mr White, my bank manager, heading along the quay in my direction and I waved an acknowledgement. Noel often visited the fish market at auction time to see how 'his' boats were performing.

In answer to his question I was happily telling him of our good fortune when Danny came running towards us. He was on his way to school via the harbour and had spotted the boat alongside the quay.

He didn't say, "hello Dad" or "did you catch anything, Dad?" His first words were, "why did Mum hit you with that plate, Dad?"

I gave him a nudge and said, "Shhh, Danny, we're talkin' business," but he continued excitedly.

"I saw it. I was watching through the window, Dad."

I turned away from my son and back to the bank manager, hoping in vain that he hadn't overheard the conversation.

Unfortunately the banker had also heard my son's story and Noel was more interested in Danny's information than anything I had to say.

"An' it broke, Dad, the plate broke on your 'ead. Was it 'ot? Did it 'urt, Dad?"

I was forced to come clean and tell Noel the story of Denk's birthday party and subsequent events, which he found highly amusing. He regularly used this tale to embarrass me whenever the opportunity arose.

* * * * * *

We'd sailed at midnight on a seventy-mile passage to the Northwest Rough, in company with a number of other vessels. It was late June and though the nights were short at this time of year, the darkening and dawning hauls were usually very good out in this shallow water, with mostly haddock but some small codling and a valuable picking of good sized, lemon sole. The daylight seemed endless and on this aptly named ground, trawls regularly became stuck and were damaged. The water was crystal clear and we'd be happy to see a kit of fish per hour trawled, though we'd see no haddock by day. Long stints of mending were fruitless and sleep robbing and if we lost any of the dark fishing, this lowered the daily average of the catch dramatically.

*Cassamanda,* the fastest boat in the fleet was the first vessel to approach the shoal ground at the northwest corner of the Dogger Bank. We'd been called out by Bluey twenty minutes from the grounds and as I entered the wheelhouse, Bev broke the radio silence. "'Ave yer seen t' colour of t' water off 'ere?" As he was the first vessel on the grounds, this was a rhetorical question to the other vessels steaming to his location. "It's like bein' in t' Caribbean; it's turquoise," he clarified.

This sounded something of an exaggeration but as the depth on the sounder reduced, the water did indeed begin to change colour. This was a peculiar phenomena, the North Sea taking on a tropical appearance. Although the water was a pale blue, when we threw the net over the side it became apparent that the water was milky, rather than clear. Normally out here we could see the whole trawl under the water but only a few feet of netting was visible. The sea was full of countless tiny micro-organisms making the water cloudy. No one in the vicinity had any previous experience of this trick of nature.

Soon half a dozen boats were towing but it would be a while before anyone would see any results and expectations were not high for the daylight. We'd only been towing ten minutes when our trawl became fastened on the hard ground. In this shallow water with tide running, it was difficult to recover gear easily and when ours came up, the net and bobbins were in a tangle and the net damaged. An hour later the mess was clear, trawl mended and we were shooting again. One or two others had become fast but most boats were getting along over the rugged ground. In no time we were stuck again. Another mess and this time the trawl would have to be replaced. The damage would take too long to repair. This further trouble meant we'd almost lost a full watch, so losing patience I shouted, "tek t' ends in." With the wings of the trawl lifted clear of the water, I set course for the deeper water to the north, where we'd made regular successful trips in the past.

We'd been steaming for about half an hour and were clear of the turquoise water which, reflecting the sun had been hurting my eyes. Bev was hauling and his report was due any minute. "Bingo," he shouted and shortly after, reported three lifts of cod. This was a big haul. The codend of our trawls held about twenty boxes of fish, about three-quarters of a ton. *Cassamanda* had lifted three 'bags' aboard. Not long after, Col also declared a bumper haul of four lifts. I turned the *Independence* around and put the throttle to full, to get back to the action as quickly as possible. Others were now recording quality hauls and soon, with a new net in place, we were shooting among the fleet again. This time things were better and we too, were amongst the fish.

We took four bags on board for a three-hour tow. "Yer fuckin' mad," was only one of the comments from my crew when, oilskin clad, I dived, landing in a belly flop onto the pile of fish, rolling on the surface of the heap. It was just a relief to be among the fish, in this case literally. I decided I'd do this in future whenever we got a big haul.

We kept up the good performance all day, but as darkness fell, the boats hauling reported poor catches. Again we hit the jackpot. Three lifts, then putting a rope becket around the remaining bag, we pulled in another ton. It had been a bonanza for all. The coloured water had made the difference.

* * * * * *

The following month, working north of Whitby we encountered more coloured water, this time not light blue, but red. There were large patches of this strange colouring, drifting with the tide and it was with astonishment that we realised this was krill. Normally, this shrimp like creature is only found in northern Arctic waters but some strange tidal surge had propelled clouds of the little crustaceans a long way south from their normal habitat. This was the food of whales but it seemed every fish in the area also enjoyed this delicacy. Useful hauls of cod, their bellies bursting with the pink creatures, were caught by boats throughout the northern North Sea. Our oilskins and gloves were stained pink from contact. The clouds of krill in the water stretched from the surface to the bottom and we aimed our boats at the blotches of crimson.

During the night and towing north, a few miles offshore from the beautiful, Robin Hood's Bay, I realised we were drawing close to a known wreck on our starboard bow. Normally this would have been easy to avoid with a slight, early alteration in course but there was an unidentified vessel, trawling on my port side, edging me ever closer to the obstacle. The 'Rule of the Road' gave me the right of way, so I picked up the handset. "There's a boat on me port side, t' north o' 'South Cheek'. Are yer listenin on this channel?"

There was no reply to my appeal. I tried again. "Boat on me port side, can yer give me a couple o' points t' port? We're gonna be in this wreck in few minutes." There was only silence in response. I had the option of stopping the boat but then we'd have to haul the net up and we'd only been shot for an hour or so. The lads below had only just turned in. How could I draw the unseeing watchman's attention to the unfolding problem? Stored in the locker under the wheelhouse console was a box of white parachute flares. If I fired one of these in the air, I'd be able to identify the intruding craft and call again on the radio, giving the vessels name. I opened the varnished door.

The power of these pyrotechnics was amazing. A few years earlier, in my previous boat *Courage,* we'd used flares to illuminate the coastline when the Whitby lifeboat was attempting to rescue the crew of a stranded trawler. The vessel had gone ashore beneath the imposing cliffs to the south of the old port.* I tried one final time. "Fishin' boat on me port side, this is t' *Independence*. Can yer gi' me a bit o' sea room. We're gonna be in this bloody wreck in a minute." Time was running out and losing patience, I removed the plastic ends from the cartridge and withdrew the safety pin. Reaching out through the port window, right hand grasping the tube almost upright, I aimed ahead of the target. My left thumb flipped the small, hinged, metal trigger upwards and I exerted pressure.

With a whoosh, the rocket shot into the black sky. There was virtually no recoil from the cartridge and the light, empty, acrid smoking cylinder was all that remained of the weapon. I threw this over the side, all the time looking skywards for the result of my handiwork. There was a far off, 'pop' as the firework exploded

---

* See Slack Water.

into life then darkness became daylight as the flare ignited and began its slow, iridescent drift downwards.

The mysterious vessel was painted green and a familiar craft but I didn't need to use the radio to draw the skipper's attention now. She was already going hard to port, much harder than necessary. Relieved, I put the helm four points to port, allowing our gear to narrowly skirt the obstruction.

The radio crackled into life and a breathless voice said, "*Independence,* what's up?"

"'Ello, Roy. Yer were pushin' us into that wreck ahead of us. I've been callin' yer on t' radio. Ah didn't know who it was. There's nowt else ah could do."

His vessel was now on a parallel course and a safe distance away. "Sorry," came back the reply. "I was sittin' on t' galley step, readin' a book. I never saw yer. Yer frightened t' bloody life out o' me when that flare went off."

His explanation was quite reasonable. Roy was an intelligent man and an avid reader who could get through half a dozen books a week. Unfortunately for him, when he hauled his trawl, the net was damaged, probably due to the radical course alteration.

We also had a problem when we hauled our net. The bobbins dropped on the deck and the headline was dragged onboard and seemed heavy. We began to pull in the net, which was deep in the water. There was no sign of any catch in the dark but in every other respect, the weight and swelling of the lower part of the trawl, indicated fish. Eventually the load was such that we could pull no more. "Can any of yer see anythin'?" I asked, peering down into the blackness.

"It's a bag of nothing," Sid said, perplexed.

"It looks like jelly," Rusty chipped in.

"That's what it is," I said, as the situation dawned on me. "It's a bag o' jellies."

The huge catch was all translucent jellyfish. There were no stinging streamers on this variety and the four small, blue rings typical of this six-inch-diameter creature were not visible in the darkness.

Bluey grabbed the line leading down to the codend and the rope was taken to the winch. A bag of mostly jelly, squelching through the meshes, was hauled up the boat's side, swinging inboard and throwing particles everywhere as the bulging sack hit the fish pound. When the bag opened, the few fish in the unwanted catch lay limp, drowned in the mass of 'blebbers', which were now slopping back and forth with the rolling of the boat.

"If we could sell the buggers, we wouldn't be able t' catch 'em," Rusty observed.

"We need a bag o' custard next," suggested Bluey.

I laughed at the wit then said, "Don't fasten the codend, Sid. Jus' let it run back overboard. We'll slip whatever's left."

The empty codend was allowed to run back over the side unfastened and we began to pull on the sleeve again. This time there was little resistance. The remaining jellies slithered down the net, flowing out of the opening to freedom and whatever purpose they served in the great scheme of things.

A noisy alarm from the wheelhouse beckoned an investigation and I hurried to the call. The engine was overheating. The machine was being starved of cooling seawater. "Well, yer don't need t' be a genius t' know what's causing that," I declared to Rusty, who'd come aft to assist. We went below to stop the engine and lift the aluminium footplates. Shutting off the seacock, I removed the butterfly nuts on the cover, passing them to my assistant, then withdrew the strainer. The foot-long, perforated tube was, as expected, totally choked with jelly. Five minutes later the offending object had been cleaned, rinsed and repositioned. As always, it was a relief when the engine fired up. The machine was seldom stopped at sea.

## CHAPTER 8

# THE FLIGHT FROM BERWICK

The United Kingdom's membership of the Common Market was making fishing more of a political issue and quotas had been introduced for each of the main species of fish we caught: cod, haddock, whiting, plaice and sole, though we were assured by glib politicians that this wouldn't be a problem for the UK fleet as we'd gained plenty of fish from the share out. It was the other countries fishing the North Sea who'd have problems with their allocation.

Wanting to know more of what was happening within the administrative regime of our industry, I volunteered to join the committee of Scarborough Inshore Fishermen's Society, attending meetings with Denk, who was the Chairman. I'd often drive him to national meetings at various venues around the north of England, and though my driving was still appalling, to his credit, Denk never once complained, though he did cringe occasionally.

Scarborough fishermen had accepted an invitation from the deep-sea industry in Hull to join their 'Producer Organisation', allowing this body to manage our catch data and administrate the new quotas, for a modest fee. We'd turned down the opportunity of membership of a more compatible body, the Anglo-Scottish Producer Organisation, following a too slick presentation by a distinctly smarmy Chief Executive, who had all the characteristics of a used car salesman.

The management in Hull were strange bedfellows, from a sector of the industry that had little in common with inshore fishing, yet the arrangement worked remarkably well. We were kept up to date with all the decisions affecting our business and of any potential developments. The PO's monthly meetings were held on Friday evenings and were attended by young, high-flying executives. These men enjoyed the informal, easy-going manner of our gatherings.

One day towards the end of the month, I was asked by Denk to attend a meeting of Producer Organisations on his behalf on the following Friday. The session was to take place in Berwick and I was telling my pals in the Sub Aqua Club of the proposed visit at the weekend. The Medical Officer, Alf, who Dotty and I had dined with on our tenth wedding anniversary, said he kept his private plane near Berwick and was intending to bring the machine south on that same day. He was planning to land on a farmer's grass strip just a few miles from town. "If you want a lift back, I'd be pleased to have you along as a passenger," he offered.

This was a wonderful opportunity, both of a special flight and an early return home and I readily accepted.

On the day of the meeting I travelled north by rail to the border town venue, ironically, at the Anglo-Scottish PO's, headquarters. This was a new experience for me but I was able to voice our society's point of view in the discussions. Starting at noon, the talking seemed to go on endlessly, with people making what I thought were irrelevant points or going over the same ground. I kept looking at my watch, aware that my lift home was at 1530 and was from a small airfield on the outskirts of town.

My own interests had been covered, so with a final glance at the time and waiting for a brief lull in the proceedings, I gathered the paperwork together, stacking the sheets noisily. Standing, I coughed to attract the Chairman's attention then announced to all, "I'm sorry gentlemen, I have to leave now, my plane's waiting." For the first time in the day the meeting fell silent. I withdrew quickly to my waiting taxi, leaving the room's occupants speechless.

The flight south was amazing. The visibility was perfect and we flew along this unfamiliar coastline at not much more than cliff top height. Within half an hour I began to recognise landmarks. First I spotted the Tyne Piers then Heugh Point at the north end of Tees Bay. Soon Whitby Harbour then Whitby High Light, nestling in the cliff, came into view. Excitedly I pointed out these distinctive features to the pilot, who though he couldn't hear me, acknowledged my enthusiasm with smiles and nods. Robin Hood's Bay, which is spectacular from both land and sea with its unique, parallel bands of rocky scars visible below the sea's surface, was beyond description.

I declined an offer to take the controls, knowing my limitations and not wanting to create a disaster. Far too soon we were flying past the Scarborough Castle Headland, with its ancient ruins. This unique perspective was breathtaking. An unexpected bonus was added to this wonderful experience when we circled the harbour and Old Town at low level, allowing me to see my home environment from above. I could see all the boats in the harbour and identify my own craft on the inside of a tier of three boats. On landing, with Dotty waiting to collect me, I thanked Alf profusely for this experience of a lifetime but he shrugged off the thanks nonchalantly, saying he was making the trip anyway and was pleased to oblige.

Though attending fisheries meetings was an unusual occurrence, two weeks later I was heading north again, this time to the granite city of Aberdeen. We'd made a midweek landing and I stayed ashore to travel to the meeting the following morning. For the first time ever, I allowed my crew to take the *Independence* to sea. As I watched her sail round the pier end, an immense feeling of guilt came over me. I felt I was malingering and should have been on board with them.

Arriving late, I stayed overnight in the conveniently situated Station Hotel and was early to the meeting at the Scottish Fishermen's Federation office, along the road adjacent to the quay. Unusually, the proceedings of this meeting were completed in less than two hours and the next train south was not for some time. It was a cold day but I felt compelled to wander round the bustling harbour, taking in the variety of craft plying their trade. The famous Shetland Ferry, *St Clair* was in port, close to some large, oil related craft and nearby, the fish quay was home to some of the renowned Scottish North Sea trawlers.

With still more than an hour to kill and in need of warmth, I wandered into the public bar attached to the Station Hotel for a beer and to while away the time. It was now mid-afternoon and the bar was almost empty. Minutes later I was sitting on a bar stool, bag at my side and a glass of 'McEwans 70/- ale' on the counter. Idly daydreaming, I looked at the dozens of different whiskies on the shelf, with little interest. To my right, the door to the street opened and I automatically looked towards the opening. The cold draft heralded the entrance of a particularly ugly woman with straggly hair and uncared for teeth. The female surveyed the sparse clientele then headed in my direction. I quickly averted my gaze, once more looking at the range of bottles, but this time in earnest, while monitoring her progress in the bar mirrors. Had the newcomer been attractive, I'd have been pleased to at least say "hello" and pass the time of day but this unfortunate apparition held no charm whatsoever.

I sensed her at my side and could now see her reflection close up, as she assessed me. Casually picking up my glass, I pursed my lips and took a long pull of the beer. "Arr ye lookin' fo' some company hen. Would ye be wantin' a wee fock." This growl wasn't so much an invitation as a threat.

The drink stuck in my throat and I coughed, releasing beer and froth, mostly back into the glass but also onto the counter. I was lost for words and if I'd had any in mind, couldn't have spoken them. Had this stranger been stunning, I'd have gently declined the invitation with a smile and maybe a joke but the thought of not only having sex with this gorgon, but that she actually expected me to pay for the experience was more than my spinning brain could contemplate.

I felt vulnerable and still coughing said, "er no thanks, ah've got a train t' catch." Slipping from the stool, I downed the remaining ale in one gulp, coughing again, unable to retain the drink. The front of my shirt caught the residue my mouth couldn't hold and grabbing the bag, I was through the door and into the street in seconds. It didn't seem nearly as cold as I headed across the road towards the station.

## Chapter 9

# New Arrivals

Harvey, the tenacious line fisherman from Bridlington who'd kept the trawlers at bay during the winter months in his little keelboat, *Wellspring* had decided to build a trawling vessel. In conjunction with Alf Goacher, the Scarborough fish merchant and Arthur Cook, the main agent, merchant and vessel owner in Bridlington, he'd chosen to build a wooden boat at the 'Jones Yard' at Lossiemouth, on the southern shore of the Moray Firth.

The uncompromising skipper had for years been one of the most successful fishers in the port. Earlier in his career he'd fished for dogfish from a coble and on one exceptional trip had filled his boat almost to sinking point with fish. He'd hung his coiled, used lines overboard to make more room for his catch, and had almost foundered getting his catch home.

Harvey was now keen to learn the trawling job, sailing on both *Our Heritage* and *Independence* to gain experience. Colin and I helped him all we could to learn our mode of fishing, even giving him our personal plotter rolls to copy, though we were aware he'd be a formidable challenge. Soon his boat would be ready to hit the water and we'd been invited to the launching of this new vessel.

We decided to drive north, taking the scenic route through the centre of Scotland, using small roads through remote villages. Dotty was now heavily pregnant and was expecting to deliver within the month. The journey was pleasant and uneventful initially. We saw some beautiful, wild scenery, though at a speed a little faster than my wife would have preferred. The reminder that we were on a mini holiday and were in no rush, occasionally drifted in my direction. Dotty was finding it difficult to remain comfortable on the twisting roads, due to the large cargo she was carrying, so breathed a little sigh of relief when a long, narrow road appeared before us.

With no traffic in view and the way ahead clear, I put my foot hard on the accelerator. The 'Maxi' picked up speed pleasingly and we were soon hurtling down the narrow mountain road. Suddenly, without warning a ramp appeared in the road and unable to slow down in time, the car left the ground. Two seconds later the four wheels hit the tarmac with a bang; the suspension bottoming out. I was sure the car must be damaged and gave a hurried glance in the rear view mirror. There were no broken pieces of vehicle in sight but the mirror did reveal four distinct piles of dry soil in the carriageway. This was the build up of muck from the wheel arches, which had been dislodged by the impact. Wrestling with the wheel to keep the vehicle on the road, I was aware of a worrying groaning from the passenger seat.

"Oohhhh, oohhhh," were the only sounds Dotty was making as her eyes rolled in their sockets and she held her swollen tummy.

As soon as possible I brought the car to a standstill, stopped the engine and turned to face my wife. "Are you alright? Do you need a doctor? Shall I find a hospital?" The questions spewed out rapidly but remained unanswered as Dotty, still holding her precious bundle, breathed deeply, her eyes eventually steadying on mine.

"You bloody stupid idiot," was her first response. "You nearly killed us. I've been telling you to slow down."

Suitably chastised and greatly relieved that she was feeling well enough to scold me, I restarted the engine then checked the map to identify the nearest large town, in case our new offspring should decide to turn up early. I drove quite steadily for the remainder of the journey, constantly enquiring after her health and comfort.

Most of the launching party had arrived at the venue by the time we turned up and having deposited our belongings, we joined the crowd in the bar, though Dotty was still a little shaken. I related some of our exploits to the group, skipping the motoring incident but embellishing the remoteness of our route, saying, "we were so far off the beaten track, when I finally found somewhere to refuel, I was asked if I wanted fodder and water."

The new craft, *Margaret H* was named after the skipper's wife. Dark blue in colour and slightly under sixty-feet in length, her construction was way behind schedule and she wasn't nearly ready, but the launch date had been set so the ceremony was to go ahead as planned. The owners had been promised the vessel would be completed as quickly as possible.

Standing with Dotty near the bar, we were joined by one of the management team from the shipyard. Holding out his hand he said, "hello, I'm Airley," then proceeded to spell out his name letter by letter, clearly something he did as a matter of course.

Dotty, obviously still not fully recovered said, "Airley, my God, what a name. Didn't your parents like you?"

Surprised at her tactlessness I turned to face my wife, raising my eyebrows.

Realising what she'd said, Dotty turned crimson, put her hand to her mouth and through her fingers mumbled, "Oh dear! Did I really say that? I only meant to think it."

Clearly insulted, Airley moved to another group where I heard him say, "hello, my name's Ai … ."

The new vessel was launched with a splash and her arrival celebrated in style as tradition demanded. Drinks were followed by a splendid banquet, then official speeches. Harvey's lovely wife, Margaret and children, David and Caroline were clearly enjoying their big day.

The prospective skipper, positioned in the centre of the top table with family, partners and builders on both sides stood up, paper in hand, cleared his throat and the room fell silent. He began by thanking his wife for naming the vessel and breaking the champagne bottle then said, "I'd also like to thank my partners, Alf and Arthur," then hesitating, stammered a little and said, "I mean Arthur and Alf." Laughter rang out round the room and Harvey coloured visibly. There was clearly a pecking order in the partnership. Picking up his theme again he continued with a toast to the builders for a fine ship then thanked the hotel for the excellent meal and the staff for their prompt service. Relieved, Harvey sat down to loud applause then other subjects worthy of toasting were suggested by the guests, starting with skipper and crew.

* * * * * *

All through Thursday night Dotty had been suffering backache and couldn't get comfortable at all. She suspected our baby was imminent and was a little pensive. Plans were already in place for my Mum to take care of Paula and Danny when the new arrival chose to appear. The discomfort continued into Friday with still no sign of the baby and late in the afternoon, radical measures were called for. We went for a bumpy drive in the car in an attempt to kick-start the launching process. This had almost worked prematurely in Scotland on our way to *Margaret H's* christening and Dotty had heard this unorthodox method had worked successfully for a friend. She was prepared to try anything to relieve her unhappy situation.

In comparison to my wife's pain I was suffering a minor, tender bursa on my right knee, the result of a fall while playing five-a-side football. The bleb didn't seem to be reducing and I was careful to avoid knocking the sensitive area.

While Patsy looked after the bairns, we embarked on a tour of Olivers Mount, the large hill overlooking the town from the South around which was a challenging international motorcycle track. We did a couple of fast laps while Dotty held her large, precious lump. From there we went down the steep road to the long, narrow, boating lake on the other side of the hill. After three circuits around the potholed, Mere path, Dotty said, "I don't think this is working. We'd better go home."

It may have been a coincidence but by Saturday morning the signs of the baby's arrival were becoming more apparent. There was no possibility of my going to sea that night so I rang Dave Normandale, a distant relative and former skipper, who'd recently joined our crew, asking him if he'd take the *Independence* to sea. This wasn't a problem for him and she was in all respects ready to go. Dave knew the area we'd been working and wouldn't have any trouble catching fish, so I could now concentrate on my family and its imminent increase.

Around eleven o'clock that night it was definitely time to go to the hospital. My Mum arrived within ten minutes of the call and leaving her with the bairns, we drove to St Mary's maternity unit, the place where Paula and Danny had been born.

Things had changed dramatically in the years since Danny was born and not only was I not dismissed out of hand, I was positively encouraged to stay. Dotty was taken to a small, single ward and assisted into bed by the midwife. I sat in a chair at her side and we talked quietly when the contractions would allow, though these were getting closer and the baby wasn't far from making its appearance. I summoned the nurse. Dotty was now in constant pain and the midwife was fussing round, preparing for the baby's delivery. "Hold her hand. Get closer. Pull your chair in towards the bed," the sister instructed.

I followed these orders immediately and a sudden, blinding pain shot through my knee. I'd banged the bursa I'd been protecting for the past few weeks on the horizontal metal bed frame. I grabbed the hurting joint and looking in the direction of my wife, called out, "Bloody 'ell, that 'urt, I've jus' banged my knee on t, be-," for a fleeting second expecting sympathy. The words died in my mouth as I saw the glazed look in Dotty's eyes and heard her groaning, in real pain. My problem fell into instant insignificance and I held her more closely.

There was another twenty minutes of groaning and pushing before the baby's head appeared and only seconds later the body slipped out, but I was unprepared for the baby's appearance. Apart from the bloody, greasy condition of the child, I didn't know it was natural for the top of a baby's head to be creased to facilitate the birth and I thought there was a major problem with our newborn. It wasn't until she began squawking healthily and the midwife carried on as if everything was normal that I realised things really were fine. We'd been blessed with another beautiful, healthy daughter. Sarah had arrived. We'd already decided on this name, should the newcomer be a girl.

I was despatched home in the early hours of Sunday morning, allowing Dotty to get some well-earned sleep and was instructed to bring Paula and Danny to the hospital soon after breakfast to meet their new sister.

Not only did I visit again early in the morning with our two bairns, I also went again on my own later in the morning to find Dotty was now in a ward with five other new mothers. The Sister suggested that I might want to bring a bottle of stout on my next visit to help build up my wife's strength, as this drink was full of goodness and would help with her breast feeding. Of course I misconstrued this message. At noon I was in the Leeds Arms, wetting the baby's head, buying and receiving drinks from many of the customers. By the two o'clock closing deadline, I was quite well oiled as I made my wobbly way across the street to the grocer cum off licence. The request for a bottle of stout had now become ingredients for a party for six new mothers and I loaded a cardboard container with a variety of bottles.

There was a look of horror on Dotty's face when I staggered into the ward with the box of booze, though I couldn't see the problem. The case was rapidly shoved under the bed until my departure and after the usual enquiries of health and family Dotty asked what I was planning to do for the next few days, as my boat was at sea. Her implication was clear. She was going to be in hospital for about five days and I was at a loose end and would probably spend more time in the pub.

In truth, Dotty was correct. I also knew I'd be bored witless with nothing to do. The weather was fine, so I said I'd try to get a lift off to my boat if there were any vessels heading in that direction. There was no swell so it shouldn't be a problem jumping from one boat to the other. I made my way to the harbour to see which craft were still in dock.

The only likely boat tied up alongside was the *Tim Windsor,* a green-painted, steel vessel skippered by Frank, who'd tragically lost his previous craft, *Admiral Von Tromp* a few years earlier under Whitby High Light. I rang Frank, asking when he was sailing and if there was any chance of a lift off to 'Bruce's Gardens', where I knew the *Independence* would be working. I told him there'd be good fishing there.

"We're sailing at ten o'clock tonight," he informed me and had no problem with taking me offshore.

When I next visited the maternity hospital, I was able to tell Dotty I'd be sailing at ten that night and wouldn't be ashore until Thursday. I'd still be back in time to bring her and baby Sarah home.

I turned up at the harbour, hoping to get a few hours sleep en route following the previous disrupted twenty-four hours, so was dismayed to find I was expected to steer the *Tim Windsor* all the way off to the rendezvous, some fifty-plus miles northeast by east. This would be a seven-hour steam.

It was a long, tiring night and daylight had broken by the time we drew close to my vessel. We'd been in touch by radio for the last two hours, so now the surprise of my appearance had worn off. It was obvious by the cloud of gulls following the vessel that her trawl had recently been hauled and re-shot.

*Tim Windsor* drew up from astern on the port side of my vessel, Frank skilfully avoided the pair of wires leading down into the water from the *Independence* and as the two vessels passed gunwale to gunwale at a distance of two feet, I stepped across the gap. The three men gutting fish grabbed and welcomed me, one of their number saying, "what are yer doin' 'ere? Yer mus' be mad."

Dave wasn't too happy when I entered the wheelhouse, as he now had to go on deck and also, though they'd been fishing for less than twenty-four hours, the fishing had been good. He would have landed an excellent trip with no assistance from me.

It was another two hours before the deck was clear and I was desperately ready for a nap by the time the lads trooped from the deck. "It's your watch now," Bluey said, laughing as he made his way from the wheelhouse to an unexpected watch below, after delivering me a much needed coffee.

At least it was daylight now and this predominantly haddock fishing was mostly in the dark. I wasn't sorry to see only seven or eight boxes drop on the deck when we hauled again. It was now midday on Monday and I'd had only a few hours sleep since early on Saturday morning. Dead on my feet, I sacrificed a meal to finally roll into my pit.

It was a very proud father that drove mother and daughter home very carefully, early on Thursday afternoon.

* * * * * *

The agreed delivery date for the *Margaret H* had come and gone but there was no sign of Harvey's boat being ready. His old vessel had been sold and the skipper in waiting was now out of work. The fishing gear for the new venture was already stored in his warehouse, ready for assembling. Unused to having time on his hands, Harvey had bought a bike. For the duration of his vessel's delay he could be seen pedalling furiously to and from the harbour, expending his pent up energy and frustrations. Eventually, months overdue, *Margaret H* was completed and ready for her delivery.

* * * * * *

Now late summer and following a disappointing auction, raising suspicions that the market was being ringed again, Col and I were having a beer in the 'Leeds' one lunchtime, discussing the way ahead. "If we don't start our own company, we're gonna get this treatment all the time. We can do it." I said with enthusiasm. Following further in depth discussions and in total agreement, we decided to pursue the matter further.

At sea the following week I worked out the figures on paper, calculating that a total first hand sale of fish, valued at half a million pounds per year would be required to make our own agency viable. Aware that we'd each grossed in excess of two hundred thousand pounds the previous year, we wouldn't need much more to be sure of our target. Meeting again the following week we decided to go ahead, agreeing to ask a couple of skippers with a smaller catching capability if they were interested in joining our project, stressing that we'd all be equal partners. Receiving positive responses, we began to harden up our plans but not until we'd discussed the matter with Noel White, whose advice and guidance would be invaluable.

The beginning of the New Year seemed a logical date to commence this exciting project but there was much to do before then. We'd need premises, boxes, office furniture but most of all, we'd need someone to pull all this together; someone who could auction fish and who'd stand up to the merchants, not allowing the sharing out of fish on the market. Time was moving on. I placed an advertisement for someone with the necessary qualities in the 'Fishing News', under an anonymous box number.

The responses were varied, including a surprising one from Barry, the salesman in our existing office. We mistakenly thought this was an enquiry to discover who had placed the advertisement and didn't consider this a genuine application. We asked Terry Pearson, a fish salesman from Hull to an interview one Saturday morning. This meeting was attended by the four, prospective directors plus Godfather Noel.

The candidate, a tall, blond-haired, bearded, married man with two youngsters, immediately filled us with confidence. Terry had a wide experience of the fish trade and was prepared to travel daily from Hull until such time as he could relocate. We discussed his suitability then decided to offer him the placement, initially on a three-month trial basis, subject to a satisfactory salary agreement. Terry declined this offer, saying he couldn't leave a permanent job to take up another for possibly only three months, so we immediately scrapped the trial period and he accepted the position.

Now confident of going into business, we had to officially form a company and think of an appropriate name. This was a poser for a week or two but my suggestion of 'Alliance' found favour with the other partners. There was still a while to go but we had a long list of things to be done, including acquiring details of the merchants we were to deal with and we had to give notice to our existing agency. Meanwhile we'd continue fishing.

For a change of scenery, Dotty and I went to the Newcastle Packet on the Friday evening and it turned out to be a special night. We'd been in the building about half an hour when the men of the Filey Fishermen's Choir came into the pub for a beer stop. They'd been performing at a venue in town and had gravitated to the harbour. Once fortified with a pint each, they were unable to resist the invitation to perform. Quickly tuning up, they burst into song. The deep, powerful voices of these eighteen or twenty men in harmony first sang of a historic storm along the coast in the days of sail and of the huge of loss of life. Another number about shoals of herring caught by drifters also brought the pub to a standstill. The choristers didn't buy any more beer. They didn't need to. The customers were only too pleased to provide their drinks to keep them singing.

The brothers, Jim and Dick Haxby, coble fishermen from the little town, standing at the back, towered above most of the other singers, not all of whom were fishermen these days. Bob 'Sugar' Mason in the front row, was one of three brothers who fished from the 'James Noble' built keelboat, *Onward Star* from Scarborough. Bob was one of the few men still living who'd 'rowed' in a Filey Lifeboat in the years before a motor vessel was provided.

The front man for the group, little George Burton, was quite elderly but a great raconteur, telling wonderful jokes and keeping the audience spellbound as he strung his stories out at length, between songs. George was still in employment for Scarborough Council as the town's rat-catcher. An attempt by his boss to retire him backfired dramatically. "I want to talk to you about your retirement, George. We don't have a need for a rat-catcher any more," he'd been told over the phone. Next day, George had turned up at the supervisor's office with a sack in one hand and politely, his cap in the other.

"As I said over the phone yesterday, George, I'm sorry but we don't need you any more. We never see any of the creatures these days," the head of department said, reiterating his earlier spiel to the little man.

"You're gonna need somebody t' catch these, ah think," George said, emptying the sack containing half a dozen live long-tails to the floor. The beasts quickly scurried to the nearest hiding places within the room, but not before the executive had leapt on his chair. His notice was rescinded on the spot, providing he removed the offending animals.

George, working alone, would occasionally lift the manhole covers to bait traps in the sewers along the promenade on Filey's shoreline. During the summer, when visitors were around and he'd finished his business below the streets, before replacing the iron cover, he'd shout down the hole, "are yer comin' up? Yer'd better 'urry, ah'm not waiting much longer." He'd listen, but obviously received no response. "Right, stay down there then. Ah don't care." Dragging the heavy, round lid back into place, he'd walk off muttering audibly, "serves 'im right." On several occasions the police or town hall received urgent phone calls from worried tourists saying a man had been abandoned down the sewers.

The old man was a fascinating after dinner speaker and particularly enjoyed talking to ladies groups, where he held his audience spellbound. "Very few people know," he'd say, "that all t' rats ah catch are recycled."

The ladies would look perplexed.

"It's true. I skin 'em an' all t' skins are used fo' makin' mittens fo' poor children," George explained.

The women would murmur surprised approval.

All t' meat goes t' factory an' is used fo' pet food," he would add.

Sounds of disgust would come from his audience, hanging open-mouthed on his every word.

He'd say, "even t' droppin's from their toilet areas are swept up an' sent t' Sheffield," then he'd pause, awaiting the inevitable question.

The ladies would again look confused and as ever, someone would ask, "what on earth do they do with the droppings in Sheffield?"

He delivered his punch line with great relish and sparkling, watery eyes. "They make ratshit screwdrivers."

Realising they'd been taken in, a combined groan would go round the room.

All too soon the Fishermen's Choir left the building following a fine, impromptu performance, shaking hands with their many friends and donning caps at the door as they left the building.

* * * * * *

*Independence* and *Our Heritage* sailed on the first voyage of the New Year, heading for Flamborough Head, but while steaming southeast, with sounders running, a mass of fish marks began to appear as we passed over 'High Rock', in the prohibited area.

"Are you mekin' these marks, Col?" I asked.

"Yeh, they look interestin'," came the instant reply.

Manoeuvring so we could tow into the tide, we shot the gear, the other vessel doing something similar. Trawling for just an hour, we hauled to assess the soundings. There were two lifts of medium codlings for the short tow, all of a similar size and I reported this to Col. He towed longer for a better haul and we continued fishing throughout the day working this ground with excellent results.

Next morning we were both tied alongside the fish market, each boat landing a catch of two hundred boxes, giving Terry a wonderful start to his new job as Manager of the 'Alliance Fish Company'. He boldly announced to the merchants surrounding our fish that they would have to bid for all their requirements and there would be no sharing fish which had not been bid for. Furthermore any challenge to the weight in a box must be made at the point of sale. No short weight would be accepted once the fish had left the market. This was the start of a new regime and the merchants were no longer going to rule the market uncontrolled.

## Chapter 10

# A Visit to the Exhibition

The town was full of rowdies, as it always seemed to be at Easter. The young yobs, occasionally with girlfriends, were all clad in camouflaged parka jackets. Many were on motorscooters, others carried bedrolls, sleeping rough and filling the pubs and streets, creating mayhem. On Good Friday evening, Dotty and I stepped out of the Leeds Arms, heading for the Newcastle Packet. As we walked out, Les was putting a sign in the window next to his other list of 'No's. This one read, 'No bedrollers, No combat jackets, No leathers'. On the bottom he'd written, PS, We don't sell cigarettes. Les was a talented amateur photographer and behind the counter where other publicans had racks of cigarettes, he had small boxes holding every conceivable type of film for thirty-five millimetre cameras.

We should have known better than to go to the 'Packet' on such a busy day. The pub was heaving with the influx of mostly unwanted visitors and after the first drink, fed up with the intrusion, we opted for an early night. A two-minute walk up the cobblestone hill and we were home. In bed I fell asleep almost instantly and slept the sleep of the dead, as I invariably did when ashore.

Next morning Dotty said, "you didn't move a muscle all night. Didn't you hear that riot outside?"

I confessed to hearing nothing at all and she described how a gang of the young hoodlums had run up the hill, chased by a posse of policemen. The thugs had smashed windows and damaged cars en route and though they'd turned off along a road before reaching our house, they'd made lots of noise. I'd slept through the entire disturbance. In the past I'd been oblivious to thunderstorms while asleep. It was different at sea, where I slept very lightly, regularly experiencing vivid, wild dreams and my ear was constantly tuned in to the engine's steady, reassuring beat. Occasionally I'd hear the machine labouring when the trawl became caught and was sometimes out of my bunk before the watchman, who was surrounded by other extraneous noises, had noticed the boat was stopped.

In my obscure dreams onboard, I'd regularly drag a trawl around the town, snagging traffic islands and bollards, banging trawl doors around street corners. I had special, secret bits of ground out in the countryside in my fantasy world where, when fish were scarce, I'd still be able to find some. After a prolonged stint of mending, following damage to a trawl, I'd often cut and stitch damaged netting throughout my next dreamtime below.

Later in the morning, I was talking to Bev in the teashop on the pier and in conversation, related how I'd slept through the violence of the previous evening, hearing nothing and how I seemed to have a two-tier metabolism.

Bev admitted he was exactly the same, confessing that once, when turned in onboard the *Utilise* as a deck hand, while trawling, he'd had such a vivid dream he'd jumped out of his bunk, dashed into the adjacent engine-room and stopped the engine. He'd known nothing of this till the skipper hurried below, thinking there was a major mechanical malfunction. He found Bev standing in the machine space with a gormless, confused look on his face. We'd both experienced crew members shouting out loudly while sleeping in their bunks.

Changing the subject we discussed the forthcoming 'Fishing Exhibition', which was to be held in a couple of weeks, in Aberdeen. Having been to a couple of these social affairs in the past, we decided to attend this year's event, timed towards the end of the week to suit fishermen and if they wished to come along, we'd take our wives.

Of course Dotty and Marion wanted to go to the exhibition, so at midday on Thursday morning two weeks later, in high spirits, with our fishing business completed and children catered for, our journey began. We were travelling in the Bevans' car, men in front and the girls in the rear seats. Our plan was to get beyond Edinburgh then take the coast road, finding overnight accommodation en route. Bev, invariably of good disposition, was at his best and I responded to his humour with my own input while our wives, pleased to be free of the day-to-day management of children, howled with laughter at the various silly things said. Early in the journey and not far past Whitby, Marion requested a wee stop. Auto-suggestion brought Dotty out in sympathy.

"We 'aven't time fo' that. We've jus' set off an' 'ave a long way t' go. Yer should 'ave gone before we left 'ome," he joked, not stopping.

The frivolity continued for another hour, Bev, keen to press on and not realising the desperate plight of his wife and the discomfiture of Dotty, still refused to stop. Marion now had her legs crossed and was unable to laugh out loud.

"Pleeease can we stop for a call of nature Dave," pleaded Marion, the urgency now obvious in her voice.

Our driver, finally realising the serious nature of the problem, began looking for a likely pit stop but unfortunately nowhere seemed suitable. It was a further half an hour before we spotted a transport café, set back on a potholed car park near Alnwick in Northumberland. The bumping of the vehicle in the holes of the plot brought little, "ooohhs," of anxiety from the back seats, so for sheer devilment, Bev drove round the site again, despite severe threats of an excruciating death, through the clenched teeth of his wife.

As quickly as was possible with their legs together at the knees, Marion and Dotty dashed into the toilet block. Bev and I passed the adjacent facilities at a less hurried pace to hear the "ooohhs" had quite audibly turned to "aahhs."

The pair of us went into the café and sat at a table to await our missing ladies, who joined us several minutes later, greatly relieved. Even the death threats had been repealed such was the sense of relief. After a light snack and drink, followed by a visit to the toilet for everyone, no one taking any chances, we hit the road for Edinburgh.

Sitting with the road atlas on my lap, I'd taken on the role of navigator, though my skills were better at navigating on the sea where, as Bev reminded me, "t' roads are wider an' there's less traffic."

My lack of direction was underlined not far from the busy Prince's Street in the capital city when, not quite sure where we were, at very short notice to our driver I said, "quick, turn left 'ere," giving Bev no time at all to question my decision. He pulled on the wheel, turning into the narrow street, only to find a car coming directly towards us. The other driver began flashing his lights and sounding his horn, signalling to us in no uncertain terms that we were going the wrong way up a one-way street. The pair of vehicles stopped within a few feet of each other and the venomous eyes of a big, hairy, gesticulating Jock met mine.

I shrugged, pointed to Bev, then mimed holding the wheel and mouthed softly, "not my fault mate. 'Es drivin'."

"Yer bastard! It was you who told me t' turn up 'ere," my erstwhile pal spluttered.

"You know that, an' I know that, but 'e doesn't," I replied through clenched teeth while smiling nervously in the direction of the big man. I tapped my head with a forefinger, pointing again in Bev's direction as our red-faced driver cautiously reversed into the busy road.

The fierceness left the man's face and he nodded sympathetically. The girls in the back thought the whole incident hilarious and just laughed throughout the entire episode while Bev muttered, "you prat, you just wait. I'll get yer back," though he didn't mean a word of it.

We cleared the city and ten miles down the road, crossed the Forth Bridge. The views were fantastic. The late afternoon sun shimmered on the water below, lighting tiny-looking navy ships, on their way to the naval dockyard at Rosyth. Downstream, framed through the underside of the monster-shaped railway bridge, a tanker was heading for the open sea. A northbound main-line train crossing the structure looked like a miniature.

Leaving the motorway, we turned off to follow the coast road heading towards Kircaldy, the fishing port with the KY registration.

It was getting late in the afternoon and we began discussing accommodation for the night. Cruising into the old town, we scanned the streets for a likely hotel or bed and breakfast residence. "What about there?" I suggested, pointing to a black and white painted building. The place in question had a large logo painted over the door saying, 'Joe's Diner, accommodation'. Beneath this sign in smaller letters were the words, 'pool room'. Even before Bev pulled up outside the establishment I'd begun to have second thoughts. "We're not staying there," our wives said in unison, looking at what appeared to be a doss house and refused to leave the car.

"Well we've stopped now. Me an' Fred'll go an' 'ave a look," was our driver's comment. We went up the tacky stairs together, though why we were bothering was a debateable point. Facing us on the landing, a door was hanging off its hinges. A toilet seat, semi-floated on the lino-covered floor. "That'll be the pool room then," Bev quipped as we turned to retrace our steps.

A door opened to the side of the flooded room and a rough looking, swarthy character appeared. Though we needed no more convincing, he completed our assessment when, in an almost incomprehensible accent said, "ye need ya fuckin' heeads testin' if ye's are thinkin' o' stayin' in this place."

We scurried down the steps to see two grinning faces in the rear of the car, both struggling not to say, "we told you so." Ten minutes later a very friendly landlady, in a small guesthouse up a narrow wynd, was pleased to welcome us to her home and following a late, boozy night in the nearest hostelry, we made our wobbly way back up the steep, narrow lane.

For Bev and me the finest ever, 'Arbroath smokie' breakfast complete with poached egg, fortified us for the day ahead. Dotty said the porridge was good too, though Marion was sceptical of both.

We were on the road soon after breakfast and followed the coast road, inspecting all the little ports we'd heard of, but never seen. St. Monance, a traditional boatbuilding town was quickly followed by Pittenweem then Anstruther as we rounded the East Neuk, passing through St Andrews the home of golf without a second thought, to cross the Tay Bridge and point towards Arbroath. We stopped briefly at each little harbour to take in the ambiance, though the girls' humour was failing now and they declared themselves, 'harboured out'. We headed for Aberdeen with a sense of purpose, making directly for our pre booked accommodation, where we dumped our gear in the rooms and headed for the bar.

Bev created controversy as soon as he walked through the door of the busy lounge bar, calling out, "who's this Ali Macleod everybody's talkin' about?" His mention of the recently sacked, Scottish football team manager, following his squad's early exit from the World Cup, brought glares from those in earshot and an immediate vocal response from the man nearest. He appeared to be a little wobbly and had probably been in the pub since the doors opened.

"Fock off ya English bastards," was his response to Bev's question.

"Shut up, yer'll ger us filled in," I said anxiously, looking at a large, staring Scotsman for a second consecutive day. Our wives were keeping back, assessing the situation.

"It mus' be my turn," Bev replied, speaking through the side of his mouth at me while not taking his eyes off the big man, only yards away. "You nearly gor us both bashed yesterday." Talking to the Scot he said, "We're not from England, we're from Yorkshire," keeping the banter going and throwing the abuser into confusion.

The Scotsman scratched his head for a minute then said, "och you's are alright then, they're nay sae baad." The man, slurring, became Bev's instant pal, which seemed to bring relief to the other customers in the bar, who were now smiling at my pal's discomfort. "We divent like the fockin' English round 'ere," the man confided to Bev in a stage whisper, hidden behind a hand raised to his mouth.

The girls wisely decided to remain detached from our company and stood at the bar several feet from us, ordering drinks. I gradually sidled in their direction, bridging the gap to pay for their delivery and pointing to Bev, who was actively attempting to extricate himself without causing offence, I said, "an' whatever, 'e wants."

I took the executive decision to order a taxi to the relief of all and five minutes later, with the new friendship abruptly broken and Bev making profuse apologies while waving goodbye and backing out of the room, we set off for the exhibition hall.

"I thought you'd 'ave brought your new pal with yer," Marion said, laughing at her husband's recent friendship.

"Don't laugh," Bev replied, though laughing himself, "'e wanted to come with us and I told 'im it was only a four-seater taxi. 'E said 'e'll see us later." Pausing he added, "but not if we see 'im first."

Traffic in the city was fairly light in the early afternoon and soon we were entering the bustling building on the north side of the city. The huge hall was filled with hundreds of exhibitors, displaying a fisherman's every conceivable requirement and many strange aids he didn't know he needed. The aisles were busy, mostly with men but a proportion of wives and girlfriends were also in evidence. Some attractive females adorned many of the stands, like bait in a pot, luring the unwary into dialogue.

Early in our wanderings, amid the maze of stalls, we found the Kelvin engine stand and were greeted by some familiar, friendly faces. Joe, Dougie and the cadaverous face of their boss Angus, known even to his workers as 'the spook', immediately made us welcome and offered us drinks. There was a host of fishermen seated around the edges of the stand and a gleaming, eight-cylinder, olive green monster was holding centre stage. This was Kelvin's latest and most powerful beast, developing 500 horsepower.

Accepting a very large Bacardi and Coke from Dougie, while Bev took something equally intoxicating, we were quickly found vacant seats in the close group and introduced to the others by Joe. Our wives, noting the measures we'd been dispensed, opted for soft drinks, then volunteered to run the bar. This offer was duly accepted by the company representatives, enabling them to socialise and talk business with their many clients.

We were introduced to John 'Lemon' Richardson,* one of the skippers of the top Grimsby pair trawlers, *Sonia Jane* and *Margarita Bojen*. He and his trawling partner, Jens Bojen were fishing legends.

---

* 'Lemon' Richardson was lost at sea with his crew when the *Margareta Bojen* capsized and sank in Southern Norwegian waters in October 1979.

Also seated was a young, tall, thin, blond-haired man, John Peter who was skipper of the recently built, Shetland-based vessel, *Altair*. We were informed by Dougie that in the six months the *Altair* had been fishing, the only times her engine had been stopped was when the oil in the sump needed changing. Next to John Peter was a big man in every sense, Bruce, also a Shetlander. We were sitting next to Bruce and Bev asked him what type of fishing he was involved in. It transpired that Bruce was bottom trawling, similar to us and he also made four-day fishing trips before landing, as we did. The similarity ended when I added that we sailed in the early hours of Sunday and finished on Thursday morning. Bruce said, "och no, ah did forty-twa days then haad a day ashore, then deed anotha twenty-eight."

We were astounded. This man and his crew had fished for seventy-two days with just a single day off.

Not to be out done, Bev said, "if we lived where you live, we'd spend all our time at sea as well."

After another, more moderate round of drinks from our new barmaids, Bev and I decided to have a look round the exhibition before being totally wrecked by the infamous 'Kelvin' hospitality. Our wives were perfectly happy to remain in their hostess role, being bored by the fishing stuff. They were looking forward to an opportunity to go shopping in Aberdeen the following day.

Strolling aimlessly up and down the aisles, we met lots of people we knew from various ports and as well as looking at the many displays and demonstrations we also managed to stumble across the bar, where we dallied for a drink or two while talking to acquaintances. Eventually, realising the time, we thought we'd better rescue our wives who probably felt they'd been abandoned by now. Wandering hopefully through the grid maze, we finally managed to locate our temporary base. We were pleased to discover that our ladies were perfectly happy and though still dispensing booze, they'd sampled a few glasses themselves and were now in charge of quantity control.

"We've been invited to a dance and you're taking us," announced Dotty, handing me another glass. Pointing to Bruce and John Peter she said, "these lovely men here are going to the Exhibition Ball tonight and they've said we can join their table."

Not wanting to miss out on a party, Bev and I challenged the maze again to find the main office of the event organisers, to buy tickets and add our names to the table plan. Looking at those already on the list, it looked like a United Nations convention. There were Shetlanders, Scots, Scandinavians, English and Bev, who was born in Wales.

Returning to the hotel, late in the afternoon, a quick doze seemed appropriate and promptly at seven o'clock in the evening, we met up again in the bar, but not before checking that Bev's pal had gone. Another taxi ride got us to the hotel, where we were soon seated in the banqueting hall. Our best, casual clothing was sufficient for the occasion and though there were partygoers in formal attire, we didn't feel out of place in our company. Our wives looked a million dollars. The food was excellent and was served quickly. All through the meal good-humoured banter flowed back and forth across the table. The atmosphere was wonderful. A kitty of banknotes in the centre of the table ensured everyone's glasses remained charged.

When the lights dimmed and the band struck up, the tall Norwegian took Dotty's hand and said, "my name is 'Last Chance Ole'. This will be your only opportunity. Would you like to dance?"

Unable to refuse the charming offer she allowed herself to be escorted onto the nearby dance floor. The tune was a fast rock and roll number and as Ole' drew Dotty towards him, he turned her three hundred and sixty degrees. When he pushed her away again he seemed to move with her. Reversing the turn, he continued spinning his partner, so Dotty did two full turns in the opposite direction. The big man was certainly a slick dancer and Dotty's arms seemed to be elastic. She spun backwards and forwards, while her partner also rotated her around the crowded floor. Everyone on our table was helpless with laughter, watching the truly amazing performance. A dizzy but beaming Dotty returned to the table with her dance partner, to be welcomed with a huge round of applause. My dancing, in comparison was totally uncoordinated but I enjoyed thrashing round the arena in a mass of waving arms and kicking legs.

The time just seemed to fly by and before we knew it, the lights brightened and the music fell silent. Some of our party made their farewells and drifted off but we still had drinks untouched and so did the Shetland lads. "Lets ha' yerr glasses noo. Ha' ye nae hames to gang tae." The bar staff, keen to get the tables cleared, were harrying those remaining seated.

"We'd better be goin'," I said to Bruce, looking at the full glass before me. "We'll be gettin' chucked out."

"Sit there an' finish yourr drinks," he ordered. "Nae one'll be chuckin' ye oot."

Looking at this mountain of a man, I was quite prepared to believe him and when the waiter came round again, wanting to clear the tables, I pointed to my companion and said, "we're with 'im."

Bruce scowled and the waiter went away again.

Marion and Dotty hit the shops immediately following breakfast, while Bev and I went back to the exhibition to take a final look round and check if there were any useful tips or gadgets that might improve our fishing. Considering our difficulty in navigating around the huge hall, we appeared to gravitate unerringly to the Kelvin stand, which we could find with consummate ease. Nothing had changed. The three company representatives were still in attendance and the two Shetland lads were sitting in the same positions as the previous day. "They can't 'ave been there all night," I thought, "'cos we'd seen 'em at t' dance."

Conversation struck up again immediately. Bev said, "it was a good night, las' night boys."

"We've nae been tae baed yet," replied Bruce. He went on to describe how they'd returned to their hotel and kept the porter up throughout the night serving them drinks. "He wasna happy, we kept him frae his sleep."

Considering their all night binge, these men were in remarkably good condition and were still totally coherent. Never lost for words, Bev said, "well you'll be used t' drinkin'. Ah don't suppose you 'ave owt else t' do where you live."

During the conversation we discovered the drinks account for hospitality on the Kelvin stand for the three-day event was three thousand pounds.

Saying our goodbyes we left to meet the girls, back at the hotel. The shopping expedition had been moderately successful, though I was pleased to see Marion carrying more bags than Dotty. We headed south again and there was no touring. Either Bev needed a pee, or he was taking no chances on upsetting his wife a second time because he found a convenience with no prompting.

We arrived home soon after six o'clock in the evening and as we parted, thanked our friends for their company. We'd only been away for two days but it seemed like a week. It was great to see the bairns again. It was only at weekends when I got that opportunity. Checking the tide times, I rang my crew with sailing orders for midnight. I also rang a friend, John Hobson, who along with his wife, Jean, a talented artist, ran the Flower in Hand guesthouse. John had long expressed a wish to go to sea with us and this looked like being a fine week.

Zany, with a ready smile, slight of stature with thinning hair and wearing small, round-lensed glasses, John was an entertaining passenger who took every opportunity to use his camera, later showing us his professional results. He told us of the outrageous letters he wrote to the local paper under a pseudonym, then of the replies he wrote to his own letters. "I used to have protracted arguments with myself in the press," he said. "I also wrote letters to the Council giving non-existent reference numbers on the headings, alluding to correspondence I'd received. The letters created major confusion at the Town Hall."

John made us laugh again when he spoke about his small hotel. "We kept a plastic fried egg pinned to the notice board in the kitchen. If anyone asked for two eggs with their breakfast, the artificial one was taken down, washed and sent through to the dining room." He said the object always came back covered in sauce, ketchup, salt and pepper but no one ever complained. "We'd wash the egg then pin it back on the board ready for the next customer."

"We had a black, plastic slug too," he went on, animatedly. "The thing was moved a few feet each day around the ornamental plate rail in the dining room. It was easy to see but no one mentioned that either."

* * * * * *

A few weeks later Bev was fishing north of the Orkney Islands and talking to Bruce on the radio. He was told the Shetland contingent had done another all night session then turned up at the airport on Sunday with luggage and drink for the flight. The hostess had informed the men that they had excess luggage and should leave the cans and bottles to be sent on a later flight. The boys had replied, "we'll tak' the booze. Ye kin send oor bags on a later flight."

## Chapter 11

# The First Wage Packet

Danny was now spending a large part of his school holidays at sea onboard the *Independence* and had gained his sea legs. He was on board when early one evening, while working on a piece of ground seventy miles to the northeast, not far from the wrecked Vulcan bomber, an unusual mark appeared on the sounder. Sitting on the edge of a small rise on the seabed, this was clearly a dense shoal of something, as the machine was having difficulty in discriminating fish from the seabed. I was sure we were in for a big haul of cod. Plotting our exact position on the 'Decca' for future reference, I despatched Danny to call the lads prematurely from their beds. "Get yerselves a pot of coffee then we'll 'ave a look at it," I informed the four men as they emerged from the cabin, heading for the galley. Twenty minutes later, oilskin clad, each with a cigarette glowing in hand or mouth, they were on deck ready to start hauling. Each one had visited the wheelhouse to inspect 'the mark', concurring that the sounding looked promising.

As the *Independence* lay across the gentle wind and swell, all eyes looked to starboard as the bridles were drawn in. Even before the net came into view there was a boiling green mass in the water, clearly visible from my vantage point above the deck. "She's gonna blow. It's a big un," I yelled excitedly from the open window. The first of the floats came into view then the codends burst to the surface, climbing out of the water like an uncontrolled submarine, the expanding air in the fishes' bellies forcing them to the surface. This was a massive haul. "Bonanza!" I screamed then realising just how much fish there was in the bulging net pleaded, "don't burst, please don't burst."

Planting feet in sea-boots I dashed from the wheelhouse, grabbing my oilskin from the peg in passing and was on deck pulling the yellow, vinyl frock over my head as the heavy bobbins came over the side. Despite their weight these rollers were reluctant to drop to the deck due to the weight overboard and remained suspended against the inner bulwarks. Had the weather been less favourable, the footrope would have jumped back over the side. It was now a race against time. We had to quickly get the entire mouth of the net onboard and stoppered off before the buoyancy of the catch was lost. The air inside the fish would be quickly expelled with the crush and the dead weight of cod would rapidly sink.

No one needed instructions. The five of us had a common goal and in a couple of minutes the thick, stern mooring rope was fastened around the upper bellies and secured to the strong, oak beam inboard. This was accomplished none too soon, as we immediately had tons of dead weight hanging from the rope down into the water and the *Independence* was listing to starboard with the weight of the haul. Now we could start taking the catch from the net. I felt a little tap on my back and a voice said, "it's a good catch Dad, isn't it?"

In the panic to secure the huge haul, I'd completely forgotten my son, who'd been standing at the fore side of the fishroom hatch, watching proceedings. "It sure is Danny, we're gonna be a while gettin' it all aboard."

Rusty heaved on the pork line, dragging the first bag to the surface; the bulk of fish running back down the sock of the bellies. I leaned over the side, forcing the lifting hook into the becket while Bluey, working the winch, hauled the first lift on board. Normally the codend swings into the fish pound in the centre of the boat, emptying as the cod-line clip releases but due to the list and sheer weight overboard, the bag opened half way and only part of the fish hit the pound. Half a ton of large cod spilled onto the starboard workspace, surrounding our legs. As the cod-line clip was knocked home again, Sid and I began throwing the dead cod across to the port side. We lifted another bag in, then two more, marginally lightening the strain on the net. The deck pounds were now full and we paused briefly to throw more fish across to the port side, making room for more to be lifted on board.

"It really is a good 'aul, isn't it Dad?" Danny said again, while attempting to throw a fish almost as big as himself across the boat.

"I don't think we've got 'alf of it aboard yet Danny," I hurriedly replied. It was growing dark now and he was despatched to the wheelhouse to switch on the deck lights.

Another four bags were lifted in and we again stopped to redistribute the fish. The list from the boat had now gone as the net lightened and the port side filled, fish flowing down the side of the wheelhouse to be packed into boxes by Sid. The next two lifts dropped in the centre of the boat and the *Independence* was clearly sagging by the head now. We began pushing fish for'ard, accentuating the dip. Now it was possible to haul the remaining fish on board, though we'd lost count of the number of lifts taken from the trawl. The boat was full from stem to stern with big cod of a size never seen inshore. We'd been hauling fish on board for more than three hours and now this huge catch had to be gutted, washed and sent below to be boxed and iced.

"We'll get t' gear back down, then 'ave a quick pot o' coffee before we mek a start guttin'," I stated. Most of the net was almost buried under fish. The stares from the crew were of consternation.

"Yer not shootin' again?" Sid said, questioning my decision.

"Only t' give us some deck space. I'm not goin' back over that piece o' ground again."

This seemed to placate him and he went aft to his galley, filling and lighting the gas under the kettle while we began excavating the trawl from beneath the heap of fish. Twenty minutes later we were towing again and the lads on deck were sitting among a mountain of fish, supping coffee and munching on thick, corned beef sandwiches with the prospect of a long night ahead.

With the boat towing on clear ground, I checked the radar then left Danny sitting in the wheelhouse chair and returned to the deck with knife in hand. The autopilot would steer the boat and my son had no decisions to make relating to navigation. His sole task was to press the red button on the bench, which beeped every few minutes when the auto was engaged. If not cancelled within one minute, a loud, constant alarm would sound. I could still keep a look out for other vessels while working on deck. My visits to the bridge were frequent to alter course, turn the vessel and check on Danny's welfare.

Now 0200 and with only a quick break for a coffee, we were making inroads into the huge catch and had cleared the starboard side and created some significant deck space to port, allowing the scupper door to be opened. Rusty was working full time below in the fishroom, while Bluey occasionally dropped below to assist him to stack the higher boxes.

All was not well when I entered the wheelhouse. Danny was now very tired and asked to be relieved of his position, but with the tremendous workload still ahead, I needed him to stay in situ if possible. "These'll keep yer goin'," I said, handing him a can of coke and a packet of chocolate biscuits. He perked up visibly and I felt able to leave him a little longer.

The deck space grew as more and more fish were gutted, washed and kicked down the chute from the washer. Cod were now being stacked on portable, wooden shelves in the emptying ice pounds, preserving the few remaining boxes for smaller fish and it was almost 0500 and daylight. Poor Danny was tearful and although now wrapped in his sleeping bag, he was still sitting in the wheelhouse chair.

"Ow can I cheer 'im up and keep 'im interested?" I wondered. "Yer can 'ave a little sleep if yer want."

His eyes lit up.

"As long as yer keep pressing t' button," I added.

His face fell again.

"Yer can 'elp yerself t' biscuits an' drinks, an' yer will get paid fo' this work, yer know."

The smile came back. "Will I really Dad?" That clinched it. Although he was shattered, he managed to keep going, not complaining when I visited his abode to adjust the course. With only a few fish remaining to go below, I left the deck to relieve the exhausted watch-keeper. The sun was climbing in the sky when Danny crawled into his bunk and after another, much-needed coffee we hauled the net again, immediately setting off for home. This catch, consisting of about five kit of mixed fish, including haddocks and lemons, denuded of scales from the long drag, was soon dispatched.

My *Independence* felt heavy and was down by the head, rising sluggishly to the swells as we steamed for home. It was easy to see over the whaleback. In her normal trim this steel shelter slightly impaired the view ahead. Danny appeared again with the other hands, all refreshed, as we approached the harbour. We'd all had at least five or six hours kip en route. The loaded vessel didn't want to stop when I put the gear lever astern as she drew close to the pier, such was the weight of her cargo and it took almost full speed astern to take the way off her.

Dad and Joxy were waiting on the pier with a stack of empty boxes and a ton of extra ice in thirty full boxes. Also standing on the quayside watching with interest were two young brothers, looking to earn some pocket money. These lads were also recruited to assist landing the fish. Sean and Kevin were still at school but were willing workers who'd helped us in the past. Armed with iron hooks the pair helped to drag the weighed containers from the quayside to the market. Due to the large size of the fish, some tails hung over the ends of the boxes, so we were unable to stack them and all had to be laid out in columns under the market. What a fantastic sight they looked when we'd finished landing. I counted two hundred and seventy-five boxes of fish, each containing seven stones, which the young lads were now enthusiastically showering with shovels of ice, prior to covering them with plastic sheeting. Dad and Joxy were restocking the boat with boxes.

Next morning, when I'd been to the office to settle our bonanza trip, I handed my restored crew fat wage packets. I also gave an envelope to Danny with his name written across the front. He ran home to show his Mum his first wage packet containing ten crisp one-pound notes.

* * * * * *

On the Saturday we were due to receive a visit from Sir Peter Vanneck, our European Member of Parliament and I'd arranged to meet him and his entourage at 1300 outside the Lifeboat House, an easy landmark. I'd agreed to show him round the harbour and onboard the *Independence*. The boat was ready for sea and we'd be sailing in the early hours of the following morning. This wasn't a particularly convenient time for me, as it conflicted with the few hours I spent with my pals in the Leeds Arms, but I was prepared to give up my time to meet a politician, who I thought could help our cause in the Common Market. I stood outside the boathouse from ten minutes to the hour until half past, looking at my watch and getting more impatient. Finally I gave up the wait and went home, angry that I'd wasted my time. I was no longer in the mood to go to the pub. Dotty was sympathetic and was preparing some food for us when the doorbell rang.

Opening the door I discovered a group of very apologetic people standing on the doorstep. "There's been a mix up in the arrangements," the politician's red-faced agent spluttered. "We've been delayed while Sir Peter opened a Summer Fete."

I was neither pleased nor placated but nevertheless invited the party in and was introduced to the great man, a former Lord Mayor of London, by his agent. Holding a potted plant in one hand and a small parcel in the other, he passed these to his minion and shook hands. In return I introduced him to Dotty.

My normally placid wife was not impressed and for once didn't hide her feelings. Turning back to his aide he took the parcel and in a very plummy voice said, "I've brought you some fi … ". The words died in his mouth. Our Euro MP must have been presented with a parcel of local fish earlier and he in turn, was about to give this carton to Dotty. It dawned on him too late that maybe it wasn't such a good idea to give fish to a fisherman's wife. He hurriedly exchanged the box for the plant, which he'd been given at the fete and coughing said, "I've brought you a 'Busy Lizzie'."

"Could you get us some tea and biscuits?" I asked Dotty, who was getting even angrier at the stupidity of our late and now unwanted guest.

"He can have some tea," came back the uncharacteristic reply and luckily for the delayed politician, Dotty left for the kitchen, where she was able to calm down.

There was no tour of the harbour or boat, just an attempt to inform our new EMP of the difficulties which fishermen were facing on the sloping playing field of Europe. In fairness to the man, he did listen to my explanation of our problems and did ask some pertinent questions, which he would later repeat on our behalf in Brussels.

Fishermen were soon to realise that Euro MPs were totally powerless, made no decisions, didn't vote and could only ask written questions. They were limited to no more than two questions in any session and written answers were received at some unspecified future date.

The VIP said his farewells and made ready to leave. Dotty, her composure restored, came to say her goodbyes and as the door closed behind the party our eyes met and she said, "what a prat." The politician must have really got under her skin as my wife always looked for the best in people.

## Chapter 12

# The Race

Bluey and several of his pals were out on the town and were on a pub-crawl. These lads worked hard but they certainly played hard too. "Taxi t' George 'otel, please," I heard him say into the public pay payphone on the end of the bar in the Lord Nelson.

"Taxi t' George?" I queried. "It's only round t' corner and up the 'ill. Yer could walk it in five minutes."

"Leave them alone," Dotty said sharply, "it's nothing to do with you. He's not on the boat now."

Ignoring my wife's wise counsel and slightly influenced by drink I said, "none o' you young uns are fit. I could race any o' yer round t' Marine Drive."

"Just shut up will you," Dotty added. "Don't you go throwing challenges out like that. You're stupid. Drink's in and wit's out," she said, pointing in my direction and speaking to the young fishermen.

It was too late to retract my words. Phil Lawrence, Colin's son-in-law took up the challenge. "I'll race yer round t' Marine Drive."

I was quite surprised at Phil's acceptance and hadn't really meant to throw down the gauntlet. I couldn't say, "I was only making a point about getting three-hundred yard taxi rides." The challenge was on. We agreed to meet at 0800 the following Saturday morning. The race was to be from the 'Corner Café' in the North Bay, around the Marine Drive to the West Pier.

"First one to touch t' crab stalls wall, on t' West Pier is t' winner. T' loser pays twenty quid to t' 'Fishermen's Wives Fund'." Phil stated.

"You are stupid sometimes," chided Dotty on our way home. "Phil's a big, strong lad. You'll kill yourself."

She was probably right. It was going to be a tough run. Phil, tall with straight brown hair was proportionate for his size with no excess body fat. He was one of Col's crew and a hard worker. The road around the Castle Headland was a mile and a half distant then a further quarter mile to the crab stalls. Word was soon on the street and side bets were being placed.

We sailed as usual at midnight and it wasn't long before I was being reminded of my challenge. Col was first on the radio. "I 'ear your gonna race our Phil round t' Drive next Sat'dy, Nommy. You'll 'ave yer work cut out. 'E's a fit lad."

I didn't need reminding. I was already regretting my outburst and wishing I'd listened to Dotty.

We fished quite well during the week and had a good landing on the Thursday but the niggling thought of the race was at the back of my mind. There were further reminders now I was back on shore. The contest seemed to have captured people's imaginations for at eight o'clock on the given day, at the start line, there were about a dozen spectators, some in cars and four or five standing on the rear of a flat-backed truck. We were clad in trainers, shorts and T shirts and shook hands before the race, wishing each other good luck. Acknowledging our readiness, someone on the back of the wagon called out, "on yer marks, get set, go."

We set off together at a good pace, one we'd have a job keeping up, I thought. I had no spare breath to talk or answer the catcalls and barracking from the back of the truck, which was keeping time with us. I heard Col shout, "yer'll never keep that pace up."

He was probably right but neither of us seemed to want to slow down. We rounded the first bend in the road at about half a mile, dead level and keeping the tempo. It wasn't long before we were approaching the distinctive 'Coffee Pot Rock' at the northeast corner of the Castle Headland. We'd done a mile. My heart was pounding but I was running within my capabilities and knew I had something left in the tank for a sprint but was sure Phil had reserves too. At the end of the Marine Drive, as we passed under the archway of the former Promenade Toll House, with its tall, pointed, red-tiled spire, someone on the back of the truck shouted, "go on Phil, tek 'im now."

Hearing the call, Phil shot off like a bullet, leaving me ten yards in his wake and it was a few seconds before I was up to his speed. Had he gone too soon? I wouldn't have sprinted from there through choice with a quarter of a mile to go, but I'd have to attempt it now.

Gradually I began to gain on him but he kept going. We'd passed the Golden Ball Slipway and were now nearly halfway along Sandside, approaching the Welcome Inn Café. We were both sidestepping to avoid early morning pedestrians who, surprised, stood still, not knowing which way to move to avoid being trampled by the racers hurtling towards them, only yards apart.

Though there was nothing left in the tank, I drew level with him opposite the Newcastle Packet and within sight of the crab stalls. I had him. With only seventy or eighty yards to go, I nosed in front but Phil never gave in. He was as shattered as I was and when I touched the brick wall of the stalls, his hand touched just seconds later.

I slumped to the floor on my back in the middle of the roadway with no idea what was going on around me, panting as if my chest would burst but still not getting enough air. A red mist was playing across my eyes and my head ached. Putting an arm across my forehead, I hoped to relieve the pain. Some kind person had grabbed a bottle of milk from a passing milk float and was pouring the cold liquid into my mouth. Although the liquid was soothing, I couldn't swallow it. My airway was taking priority and the white juice spilled down the sides of my mouth.

Gradually, very slowly, my strength grew. I sat up, resting against the brick wall. My eyes began to focus and I was able to take the bottle of milk from Rory, one of Bev's crew who was standing over me concerned, fully expecting to call an ambulance at any time. It was small consolation that Phil had fared little better.

Five minutes later I was able to stand, on wobbly legs. My sporting opponent came over saying, "well done Fred, t' best man won," shaking hands once more.

"He didn't Phil," I assured him, still breathless. "You jus' went too soon. If you'd 'ave waited for another couple of 'undred yards, ah'd never 'ave caught yer." I knew this to be the truth. Whoever had encouraged him to make his early burst had lost him the race.

I'd recovered sufficiently to make my way up the hill home and tried to walk into the house nonchalantly but there was no fooling Dotty. "You look terrible, you're ashen. Sit down before you fall down. I'll get you a glass of water."

I followed instructions and slumped onto the settee. As she made to leave the room I said, "nex' time I start throwin' challenges out, smack me in the mouth."

She promised to do exactly that.

I lay on the sofa for the next few hours dozing and feeling as weak as a kitten. I did recover sufficiently to go to the Leeds Arms for the usual Saturday gathering, though I still wasn't one hundred percent. Before setting off for the pub I put two ten-pound notes in an envelope and marked it, 'Fishermen's Wives' Charity Fund.' I might have won the race but it didn't feel as if I had. There was no feeling of euphoria.

* * * * * *

Fishing onboard the *Independence* had been good these past few years and she was now almost paid for. In the wheelhouse, during quiet tows and with lots of time for contemplation, I began to think ahead. In my early thirties, maybe I should look into the possibility of building another boat. I wasn't going to do anything in a hurry but the seed was sown and this was something I should be exploring. There was a nasty surprise however, when I arrived home. A letter from my accountant said the Tax Inspector was seeking an interview to discuss some undisclosed business and required me to make an appointment to address the outstanding matter soon. I didn't like the sound of this but a date was set for the following Friday, which came round too quickly.

Sitting in the accountant's office with Ray, who'd looked after my tax affairs since I'd been a deck hand, I was pensive. His huge desk, where a cigarette permanently smouldered in the ashtray, was piled high with papers. Every level surface in the office was stacked with files and there were documents in heaps on the floor. How he was able to find anything with this chaotic filing system was a mystery to me but it obviously worked for him.

Ray, a keen golfer who enjoyed his beer, was of medium height, had a ruddy complexion and straight, combed-back, thinning hair. He was full of nervous energy, forever on the move and constantly wiping ash from his suit. We were waiting for the inspector and his assistant to reveal the purpose of their visit. The bespectacled man, who'd clearly found his vocation in life, was devoid of humour and avoided any attempts by me to lighten the heavy atmosphere in the room. The small space he was using on the desk had been made when Ray stacked even more client files on the floor at his side.

The revenue man, enjoying my discomfort, eventually finished shuffling and rearranging his paperwork, cleared his throat and looked in my direction with steely, unblinking eyes. He said, "Mr Normandale, I have reason to believe your income tax return is incorrect. Do you have anything to tell me? Is there anything you may have omitted in your tax submission?"

I looked from him to Ray, wondering what I should say.

"As far as I'm aware, Mr Normandale's tax return is in order. Can you give us more information?" Ray said on my behalf.

Mr Charisma looked back at me and said, "have you been receiving cash for fish from a Scarborough fish merchant? I have information, which I believe to be correct, stating that you have received substantial amounts of money on a weekly basis." He went on to say the trader in question had done nothing wrong. Though he'd paid for his supplies with cash, getting his fish cheaper, he'd put this stock through his sales ledger. The inspectorate had become aware of these unusual transactions and obviously wanted to know who'd received these funds.

"The bastard, the bastard," was all I could think. "I've been shafted by that bloody twat." How could someone do that when dealing with you face to face, regularly? He must have known this investigation would inevitably take place at some point but had given me no indication.

I was stunned and Ray could lend little assistance. He'd not been aware of this unrecorded arrangement. He tried to help nevertheless. "Have you any details of the amounts involved?" he queried.

The inspector was having none of this. "I rather thought Mr Normandale might tell me how much he'd received, providing he now agrees that his tax return is incorrect."

I nodded and reluctantly muttered, "yes I 'ave 'ad some cash from that person." I couldn't bring myself to say the merchant's name, I was so annoyed with him. "Ah don't know 'ow much 'e told you 'e gave me. Ah don't know 'ow much I've 'ad meself, without workin' it out."

There was more to come. "Have you received any other amounts from other merchants or other sources that you might like to tell me about now Mr Normandale?" His piercing stare was once more holding steady in my direction in an uneven contest. "If this is the case, now would be the time for you to disclose it. You are already in serious trouble and withholding further information can only compound the matter."

"Shit! Shit! Shit! What am ah supposed to say to that? What does 'e know?" I thought, racking my brains, expecting more bad news and feeling his unflinching gaze burning into my brain.

What about t' few quid we occasionally got from 'Uncle' Bob Wheeler? Does 'e know about t' bits o' stocker we sometimes got fo' lobsters or queenies? "No I 'aven't 'ad owt else," I croaked, dry-mouthed, hoping there was nothing more he was aware of.

A master of psychology, the man said nothing for several seconds, waiting for me to reconsider. Time stood still and I was sweating profusely, feeling my face going red, despite wearing a light cotton shirt. It was a relief when he eventually spoke again, explaining in no uncertain terms that via Ray, I was to inform him, as soon as possible how much I'd received from this illegal source. Meanwhile he would write to me explaining the seriousness of the situation and proceed from there.

Fresh air never tasted sweeter as I walked down the steps from the inquisition, making my way to the harbour to seek out the prat who'd got me into this fix. When I found him on the pier and angrily confronted him, he of course denied any wrong doing; said it was purely a business deal as far as he was concerned and that his accountant must have given the revenue my name. He was so glib and smug, having all the answers off pat. I felt like punching him, but knew this would only compound matters. Instead I told him in very few words, what I thought of him and his dirty trick.

I'd no idea what sum was involved and spent most of the following week at sea, attempting to guestimate the total. The amounts were usually between fifty and a hundred pounds a week. I calculated that as near as possible, the true amount was about three thousand pounds in total. I didn't want to prolong any investigation and declared this sum to Ray when I was next home. Of course my crew had received a fair share of these proceeds and were therefore implicated but I volunteered to pay anything due without naming them, hoping for a swift resolution.

If I thought the situation would be brought to a rapid conclusion by my willingness to co-operate, I was woefully wrong. The next few months brought frequent anguish when worrying letters dropped on the mat and threats of court and possibly jail were communicated. All thoughts of building a new vessel had completely gone from my head. Eventually my tormentor was forced to agree that I'd told the truth and three thousand pounds was the correct sum. His final message, which I opened with trepidation one Saturday morning, stated that though he now accepted my calculations, he was imposing a one hundred percent penalty plus interest of eight hundred pounds. The total sum due to the Inland Revenue was six thousand eight hundred pounds. Interest would be chargeable on any outstanding amount forthwith. Ouch! I was also required to sign a declaration saying I would not undertake such practice again. There wasn't much chance of that.

There was a pleasant end to the week. We'd been invited out for the evening. Noel White was due to retire soon and had announced he was holding a few little parties for his various clients.

He'd decided his fishermen customers and their wives were to be invited to the Central Hotel, owned by Conrad, a small, black-haired, flamboyant Spaniard. His hotel and restaurant was one of the most popular establishments in town and his grilled steaks were legendary. Conrad also banked with Mr White.

Behind the bar in the 'Central', in order of ascendancy, stood a range of 'Moet and Chandon' bottles of champagne. Unknown to Noel, the previous week, his fishing clients had clubbed together, buying two of the larger bottles, which Conrad informed us were a 'Jeroboam' and a 'Rehoboam'. The bottles were buried in a wheelbarrow of ice, in preparation for the banker's arrival. The welcome and look of surprise on his face when he walked through the door with his wife Mary, was wonderful to behold. He'd clearly not only been my Godfather.

## Chapter 13

# Progress

I'd thought more positively about building a new vessel recently and had decided to go ahead, subject to grant and loan assistance from the White Fish Authority and wrote to this body applying for approval. If consent were to be given, this government funded organisation would grant twenty-five percent and loan fifty percent of the cost of the new build at a fixed rate of interest. The paperwork stated that the grant element of the contract was subject to tax. I shivered when I read this section, my recent ordeal still dwelling on my mind. If the project went ahead, the WFA surveyor would also undertake supervision of the construction to ensure all work was to specification. This was of huge assistance, considering the location of the builders.

James Noble's Fraserburgh yard had closed since the *Independence* had been built so I'd chosen the J and G Forbes yard in Sandhaven as the potential contractor. Forbes boatyard was only two miles from Fraserburgh and the company had a reputation for building well-shaped, successful vessels. I'd seen new craft on the Forbes slipway when I'd been in the area in the past.

A phone call to the shipyard found me talking to Derry Forbes, the Managing Director of the company. I was sent a specification document, which I deliberated over throughout the next two weeks at sea. I had a better idea of what was required this time, having been through this detailed process before. Anything needed and not listed in this document would be charged as extra. I knew for sure that I wanted a Kelvin main engine and for the deck machinery package, North Sea Winches was a must. This Scarborough company, whose reputation for building powerful winches was second to none, was on my doorstep and I knew the people at this factory, so would be able to talk with their designers face to face. There was the myriad of minutiae, which needed concentrated thought.

The quotation from Forbes, when costed and returned to me was a big surprise. I opened the envelope with excitement on arriving home from sea but then gulped when I read the bottom line. The price to build a new vessel had more than doubled since I'd last been down this road. The three hundred and eighty thousand pound figure made me think long and hard whether this was a good idea. There were two other quotations to come in, which would give me a comparison, though in truth these would probably be similar or higher. Derry Forbes would have communicated with these other yards, knowing he was the preferred builder.

I could always sell the *Independence* to assist with the funding of the new project if strictly necessary but then the dreaded taxman would be back again, taking most of the proceeds and I did have a great deal of affection for this fine craft. She'd served me well these past years and I was reluctant to part with her. This would only be a fallback position.

It was with delight that my request for government assistance was approved and I was now convinced this was the route I wanted to take and was hopeful of success. The following week when back in port, I received two visitors at home. Derry Forbes, small in stature, stocky with square features and silvering hair was immaculately turned out in a light grey suit. Accompanying Derry was Joe Taylor, the installation engineer and Kelvin agent. Joe, taller, rotund, red-faced, bespectacled and balding, was also wearing a grey suit though this was crumpled and his woollen pullover added nothing to his appearance. What both men had in common were brown, nicotine-stained fingers, underlined when an ashtray was requested, immediately following introductions. This, along with a tea tray was provided by Dotty who, not wanting to be involved in the business dealings, was pottering in the kitchen.

We discussed various aspects of the proposed new vessel, Joe quickly expressing concern that the new type of variable, stern gear I'd specified which allowed a different propeller pitch for steaming and trawling, could be suspect. Since completing the specification, I'd also heard unfavourable reports of this system and had already decided not to install this machinery, intending instead to stay with a conventional, well tested, fixed propeller.

"Ye could hae saved me the jourrrney," Joe growled. He'd made the trip south with the sole intention of dissuading me from my choice of this revolutionary mechanism.

Minutes later, from his inside jacket pocket, Derry produced the all-important contract, which was a White Fish Authority approved document. Drawing his fountain pen from the same source and removing the top, the builder handed the implement to me. I'd already made my decision and without a second consideration, signed on the dotted line. A cheque for ten percent of the total cost was required to complete the deal and this too was promptly signed and handed over. Other stage payments would be due as the vessel progressed. Godfather Noel had now retired from the bank but he'd introduced his successor, who was keen to see the project go ahead and had approved the shortfall in funding. My contribution to the project had to be paid first. Dotty joined us as we shook hands on the deal and the men, their cups drained and business done, refused an offer of a meal and left to head north again.

The stale fug hung heavy in the room. Its source, a collection of stubbed cigarette butts and a pile of ash in the repository were swiftly disposed of and the perpetrators' departure signalled the appearance of a canister of air freshener.

Although Noel had now left the bank, he still kept his regular, Thursday evening rendezvous in the Leeds Arms with the usual crowd and was as quick and witty as ever. Tonight though, with Dotty in close attendance, I had a serious question for him. "Noel, you've always been my unofficial Godfather, ever since we first met. Would yer be a real Godfather now t' little Sarah. She's due t' be christened in a few weeks."

He was silenced by my request but quickly regained his voice. "Nay lad. I'm sixty now. I'm far too bladdy old for that role. I'm supposed to have the child's welfare to consider until she's eighteen years old. I might not live that long."

It was my turn to think fast now. I dearly wanted Noel to be one of Sarah's moral custodians, even if tenuously. He'd been a true benefactor and guide to me by his integrity and faith when I was struggling to progress, years earlier. "Take the job on, an' if yer snuff it before she's eighteen, we'll let you off wi' t' balance."

He wavered and Dotty, putting her hand on his added, "please, Noel."

Acquiescing, he held up his forefinger and announced, "I'll take it on those terms," and received a big hug from Dotty for his agreement.

We were also fortunate to enlist the services of the vicar who, years earlier had christened Danny. Although Reverend Charlie Bubbins had now relocated to a run down area in Teesside, with the permission of the local vicar, he willingly came along to conduct the service at St Mary's. He swiftly waved off any offer of payment for his travelling expenses. Charlie intended to renew acquaintances with old friends. When he lived in Scarborough he'd occasionally sailed on the lifeboat and regularly had a pint or two with Bill Sheader and other fishermen in the 'Leeds'.

* * * * * *

The tide was turning against fishermen attempting to work within the Common Fisheries Policy. The fish quotas we were allowed to catch were tighter this year, especially whiting, which the smaller, inshore boats relied on. These voracious feeders had been particularly abundant and were now strictly rationed. The problem was, there wasn't much of any other species close inshore to catch at present as an alternative. This wasn't an issue for the bigger boats that could fish further offshore and find cod and haddock. The matter was to be tabled on the agenda at a fisheries meeting for Producer Organisations in London and I'd volunteered to attend. Bill, skipper of the *Success II* said he'd like to come along too and his offer was accepted. This was unusual as Bill, who'd been my right-hand man and a stalwart when we were in the

*Courage* together, though intelligent, was usually a quiet man, who kept his opinions to himself.

Dave Normandale had left the *Independence* with plans to emigrate and had been replaced by Mick, an experienced hand who would be a major asset to our crew. I asked Bluey, now in his mid-twenties, his shock of blond hair, slightly thinning, to take the boat while I travelled to the meeting. At some point, if I was to keep her, she'd need a skipper and this was an opportunity for him.

I met Bill at the station and we travelled south together. Dressed in his normal working attire of shirt, jeans and slip on, wooden soled clogs, he'd made no concessions to the formality of the venue, the Ministry of Agriculture, Fisheries and Food in Whitehall. He was pensive throughout the journey and said little on the train. I wondered if he was composing his thoughts.

There were many representatives from organisations throughout the country seated at the table, when the numerous men from the Ministry trooped into the room. They arranged themselves at the opposite side of the room and I could sense Bill at my side, bristling with anger at his first sight of the perceived foe. The Chairman, a Ministry man, started the meeting by asking those present, clockwise around the table to give their names and the body they represented before the main proceedings began. These introductions were delivered in a rich variety of dialects. We were from the smallest group, the Scarborough and Bridlington PO.

Half an hour into the meeting, when whiting were mentioned, Bill could stand the pressure no longer and stood, pointing with a shaking hand to the men opposite. "You lot are the enemy," he said in a tremulous voice. "The amount o' whitin' quota ah'm allowed t' catch won't even pay me fuel bill. There's nowt else t' catch jus' now. Whitin' is all there is. As far as ah'm concerned, yer can stick yer quotas up yer arse." He sat down, drained, having spoken with real passion, from the heart.

For a few seconds there was a stunned silence and the officials looked extremely uncomfortable. Compounding their discomfort, a spontaneous round of applause in support of this straight speaking, honest man, filled the room.

Bill remained silent for the remainder of the meeting and most of the journey home but he'd achieved his objective. He'd not just accepted the will of faceless bureaucrats. He'd been to London and told the politicians and civil servants what he thought of them. Of course nothing changed. The inshore men were forced into criminality, landing whiting under cover of darkness when the inspectorate had gone home. Little did we know how this practice would escalate for everyone.

For the remainder of the week I was concerned that Bluey might be struggling to catch a trip but my fears were groundless. He'd managed perfectly well and was back in on Thursday morning with a big shot. This was a cause for optimism.

* * * * * *

It would soon be time to lay the keel of my new vessel and knowing this was imminent, I had a request for the builders. I had recollections from my younger days, of some wonderful looking herring drifters, built by the Forbes Yard in the 1950s that had full, flared, bluff bows. The vessels I remembered, the *Silver Wave, Prospective, Forethought* and *Prevail,* all painted black, were special and I wanted my new baby to have this characteristic. Derry Forbes was surprised that I was even aware of these craft from the stocks of his family's Sandhaven yard and assured me I'd get my wish.

## Chapter 14

# The Diving Trip

During my time ashore in the past few weeks I'd managed to get some diving in on the wrecks off the coast with the lads from the Diving Club. These pals were great company and skilled, knowledgeable divers who kept an eye on inexperienced novices, including me.

Friday evening found us hauling up the grapnel from a wreck we'd dived on five miles from home. A Grimsby vessel came in sight from the northeast, heading towards Scarborough. As the distinctive, pale blue vessel drew closer, I recognised her as the *White Bank*, the wreck fisher, skippered by my pal, Olaf. Contacting him on the radio, he was surprised to hear the small diving vessel, *St Hope,* on his beam, calling his boat's name but then recognised my voice. He said he'd shot his nets on several wrecks between twenty and forty miles off and was going to spend the night in Scarborough, intending to sail early the following morning to haul them.

Olaf was one of several gill-netters operating from the Humber port that occasionally called into our harbour while tiding their nets or to make a mid-trip landing. Eric Lose of the *Wardley* and Billy 'Wiggy' Hardy skipper of the *Christine H* were others. I'd known these fishermen for several years and all were friends.

It was inevitable that we'd meet up in the pub and Olaf, big, rotund, red-faced and bearded was his usual, larger-than-life self.

He and his crew had been in the Newcastle Packet most of the evening and had made their way to the Sub Aqua Club just before closing time, knowing if they were inside when the door was closed, they'd be in for an extended session. They'd been locked in the 'Sup After Club' before.

"You lads should try diving out on the Well Bank," Olaf said, downing half his pint of lager in one, large gulp. His capacity was immense and seemed to have little or no effect. "There's dozens of wrecks out there. They're all close together and it's shallow. The water's as clear as gin." He was describing an area south of the Dogger Bank, about seventy miles to the east, a place unfamiliar to me as a fishing ground. The 'Decca' system was less accurate further offshore but was sufficient to find the approximate wreck sites. These netting vessels were fitted with sonar, so could locate iron shipwrecks precisely at three-quarters of a mile or more.

Those remaining club members were getting excited about this inaccessible graveyard for ships, which was every diver's dream, though this may have been slightly drink-induced. "What about going in the *Independence*?" someone asked. "We could charter your boat for the week. If twelve of us went, we could afford it."

The speaker clearly didn't realise the earning potential of my vessel but he'd sowed a seed that would bear fruit. I began to consider the logistics of getting off to the Well Bank between fishing trips when the *Independence* would normally be in harbour and realised this was a possibility. We usually landed our catches on Thursday mornings and my crew could get their normal time ashore. The boat would sail on Thursday evening with the divers and steam overnight. We could dive on Friday and Saturday and be back in port in the early hours of Sunday. When the dive crew disembarked, the *Independence's* crew could take on the week's supply of food and make a quick turn round. I ran the plan through my head again quickly, then mentioned the scheme to those present, finding unanimous, excited support.

Olaf, joining in the conversation with enthusiasm, offered the wreck readings we'd need and Pete, the most enthusiastic of all, contributed, "we could get some information for the area from the Hydrographic Department."

This was news to me. I had no idea the Royal Navy had information they'd divulge on a commercial basis. If we did undertake the trip, it would be even better to have some idea of the identity of the wrecks we wanted to dive on. It seemed probable we were going on an expedition.

Changing the subject briefly, Olaf pointed to one of the club members, standing at the bar. "That fella over there," he said loudly, the lager finally working, "he's got half a red face and half white one. What's wrong with him?"

All eyes turned in the direction of Roger Flower, a heavily built man, well dressed, with short, blond hair and normally a round, pale face. "I've been sailing with Arthur on the *Mekong* and we've just come back from Holland," he explained, a little embarrassed. "He told me to steer a straight course and not take my eyes off the compass, so that's what I did. I was steering the boat for four hours and the sun was very hot. Half of my face got sunburnt."

The diving plan would come to fruition in a few weeks and we'd work on the detail meanwhile. We set the limit at twelve divers plus skipper and a cook. The voyage would be by invitation, as diving from a trawler was never going to be easy. There were lots of considerations, not least, where were fourteen people going to sleep? There were only six bunks on the vessel and one of those was mine. Meanwhile there was some fishing to be done and we'd be sailing again on Sunday morning.

The new vessel's keel was laid and her frames in place. She was given, 'Yard number 305', indicating the contribution J & G Forbes had made to the fishing industry in almost a century of boat building. I wanted to see how my new baby was progressing so decided to visit the yard, flying from Kirmington, south of the Humber, as I'd done a few years earlier. I was intending to stay overnight and though not needing to take much in the way of clothes and only a small toilet bag, I was dismayed when Dotty handed me a plastic shopping bag with the words, 'Tesco', emblazoned prominently.

I said nothing, knowing she was busy with three small children and was preoccupied.

It was surprising how this previously, quiet little airport had advanced in the few years since I'd last flown from Humberside. There was now a bar and lounge, when previously I'd watered in the local flying club whilst waiting for my delayed flight. Now a steady stream of helicopters were landing and taking off, servicing the rigs in the expanding, offshore oil and gas industry.

The flight was full with workers, returning to the offshore industry in Aberdeen, which was also booming from North Sea oil exploration and production. Normally I'd have been quite excited at a flight along the coast but after my cliff high passage with Alf, this seemed quite pedestrian. More choppers were present here, flitting to and fro, supplying the needs of the northern oil business.

Derry had sent one of his workers to collect me. The boiler-suited driver nodded in my direction, acknowledging me, as I left the arrivals gate. Without a word I followed him to a waiting pick-up truck. Conversation was stilted on the hour-long journey to the shipyard, the morose man resisting any attempts I made to make conversation, answering my early questions in monosyllables or grunts. His body language spoke volumes. "Why the resentment?" I wondered. "Was he still fighting long forgotten wars?" Ignoring his surly attitude, I opted to look out of the window, admiring the flat, fertile land, contrasting to most of Scotland's terrain. I knew this man wasn't representative of the people in the northeast, as I'd been visiting this part of the country since my teens and was aware how hospitable these friendly folk could be.

I didn't want this man collecting me again when I next came north to monitor the progress of my vessel and made a mental note to tell Derry Forbes this. We pulled up outside the rectangular, single story office building with J & G Forbes fixed in red, formed letters, high on the front. Across the road were two huge wooden sheds, where my baby would be taking form. My reluctant chauffeur left me standing on the pavement, begrudgingly directing me to the office door, at the back of the building.

I knocked and entered, finding Derry at his desk in a fug of smoke. He greeted me, but before I was able to complain about my driver, he apologised for not collecting me, blaming the pressure of work. His smart Jaguar, parked outside, would have made short work of the distance. The boss took me across the road to the yard and we entered the massive building through a small, side door. The smell of new wood in the air instantly hit me, with effect. The warm shed was a hive of activity and the noise of electrical machinery, deafening. Steam was emitting from a long, horizontal box, where planks were softened, making them pliable before being bent into place on the frames. The skeleton of my new craft towered overhead, almost reaching the rafters and she was certainly full in the bow department. Her ribs, even without planking, indicated she'd have a spectacular shape. She may have filled the shed vertically but in length there was plenty of room available. My new baby was slightly less than sixty feet and there'd been much bigger vessels delivered from this place.

I walked round the growing, living entity slowly, several times, awed by the thickness of her oak keel, stem and sternposts. There were only a few planks in place, attached to the keel at deck level, but enough to give an impression of the depth of the vessel internally. She was going to be some boat.

I'd forgotten Derry was in the shed with me till he patted me on the arm, breaking me from my reverie. "I'll tak ye tae the Cliff," he said. This was an instruction not a request and I followed him outside. He collected his car keys from the office, passing me my plastic bag with a smile, indicating I should get in the car. Setting off slowly, we rounded the bend out of the village to head west in the direction of Rosehearty. A long, straight road lay before us. To the left were fields and on the other side, surf was breaking on the rocks. This was a really attractive, pleasant drive, or was, till unexpectedly, the driver hit the accelerator. I was thrown back in my seat by the G force as we went from thirty to over a hundred miles an hour in seconds. My face must have turned ashen but Derry just laughed at my startled expression.

The few miles were eaten up in no time and there was no chance of enjoying the view. He slowed down as we approached the sharp bend turning into Rosehearty. I recognised the Masons Arms, the first building on the left. I'd been in there often in the past with Dennis, my old school pal and his wife Vera, who lived in the village. Dennis had worked on the nomadic, Scottish herring drifters sailing from Scarborough when he first left school. He'd moved north to settle while still in his teens. Now he was one of the shareholders of the seventy-five foot *Kimara,* also a Forbes vessel. They had two young sons, Derek and Paul, now at school. I'd stayed with him on a couple of occasions during the building of the *Independence*. I'd ring him later and arrange to meet up for a beer and an update.

We passed the Forbes Arms, near the centre of the village, then his son Rory's house. Next we went by his own house on the way to his brother-in-law's hotel, restaurant and bar, The Cliff View. There was no doubting this family's influence in the village. Edna and Billy were good hosts and the lady of the house was also an excellent cook. Dennis and Vera turned up for drinks and a superb meal at the 'Cliff'. Dennis, tall, curly-haired, sparkling eyes and a ready smile, now had an accent thicker than most Scots, his Yorkshire twang long gone. Vera, vivacious, tall and thin with a fresh complexion had straight, long, raven coloured hair and wore large, gold looped gypsy earrings.

Following the meal we sat at the bar reminiscing and joking, though it was long after midnight. Billy, the landlord occasionally joined in the conversation, though his broad Scots tongue was difficult to understand. He frequently added, "ye ken," at the end of sentences to emphasise a point. We were drinking after time but this didn't seem to bother Billy, the fact that he was a magistrate in nearby Fraserburgh was conveniently forgotten.

I was nursing a hangover next morning when I was collected to be taken back to the airport. Again Derry was busy but at least my former driver was also unavailable.

* * * * * *

A couple of weeks later at noon on Saturday, the twelve chosen divers gathered in the clubhouse to discuss requirements for the forthcoming expedition. There were many tasks to undertake and jobs to delegate if we were to get *Independence* turned round the following Thursday. Pen and paper were produced and a list was compiled. Charts, readings, hydrographical data, inflatable hulled craft with outboard motor, compressor, buoys, ropes, grapnels, food and a cook, beer, fishing rods, goody bags, lifting bags, sleeping bags. The list was endless. Satisfied that the main necessities had been covered, we began to address each item in turn.

Admiralty Charts, with 'Decca' lattice overlay for the area and the wreck positions were my department. I had a chart catalogue and would have the necessary charts sent by overnight post, from 'Cooks' in Hull. This firm, supplying all precision navigating instruments, books and charts, was an institution and sadly, now a shadow of its former glory. When Hull was a huge port for merchant ships and sent trawlers all over the western, high latitudes to hunt cod, Master Mariners, Officers, Cadets, Skippers and Mates, all used this establishment for their many professional requirements.

I'd also get the all-important readings from Olaf or one of the other gill-netters during the week at sea, by radio. These would be 'Decca' readings. Pete had already acquired a printout from the Royal Navy for an extensive area to the east, with scores of wreck positions, though most were listed as unknowns, with a few interesting exceptions. All these positions were in latitude and longitude fixes and would have to be plotted on the chart along with the 'Decca' readings.

The Diving Club had its own small, orange, inflatable craft, fitted with an outboard engine and also owned a portable, petrol driven compressor. Two members were detailed to deliver this equipment at the time of sailing and these essentials were quickly ticked off.

We had inflatable fenders onboard the *Independence* that would double as marker buoys. Plastic bins of light rope from the *St Hope* would attach to these floats and could be supplemented if necessary with coils of similar material that we used to fasten our trawl to the bobbins. Richard 'Dick' Sellars, one of four divers on the expedition who lived in the countryside, collectively known as the 'Emmerdales', volunteered to make the grapnels or plonkers, as the lads called them. Dick, thin, of medium height with fine, blond hair had been an RAF mechanic and was now a village blacksmith, making and repairing agricultural implements for the farming community. He could manufacture virtually anything, working with metal. It was Dick Sellars who'd installed and piped up the club's main compressor and a bank of storage bottles, enabling members to fill their tanks at any time. He'd cut and shaped girders for major club alterations, made railings, boat ladders for divers' exit from the water and even brackets for trophies on the club wall. Knocking a few plonkers up would be childs' play for Dick.

I'd ask around the harbour to see if anyone wanted to sail on the trip as cook. We reckoned a fee of a hundred pounds for the trip should get us a willing hand, meanwhile Colin, the Chairman would compile a food list and organise the kegs of beer, gas propellants and plastic glasses.

Everyone was to bring a fishing rod. There was sure to be lots of cod on the wrecks. We'd need plenty of tackle and one of our team, Brian, a keen angler, undertook this task. Any out of pocket expenses incurred would be reimbursed. All the divers possessed goody bags for any small finds or the occasional lobster. Some possessed lifting bags, which could be inflated on the seabed to raise heavier, non-ferrous objects from the bottom.

The nocturnal arrangements would be more difficult. With only six bunks, sleeping would at best be rudimentary. The bunks would be on a first come, first served, basis and would be rotated when empty. Camp beds, sleeping bags and even a hammock would be deployed. There was space on the seat lockers in the cabin and on the mess-deck and though cushioned, these were not ideal. There was also space for'ard in the fo'c's'le, where we stored spare fishing gear. It was all systems go.

We landed in the early hours of Thursday morning and I managed a few hours in bed before breakfast. I was able to see the elder bairns off to school and spend some time with Dotty and baby Sarah before going down to settle our fishing trip. I boarded the *Independence* to retrieve my job list, the compilation of work required and spares needed while the vessel was in port. I was surprised to see diving bottles and bags already stacked on the deck. Below, in the cabin, name cards were in each of the five spare bunks, claiming them for the more astute members of the forthcoming voyage.

Inspiration made me ask Maurice 'Slack' Harwood if he wanted the cook's berth as I passed him on Sandgate Corner. Maurice was from a longstanding, Scarborough fishing family and operated a motorboat from the slipway. He took passengers and worked crab pots from his small boat but was pleased of the chance to sail with us. Maurice would be a good man to have on the expedition.

It was like a schoolboys' outing when we sailed at eight o'clock that evening, the sun still shining over the land astern of us. There were men standing on the whaleback, on the deck where the inflatable was stowed and posing at the stern as we headed east into a flat calm sea. All were enjoying the alfresco beer. I'd insisted on an empty wheelhouse until we were in open water but now I had half a dozen bodies invading my space, wanting to know where we were going and what the plan was. "We're 'eading east by south," I said. "We'll be about nine hours steamin' an' we'll set t' watches soon." The squad had paired up and drawn for time slots. The teams would do an hour and a half each. I set the range ring on the radar at two miles. When I turned in I'd be on call throughout the night to deal with shipping or static rigs, should any encroach this zone.

I was summoned several times to give advice or alter course during the passage and eventually, an hour before the estimated time of arrival, was called to take over. Plotting our position, I altered course slightly and switched on sounders and sonar. The loud, slow ping, ping, ping as the sonar step scanned ahead across both bows was reassuring. Maurice, who'd been dozing on the seat locker in the galley, produced a welcome pot of coffee.

All hands were called with fifteen minutes to go and I noticed the four country lads coming aft from the fo'c's'le. It must have been a little cramped down in the forepeak. "There's barely enough air down there to sustain life," one of them called to me, grinning as they spotted me through the open window. These four, the more awake members of the expedition, opted to prepare a plonker with twenty fathoms of line and a buoy, ready for deploying. The wreck we were looking for was one of several in close proximity and all were listed as unknown on the printout. Maybe we'd shed some light on this sunken craft in an hour or two, literally.

Following a green line on the 'Decca' chart for a few minutes, with an audience of two interested observers at my shoulder making me nervous, there was a sudden faint echo on the sonar. "There she is," I announced, easing back the throttle and becoming more focused. The onlookers could see nothing and had missed the phut, as the signal bounced back from its target. The sonar was now pointing to starboard, away from the wreck. Freezing the beam in the direction of the echo, fifteen degrees to port, there was now a constant echo, ping-phut, ping-phut, ping-phut. Gently easing our course towards the wreck and adjusting the beam to follow, the object was now dead ahead at a distance of seven hundred and fifty metres and was marking clearly on the wet paper recorder. The pair at my shoulder now had something tangible to see. The time lapse between the ping and echo grew shorter as we approached the location and the recorder showed the dark brown stain coming closer along the scale. "Stand by!" I yelled to the men at the stern, from the window. The heavy grapple was balanced on the transom ready for a push. The line and buoy would automatically follow.

Lowering the angle of the beam, as the target grew ever closer, I followed the direction of the target but at two hundred and fifty metres, I could track the object no longer. This was expected. The echo was lost as the beam was now passing over the top of the wreck. Turning to the sounder, marking soft ground in eighteen fathoms, I held the course, watching the screen, willing the stylus to scratch the wreck's shape on the paper. "There she is," I repeated and leaning out of the opening yelled "leggo!"

The lads were on a hair-trigger and the metal bar, with its curved prongs, shot through the air, entering the flat surface with a pleasing splash. The rope ran smoothly out and even before it had reached its end, Pete had thrown the buoy over. "That should be in the wreck," I stated confidently for the benefit of my audience, though I was far from sure. The noisy sonar, no longer needed, was now turned off.

The buoy was riding at what little tide was evident, so dodging into the direction of the gentle current, passing close to the surface marker, I looked for confirmation of a hit. The line from the buoy was visible a long way down into the deep. "Look at the vis," several of our number on deck enthused, commenting on the underwater visibility. The water was very clear indeed, though this wasn't always the case on the bottom. Once clear of the buoy, the sounder began to show the wreck with greater definition. Standing more than two fathoms high and appearing intact, this was very interesting.

The inflatable was lifted outboard with the winch and secured by its painter to the stern then divers quickly began kitting up. Wetsuits, buoyancy aids, masks and fins appeared from bags and with so many rushing to kit up at once, the foredeck looked like a divers' jumble sale. Soon there were several pairs of black suited frogmen, sitting with legs dangling inboard along the starboard side. A plastic sheet, tucked down the edges of the net compound, covered the trawl stowed beneath. "Stand by!" I called as we approached the buoy again. A quick blast astern stopped the *Independence* alongside the orange float. "Go now," I instructed loudly, for the benefit of ears buried under neoprene hoods and mask straps. Three pairs of frogmen dropped into the water, falling several feet before hitting the surface. Each had the palm of one hand holding his facemask in place. All were armed with powerful torches; goody bags were clipped onto weight belts. Some entered the water vertically, others on their sides, the heavy diving bottles unbalancing the unwary and creating large plumes of spray. Once in the water the divers quickly swam for the buoy, grabbing the line before the tide carried them downstream. The uninitiated quickly learned that even a gentle current is difficult to swim against.

Soon all had disappeared below the surface, leaving only bubbles to mark their presence. The divers' names and times of entry were noted on a printed form by Dave, one of the four men remaining on deck. Dave Jackson, tall, thin, bespectacled was an electrician by trade and like many other members, gave much of his time to maintaining and improving the club premises, free of charge.

Though I knew these men were all experienced divers, this was a time of anxiety. No one knew what was waiting, below in the depths. Maybe the wreck would be cluttered with fine, tangle netting and would trap the unwary. Colin manned the small boat, tying onto the buoy with the painter and I stood off in the *Independence*, not wanting to be near any surfacing divers.

"Bag up," I bawled to Colin minutes later. He was lying horizontally in the bottom of the rubber craft, enjoying the sunshine. Looking up, he acknowledged my pointing finger and started the engine with a single pull of the cord. A yellow lifting bag had surged to the surface, carrying beneath it some object too cumbersome or heavy to be dragged around the bottom. This was exciting stuff, like waiting to see what was in a parcel at Christmas.

The boatman steered close to the vinyl balloon, stopping alongside and precariously reached for the bag. If he spilled the air from the opening at the bottom, without having a firm grip, the object would quickly sink and be lost forever. There was no cause for concern however; Colin had retrieved bags before and knew the dangers. I watched through the binoculars as he took hold of the envelope with both hands, dragging bag, harness and artefact inboard in one smooth movement. Unfastening the sling, he held up an almost black, tarnished ship's bell, still mounted on its bracket.

"A bell! " I shouted to the four divers, leisurely kitting up on the foredeck. "They've found the bell. Wow!" This was the most coveted of all trophies and we'd found one on the first dive. I couldn't wait to get in the water. While Colin was waiting to collect the first wave of divers, I took the opportunity to open my kit bag and don my two-piece wetsuit. Bottles and regulator were assembled for quick deployment, so I could kit up easily when the first team had re-embarked. A wonderful smell of grilling bacon was permeating the air, making me feel hungry.

Twenty to thirty minutes later the explorers began surfacing, each holding an arm aloft, thumb and forefinger together, signalling they were OK. This was acknowledged and repeated by the boatman, who headed in their direction. The divers, one hand holding onto the side of the inflatable, removed their cumbersome, heavy tanks and weight belts, passing straps to the boatman to haul onboard. Several divers passed goody bags containing small keepsakes up to the excited boat handler, now also keen to get into the water. A mountain of gear was piled high in the centre of the vessel and divers were sitting in equal numbers on the sponsons, as she slowly headed back to her base. The wetsuited figures climbed on board, timing their jump as the *Independence* rolled gently to starboard, then the used equipment was hurriedly transferred to the mother ship, again on the roll. The second wave were keen to get going. It was slack water, the slight drain of tide had ended so the second drop would have an easy dive.

Now back on board, all were attempting to relate their experiences, clearly excited by the adventure. The expression, "did you see?" prefixed every sentence.

"What was it?" I asked Pete when he came up to the wheelhouse to take over the helm. He would drop the remaining six divers at the buoy.

Pete delivered an excellent appraisal of the wreck. "It's an old steam trawler," he reported with pleasure. "I saw the winch and a gallow. The vis' is superb. You won't need a torch. You can see virtually the entire ship from the shot rope. The plonker is on the stern. She's intact but the wheelhouse has gone. It's absolutely teeming with cod. There's a wall of fish down there." His enthusiasm rubbed off instantly and I went to the deck to join the other pairs kitting up and who were almost ready. My buddy was Brian.

We hit the water and set off down the line at speed. Our immersion time commenced as soon as we entered the water. The dive tables didn't give us long without decompressing, so every minute counted. Pete's report was correct. We could see the wreck laid out before us long before reaching the bottom. The clarity of the water was incredible and it didn't seem at all cold. Looking out into the blue, away from the wreck I could see a shimmering, silver green. The fish, which the first divers had seen, had moved from their habitat, frightened by the noise and bubbles but they hadn't gone far and would return when we departed. This would be good sport with the rods later.

Now on the bottom we relaxed, conserving air and gently finned along the port gunwale, navigating round the sunken ship. A step down in the gunwale leading from aft to the main deck was evident. The winch, with its distinctive, twin barrels was clearly visible amidships and was being examined closely by the other divers. There was plenty of lost tangle net strewn around the wreck but this had mostly spun up with tidal action and now had the appearance of rope. A small arc of metal near the winch attracted my attention and I reached for it, pulling the object from the sand, causing a small plume of silt to rise, briefly impairing the visibility. Holding the find up from the cloud, I was delighted to see a six-inch porthole with glass intact; a pleasing discovery that was soon in my goody bag. Moving further forward, we approached the pointed stem where a square hatch had at one time been the entrance to the crew's accommodation. This was now totally filled with sediment and the cabin was no longer accessible. A feeling of great sadness swept over me as I saw this small inlet. In all likelihood there would be the remains of some of the crew buried there. Who were these fishermen? When were they lost? What ship was this? What port had she sailed from? There were so many unanswered questions. The poor wretched men below must have died a horrible death with no possibility of rescue.

Swimming down the starboard side, leaving my gloomy thoughts behind and giving Brian the OK sign, I was aware of the tide beginning to pick up. We were finning harder now and grabbing handholds to assist our passage along the edge of the vessel. Rather quickly, I became aware that I needed to pee. Whether from pressure of water or change in temperature I wasn't sure but it wouldn't wait. With difficulty I forced my body to do what should come naturally and a warm glow filled my suit. Unfortunately this soon cooled and ran down the suit into the boots. This was common practice and the suit would be hosed and hung up to dry when back on board.

I looked at my watch. We'd already been underwater fifteen minutes and it was time we were leaving. The other divers were visible on the other side of the wreck, also making for the stern. Minutes later we were on the shot rope. One of the other team had thrown the grapnel clear of the wreck, making retrieval easier. Our ascent was deliberately slow, hand over hand, allowing the nitrogen to leave our bodies without damaging tissue. Monitoring the depth, we stopped at ten feet for a few minutes to decompress, joining another pair of frogmen. Two others were dangling from the line immediately below us, the underside of the orange craft clearly visible above.

We broke the surface to see Ian Robinson beaming down at us. Ian, one of the younger club members, was the finder of the bell. He was totally deaf but in no way was he handicapped. Ian was an amazing lip reader and spoke quite clearly. Underwater he was better than most and when occasionally, he dived with a deaf friend, they had the advantage of using sign language. Ian and the boatman relieved us of our heavy gear, allowing us easy access into the boat.

Back alongside the *Independence,* the compressor was already in harness, clattering away loudly, recharging bottles ready for the afternoon dive. We passed our gear from the rubber boat to the divers who'd changed from their wetsuits and already eaten a hearty breakfast. The rubber suits were now turned inside out and hanging from the landing pole, making my vessel look like a laundry. Maurice, standing on the galley step with pot of tea in one hand and cigarette in the other looked content but bemused by these grown men at play. "Are yer ready fo' some breakfast?" he asked as I walked aft, still in my wetsuit. "It'll be ready in about five minutes."

"Ready? I'm bloody ravenous," I replied. "I could eat a horse." The early morning dip had honed an already sharp appetite.

Lots of interest was shown in the bell, usually identifying the vessel's name but in this case there was no lettering visible. "Just my luck," Ian said, in the slightest of nasal tones. "I find a bell an' it's a blooming bald one."

Shortly afterwards, we remaining hungry crew, now changed into casual wear, were seated round the mess-deck table. Our diving suits had been hosed and added to those drying on the line above the deck. Fishing rods, in various states of assembly were now in evidence through the galley window. A full fry up of bacon, sausage, eggs, beans, tomatoes and fried bread with toast and tea or coffee was quickly served up with little ceremony and few words by a still smiling cook, who occasionally shook his head in disbelief muttering, "ah've never seen owt like it."

The breakfast was rushed and I was soon back in the wheelhouse to discover Pete had kept the *Independence* on station with the buoy and tide was now clearly evident, streaming past the anchored position. Thanking him for his support and confirming his wreck analysis I said, "go an' get yer rod ready. T' troops are fishin' keen." Dodging the boat up tide, past the floating wreck marker, I stopped her dead in the water with a touch of stern gear then shouted, "drop 'em down," to those with tackle ready.

Half a dozen reels were released within seconds and the weighted lines sank to the bottom. The boat quickly drifted back over the wreck, where lures attracted the ever-hungry cod. Only seconds later, every rod was bent double. Cries of "fish on!" "Gotcha" and "gaff!" encouraged those not yet ready to double their efforts of preparation.

Brian, whose line had been first in the water, was also the first to reel his catch to the surface. Two writhing cod, one on each hook, were being held just below the surface. Maurice, grasping a long pole with a large, barbless hook lashed on the end, was rushing to the boat's side. He quickly assessed that one fish was lightly hung, the hook clearly visible through the lip and the other one had been swallowed. He stuck the gaff accurately in the belly of the loose fish, lifting the wriggling creature, along with its attached companion, cleanly out of the water and onto the deck, detaching the gaff in the same movement. Unceremoniously, he unhooked the lightly hung fish then wrapped the nylon line around his hardened hand and yanked the hook free from the second fish's throat. Though this had taken only a few seconds, the other fishers were already clamouring for his services. A second gaff was deployed in answer to an earnest plea of, "will somebody come an' gaff this big bugger please. I'm gonna lose it." A large cod, weighing around fourteen pounds, suspended in the water, was hauled onboard to the relief of the rods-man. This specimen could feature in the heaviest fish competition. A pound a man was riding on this sweepstake.

There was no time for the anglers to drop their lines down again. We were already down tide from the wreck and I'd have to take the vessel back upstream, repeating the manoeuvre. This time there were eleven fishing poles, the owners unevenly spread around the deck, eagerly awaiting the word. "Where's your rod, Vinny?" I asked of the man holding the gaff.

Vinny, a tall, pale, craggy-faced man with tufts of curly hair on the sides of a balding head hadn't been a club member long and clearly hadn't understood the importance of the fishing aspect of the expedition. The proceeds of this sport would contribute largely to the running of the trip. He'd never caught a fish in his life but he'd have been sure to change this record if he'd brought a rod. This was the nautical equivalent of shooting fish in a barrel. "If ah want fish, ah go t' 'Donny Market'", he called out in his broad, South Yorkshire accent. According to Vinny, any of life's requirements could be obtained from Doncaster Market.

Wooden fish boxes were distributed around the deck in key locations, ready for the prospective catches. Some were already in use. "Stand by!" I called out, preparing the anglers for the next drop. The engine revved in stern gear again and I yelled, "go on then." This second call was unnecessary for some. The slicker fishers had taken their cue from the distinct change of engine sound and were already lowering their tackle.

The wreck again began to mark on the paper and even though the lines, trailing up tide had yet to reach the location, rods began bending again. "Fish on!" was heard in several locations at once and Maurice excitedly began running towards the nearest with the gaff. Once the boat was drifting on the tide I could do nothing, so went on deck to assist with the fish handling. There was a chance the first catchers could get their lines back down again into the wreck if we could get the fish off the hooks fast enough. There were frequent tangling of lines and men hurried to unravel them. When there was a fish involved in the mix up, good-natured banter could be heard contesting ownership.

Everyone was using two hooks and almost all were taking fish on both, though unlucky ones occasionally caught the wreck and were compelled to tie their line to a fixed point on the boat until the stretching thread parted. The alternative was a broken rod. Brian even though he was a keen angler, had never experienced fishing like this and now had three hooks on his line.

The pattern was repeated on numerous occasions over the next couple of hours, though I occasionally missed the wreck. The tide was now racing and the surface marker gave the appearance of surging through the water. We were only managing brief seconds as the fishing tackle whizzed across the target and we were losing gear, sometimes on the rope. It was time to call a halt.

The plonker was hauled up and some of the lost perks and hooks recovered, including a couple more fish, ownership again heatedly debated. Maurice took charge of the gutting operation, teaching willing pupils how to disembowel the dead fish, efficiently. These dressed fish were thrown into the washer to port and the hose held by another volunteer, washing caked blood from the bellies. Chute attached, the catch was sent below to the fish-hold, propelled by the hands and feet of yet another diver, standing in the washer, wearing thigh length boots. The temperature was almost at freezing point in the fishroom, where metal plates on the deckhead were caked with frost. With some assistance I sorted the cod into sizes before boxing and icing them.

Not long afterwards, the sonar was again switched on and we began scouting for the next wreck. There were few of the diving team to be seen now. Most were below dozing, with the exception of a couple of the 'Emmerdale' lads, still refilling bottles.

The sonar was soon banging at another solid object and this too was located and buoyed, but with plenty of tide still running, there was little to do but wait for the six-hourly cycle to ease.

There was more fishing to be done, then more diving. This time Brian and I were in the first wave of divers to enter the water, to discover another trawler, in virtually the same circumstances. This vessel was clouded in cod but was lying over to port, with her gunwale almost on the seabed. I couldn't believe my luck when, following slowly behind Brian, I spotted the ship's bell. My buddy had swum over the top of the find. The wheelhouse must have collapsed over the years and the attached bell and bracket dropped into the scuppers. I couldn't believe my luck and began pulling and twisting the bell, attempting to wrestle it free of its fastening. This wasn't as easy as I'd hoped and with the cloud I'd created, Brian had no idea what I'd discovered.

My find came free of its fixture and I held it up triumphantly. My buddy gave me the thumbs up and even with the mask covering most of his face and regulator in his mouth, his pleasure was plain to see. The bell, detached from its bracket, wasn't too heavy and fitted in my goody bag, so we continued our dive, though in truth I was so excited now, I was just filling in the minutes before ascending the line again. We were first to the surface and as we'd done a shorter dive than the others, needed no decompression.

Greeted by Vinny's grinning face, I passed the precious bag inboard to his obvious approval.

As we were back early, we were taken to the mother ship, allowing the others to prepare for their dip. The dive resulted in some collectable trinkets, a brass lamp, small porthole and a steam gauge. It was evident there was lettering on the little bell but the years of marine growth was obscuring this and I was desperately curious to discover the name of this mysterious vessel. My rough, enthusiastic handling of the object on the seabed had resulted in the lug on the bell breaking off where it joined the bracket. Had I been more careful, perhaps I might have retrieved the mounting too.

After tapping at the obscured name and frequently washing and scrubbing, the letters Leo—ra Grimsby became legible, though the remaining part of the title had worn away completely. At least I had some evidence to work on. She'd sailed from Grimsby.

More fish were taken following the diving, then our sport was done for the day. Maurice had cooked up a wholesome, simple meal from Colin's ingredients and everyone ate their fill, washing the feast down with plenty of beer.

It was Friday evening, the sun was setting and the weather glorious. There wasn't a ripple on the sea or a breath of wind. We stacked lots of fish boxes around the deck to form a semi-circle, which Pete named, 'The Well Bank Arms'. It was Ian's birthday and his Mum had supplied him with a cream sponge cake to celebrate. She'd also sent an aerosol canister of cream to add to the proceedings and everyone was given a piece of cake and a blob of cream on a paper plate. A rousing chorus of 'Happy Birthday' was sung, then totally unexpectedly and probably drink induced, someone hit Ian in the face with a portion of cake. In quick succession others joined in and the birthday boy was immediately blathered in cake and cream.

Ian was not one to take punishment lying down and promptly scattered everyone in range with the remains of the dessert. The next few minutes were pure slapstick. Everyone was hitting everyone with gunge, even reusing the stuff splattered round the deck. Eventually, at about 2200 the improvised seating and deck were hosed down and the Well Bank Arms closed and dismantled. Watches were set for the night, though we didn't expect to see much traffic, apart from the odd fishing boat.

Another dive early next morning was also on a small wreck, marked 'unknown' in the survey. While the first of the divers were underwater, I became aware of a fishing vessel a couple of miles from our position, heading in our direction. I identified her as the *Christine H.* Bill Hardy was working the wrecks in this area and was intending to shoot some nets on the one we were diving on. Raising him on the radio, Bill obligingly said he'd leave this target and our next proposed location until tomorrow, altering course for another prospect.

Expressing thanks, I chatted for a while, then at Colin's suggestion said, "stop yer boat for a few minutes. We 'ave a present for yer. 'Ow many crew 'ave you onboard?"

"Six of us aboard, including a trainee," came the reply. "What have you got for us?"

Colin pulled twelve pints of beer from the aluminium keg into plastic glasses and stowed them in a cardboard box, preventing movement. With Pete's assistance he carefully transported the ale across in the inflatable boat to the stationary vessel, half a mile away, to be met with looks of incredulity. The number of days in a year an operation like this could be undertaken, could probably be counted on one hand, if anyone wanted to undertake such a transfer.

"Cheers Freddy," came the message over the airwaves as his vessel began to move away. "That's the last thing I expected." We selected a little used VHF frequency and agreed to stay in touch.

The first returning divers reported the site to be almost unidentifiable as a ship; most of the vessel was buried under the sand. The only object surrendered by the wreck was the builder's nameplate, covered in marine growth but with small flakes of red paint in one corner. The information yielded, said she'd been built in Sweden. The rectangular, fifteen inches by nine brass plate read, No 27, Aktiebol, Lodose Varf, Goteborg, 1908. This must have been the twenty-seventh ship this Scandinavian shipyard had built. Due to its size, this wreck was difficult to hit with the fishing lines without tangling the buoy rope, so recovering the plonker we moved off, looking for the site of our afternoon dip.

A solid sonar contact, a few miles to the south looked promising and in short time the position was marked. We were getting quite slick and blasé in the matter of wreck finding, the earlier anxieties now long forgotten. As the tide eased, fishing rods re-appeared; the fierce competition was about to resume. The heaviest fish so far weighed about twenty pounds.

Brian now had six hooks on his line and was going for broke. Closing slowly, I marked the target and went astern. The lines dropped and all hit fish. Rods were bending the instant the lures hit the bottom, the fishers leaning back then quickly winding up the slack as they bent forward again. Brian's rod was almost curved double and he could hardly turn the reel. Sweat poured from his forehead as he gradually pulled his massive catch towards the surface. All the other rods were out of use now, their catches onboard. We were off the wreck and couldn't move back towards the site until this haul had been landed. Both gaffs were poised in readiness as the line, very slowly, mounted on the smoking reel. Brian looked totally exhausted but the encouraging cheers and goading from his mates kept him working.

"Go on Bri', you can do it. Keep pumping."

"Have you caught a whale? Maybe you're pulling the wreck up."

"Come on, what are you messing about at? Pull 'em up. We want to get our gear down again."

Brian was grunting expletives when his breathing would allow, his cranking now very slow but still drawing his pray closer. Leaning over the side I glimpsed six fish shining in the depths. Within feet of the surface and with everyone onboard in attendance, the line snapped and Brian fell backwards. A universal groan filled the air and six fish, now joined together for life, dived for the bottom leaving the angler a broken man.

The fourth dive site inevitably revealed another sunken fishing vessel. This seemed to be a trawlers' graveyard that we'd discovered. What was unusual about this wreck was its peculiar shaped stem and each pair, as they entered the pick up boat said, "did you see the curved bow? It was like those on old clipper ships." This was most unlike any fishing vessel I'd ever seen. A few brass souvenirs were given up by the old vessel but sadly, the bell remained elusive.

A little more fishing took place, then we recovered the buoy, hauled the rubber craft onboard and set the course for home. A slight, westerly breeze caused the Well Bank Arms to be relocated to the stern of the boat.

Arriving back in port at 0400 from the ground-breaking trip, the landing gear was topped to haul not only the diving gear but also eighteen boxes of cod, weighing well over a hundred stones. The heaviest fish, weighed on the market scales, was a twenty-one pound cod, winning Brian twelve pounds. Vinny paid his contribution by default.

Following a team photo, there were handshakes all round and thanks to Maurice for his culinary efforts, then the twelve intrepid, sunburnt pioneers departed the pier for home. Their dive bags and related gear, plus a large fish each were stacked into numerous vehicles. The dive trip was over and it was time for fishing again but with the information gained, there was plenty of research to be done.

The following weekend I borrowed an old, pre-war, 'Lloyds Register' from Arthur, who together with Pete had written a popular book on shipwrecks. This register listed every ship insured through this august body and I began working through the Ls. The search didn't take long. The name jumped out at me. *Leonora,* Built at Cochranes, Selby, 1904, 217 tons.

Armed with this information I wrote to the Grimsby Evening Telegraph, asking if they had any information in their archives, relating to this ship's loss, not knowing what a can of worms I was opening. I also enquired by post to the Maritime Museum in Gothenburg, asking if they had any information in their possession relating to the yard plate that had been recovered.

The banner headlines in the following day's Grimsby paper read, 'Wreck found after 42 years', with a cutting from the original paper, published on the seventh of May 1940. Along with two other trawlers, *Penn* and *Hercules, Leonora* had failed to return from her fishing trip. The sub-headline said, 'Hope given up for 27 Grimsby fishermen'. The article listed the names of all who'd been lost on these vessels and speculation as to their fate. Had they been torpedoed? Maybe they'd been captured and taken to Germany. This had happened to trawler crews in World War I.

During the next week I received several letters from relatives of the lost men, thanking us for our discovery and saying, "at least we know now."

In subsequent weeks, photos of the *Penn,* with a step in her gunwale and the *Dorando*, sister ship of the *Hercules*, a vessel which had subsequently been scrapped, were found. *Dorando* had an unusual, clipper bow. We'd found all three of the vessels, lost on that fateful voyage. Strangely, none of these ships were featured in a book Pete had researched titled, 'Vessels lost by Enemy Action, 1939-45'. Had these trawlers been lost in a British minefield? Were they fishing? Were they on passage? We'd never know the circumstances of their loss.

A letter from Gothenburg Maritime Museum said they hadn't much information on this shipyard and had no details of individual vessels but said there was only one ship registered from this yard in 1908, The *Sita*. She was subsequently sold to Norway and left the register in 1918. Had we found the last resting place of the *Sita* and her crew? Was this area a minefield in the Great War too? There were other wrecks in this area yet to be investigated. These would keep for another time.

## CHAPTER 15

# A NEW VESSEL

The new boat was now planked and decked and I'd decided to call her *Emulator*. In my younger days, a steam trawler of that name still operated from Scarborough and in her time had been a very successful vessel. She'd been built before the turn of the century and when taken for scrap in the early 1960s was more than sixty years old. *Independence* had been a lucky boat for me so if this new craft could emulate her performance, I could wish for no more. She was due to be moved out of the shed down the ramp so her machinery and superstructure could be fitted and I wanted to see her progress to date. Dotty handed me my 'Tesco' bag, much to my dissatisfaction and I departed for the airport. Met by Rory Forbes, son of Derry, I was given a progress report and taken directly to the yard. The vessel was already outside the huge shed and was clearly visible from the approach road. My *Emulator* looked spectacular in her first coat of blue, contrasting with the maroon, anti-fouling bottom paint.

Again I walked around my new baby, climbing onto the stocks and standing inside her 'Kort' nozzle, which would house the propeller. I was stooping but this was a measure of the size of her propulsion unit. Looking up at the waterline, it was incredible how much of the boat was going to be under the water. I climbed the extended ladder to the deck where, apart from the gaping hole in the centre, her decks were smooth and the gaps between each thin plank caulked and pitched.

Descending to the fish hold, which seemed cavernous, I stood on the bottom boards and looked aft through the opening in the bulkhead to the engine room, where as yet there was no machinery. The polished flange of the propeller shaft, which the engine would eventually be coupled to, reflected in the glow of the various cluster lights dotted around the open space. A pair of solid looking, parallel, angled steel bars stood waiting to support the eight-cylinder, Kelvin engine. I could already envisage the layout of the machinery space. The fuel tanks would be installed first, then the engine would be slotted between them. At the fore end, before the bulkhead was closed, would be the hydraulic pump in the centre, auxiliary engine to starboard, two banks of batteries to port, plus electrical generating gear and switchboards. The bilge/deck-wash pump would be driven from the main engine.

The secondary engine, though only 22 horsepower, would, when required charge the batteries, pump the bilges and even slowly drive the trawl winch. This was the work of the Kelvin in normal circumstances but the little workhorse stood ready for emergencies.

Another, quieter night was spent in the Cliff View. Dennis was at sea so after dinner I sat at the bar, listening to Billy and his frequent, "ken this" and "ya ken," as he imparted information.

Before heading for the airport I wandered to the top of the road, overlooking the coast. The morning was cool and sunny with a light, autumn breeze coming from the Moray Firth. About half a mile from the shore, a series of yellow marker buoys seemed to form the shape of a large ship. As I pondered the significance of this strangely marked zone, I spotted a jetfighter almost at sea level, screaming in at high speed, thick, dark vapour emitting from its engines. Suddenly the plane altered into a vertical climb showing its underbelly. What an amazing manoeuvre and I'd had no one to share the experience with. Minutes later another, then a third followed the same track, each stalking the mock vessel.

Several seconds after the noise of this fighter had died I noticed a white splash near the buoys. This couldn't be a bomb from the plane. The flying machine was nowhere near the zone now. When a fourth aircraft flew in, again at low level, I watched carefully, though never saw any missiles leave the plane prior to the climb, but again there was a splash when the craft was miles away. It suddenly dawned on me that the bombs were not being released until the jet was in the vertical position, then the explosive was released upwards and lobbed at the target. What great sport this was to watch and all at the taxpayers' expense.

Looking at my watch I realised I should have been on my way to the airport by now and ran back to the hotel to find a perplexed Rory looking for his charge.

* * * * * *

Back at home on Friday evening and looking at the forecast, it was evident that we were not going to be at sea on the following Sunday. The outlook was for strong, northerly winds. Dotty suggested that we invite our friends Syd, his lovely wife Ann and their two girls for Sunday dinner. Syd enjoyed the atmosphere in the Leeds Arms and regularly joined our Saturday group. Ann, originally from Wales, was a schoolteacher and equally companionable, though would blush and pretend to be embarrassed by the risqué humour in the pub.

"I'm sure I don't know what you mean," she'd say coyly.

The family arrived slightly before midday and I suggested to Syd that we went to the pub, leaving our wives chatting, preparing the food and enjoying a glass of something while the youngsters played together before eating an early meal.

"Dinner is at two o'clock," Dotty said as we prepared to leave.

"Oh come on, Les calls time at two. Can't we make it two-fifteen? We need a little bit o' drinkin' up time."

"Two o'clock," was her intransigent reply. "The Yorkshire puddings will be coming out of the oven at two o'clock." This was her last word on the subject. Why she'd adopted this stance was uncertain but at this point the matter was neither open to debate nor question.

It was a very busy lunchtime session in the 'Leeds'. The bad weather had arrived on cue and kept the fleet in port. There was lots of joke-telling, talk of fishing and Col was relating how his wife Rachel had recently been to Whitby and had taken up a drinking challenge from Billy Storr, one of the keelboat skippers in the busy river harbour. Billy was renowned for his capacity but Rachel had drunk him under the table, literally.

Of course, the time flew by. At ten minutes to two, Syd said, "isn't it time we were going?"

"Naw, it'll be alright. She was on'y jokin'," I assured him, feeling brave in the company of others and fortified by beer. "We've time for another," and though Syd declined the opportunity, I ordered another pint.

The foaming glass was delivered by Les, who then immediately bawled, "tiiime, let's have your drinks off please."

I couldn't down the pint instantly so was taking a little time, much to the landlord's displeasure. Syd, constantly looking at the clock, was becoming increasingly agitated and my reluctance to be concerned at Dotty's instructions wasn't helping. He'd finished his drink and was waiting by the door. It was ten past two. "Come on, we're late already," he urged.

Downing the remains of my drink, I joined Syd and we set off for home, only a few minutes walk away, though I had a hard time keeping up with him, such was the pace he was setting. Outside the house he stopped, allowing me to lead the way as we stepped through the back door into the kitchen. Both wives were present and I was delighted to see Dotty drawing a dozen, magnificent, golden Yorkshire puddings from the oven. The delicacies looked so light, they were almost levitating from the tray.

"Just in time," I enthused. "They look fantastic."

Without a word but with a scary look in her eye, Dotty crossed the kitchen, tea towel protecting her hands, and tipped the entire contents of the oven tray into a sink full of hot, soapy water. There was a gasp from Ann, who, hand to mouth, couldn't believe what she'd witnessed.

"When I said two o'clock, I meant two o'clock, not a quarter past. Next time you'll listen," came the angry retort from Dotty, now back at the stove.

"I told you we'd be in trouble," said the six-foot plus, ex-sailor, absolving himself from any blame by association, but I wasn't listening. I was already at the sink, fishing out the puddings, floating high among the suds. I wiped the first two or three on my sleeve and said, "quick, they're not too bad, come an' get some."

Syd quickly responded, joining me at the sink, plucking a few more of the golden orbs from the foam. We stood at the sink, oblivious to the open-mouthed, incredulous stares from our wives, comparing our salved puddings. "This one's alright," I said.

"Just a bit of froth on that one," Syd replied, quickly picking up his cue.

Ann began to laugh and despite her initial wrath, Dotty also began giggling at our behaviour. I placed the recovered puddings on a plate in the top of the oven, pending the serving of the other delicious component parts of the meal. When we were seated at the table and the Yorkshire puddings passed round, it was noticeable that the ladies declined the invitation to take one. Both Syd and I took three puddings each and with full plates, including beef and roast potatoes, tucked in. Despite the early rescue, the taste of soap was all too obvious and we exchanged glances, but said nothing. Our movements and responses were being observed, so manfully we ate the detergent without a whimper, though as was obvious to the girls, the things tasted foul.

"There are a few left if either of you want any," I offered, but the invitation was declined. Even drowning the delicious looking puddings with thick, rich, onion gravy didn't completely disguise the taste of soap and having eaten two, plus everything on the plate a single orb remained on my plate.

Syd had somehow devoured his allocation entirely and his platter was clean. "Delicious," he exclaimed to Dotty, though I half expected him to blow bubbles as he spoke.

"You've left one," Dotty challenged me, her eyes full of mischief.

"I can't eat another thing," I replied, holding my not completely full stomach to accentuate the message.

"That's strange, you usually eat everything placed in front of you. Were the puddings alright?"

"Delicious," we said together.

"Humph!" was her reply. "I don't think you'll be late for your dinners in future."

* * * * * *

Christmas Day and Boxing Day with all the usual manic goings on, came and went then we managed a few days of fishing before the New Year. Fish prices for the first market in January were excellent as the huge Scottish fleet was either still tied up in port or had just sailed. Following another trip we were back in our routine and the shipbuilder asked me to pay another visit to discuss the wheelhouse layout and several other outstanding matters.

Bluey was keen to take the *Independence* to sea to gain more experience and we'd already agreed that when my *Emulator* was ready, he'd take command of the old boat. We'd also decided if he made a success of the new role he could purchase shares in the vessel and be a part owner. The down side was, if he failed to make her pay financially, the *Independence* would have to be sold. He was itching to prove his ability.

On Monday morning, intending to spend most of the week north of the border, I made ready to leave home. Dotty handed me four plastic bags with my supply of clothes and toiletries and I looked at her in total disbelief. "If you think fo' one minute I'm takin' them on an aeroplane an' then livin' in an 'otel, yer can think again. Ah'll look more like a tramp than a prospective new trawler owner."

For the first time Dotty looked at her packing arrangements. Spending most of her time looking after three lively youngsters, her brain was on automatic and she laughed at the potential scenario. A small handgrip was located and my necessities transferred. A kiss on the doorstep and I was on my way north again.

An amazing transition had taken place since my last visit. From the approach road *Emulator* looked ready for sea with her wheelhouse, whaleback and masts in place. This wasn't the case when I climbed the long ladder. Her decks were strewn with electric cables, wires, rubber welding hoses and all the related tackle from the varied trades-people involved in the fit out. Now the engine was installed, the gaping hole in the deck had been closed and become a smaller, more recognisable, fishroom hatch. The flat top of the whaleback in the fore part of the vessel was lined up to meet below the wheelhouse windows in the event that the vessel would, at some point in the future, become fully sheltered. Derry had already predicted this would happen, but I had my doubts.

The central section of the bulkhead, below in the hold, was still open and would remain so until her completion, allowing easy access to the machinery at the fore end of the engine room.

The wheelhouse arrangement wasn't too difficult to sort out. Minor modifications to the array already on board the *Independence* were all that was required. The gallows, winch and deck bollards were also positioned and several other one off decisions made in the days spent in the shipyard. There was also time to meet up with friends, George and Hazel McLean and their family in Gardenstown. I'd known these people since my school days, when I'd sailed on the herring drifter, *Hazael III*, which George was a shareholder in. I'd travelled north for a weekend during the summer holidays with her crew. We'd remained in touch over the years and I spent a very pleasant evening with the family and some of their friends in the village, before being driven back to the Cliff View.

Back home, Bluey had again landed a good trip on the *Independence* and it looked like he'd have no trouble making her pay. My days aboard her were numbered and he already had his crew lined up, including brother-in-law Barry, who would remain on board this vessel when the *Emulator* was ready. Meanwhile I still had a few trips to do.

The strong, spring tides were easing and during the previous neaps there had again been some good fishing south of the Humber, off the Lincolnshire coast, so along with boats from Whitby and Bridlington, we headed in that direction. The huge fleet was scattered over a wide expanse of sea, from close inshore between the towns of Mablethorpe and Skegness, out to the edge of the deep-water trench of the Yorkshire Hole, fifteen miles distant. This wasn't an area to be in when the tides were strong.

The water was only between six and ten fathoms deep and ran like a millrace across these shallows.

Fishing was good and the boats, over the wide area, were reporting bags of anywhere between five and ten kit each haul. This was mostly good quality, half-grown, fat cod, with a smattering of dover sole and large skate mixed among the green fish, adding value to the catches. When fish marks were encountered on the sounder, it was easy to turn the *Independence* round in the shoal water, where only forty fathoms of wire were required between the boat and the trawl doors. Ninety or a hundred fathoms was the norm elsewhere. The angle between the warps at the stern was huge. An added bonus was the ten minutes less it took to haul, empty and redeploy the trawl.

The seabed was mostly sand, though there were several wrecks littering the grounds, mostly sunken merchant vessels, the victims of enemy action in the approaches to the busy river and its associated ports. These wrecks had been dispersed postwar, as hazards to shipping in the shallow waters and some were spread over a wide area. If these fasteners could be avoided, there was little to trouble the boats while the tides were slack. This was sleepy valley.

Catches remained good for a few days and doing five-hour tows, life was easy. We were putting a good catch together until we snagged one of the wrecks while towing before the tide, with the 'Decca' playing up. The bang, as the boat came to a sudden stop, shook her from stem to stern. I thought she'd broken in half, such was the noise and I hit the throttle, dropping the motor to dead slow. Luckily the wires connecting to the trawl remained intact. The lads tumbled from their bunks and were on deck in seconds, two of them running for the winch. Heaving gently, the towing bridles were unhooked. "'Eave for'ard, slack aft," I yelled, though this instruction was expected and the manoeuvre already underway. The vessel quickly turned through a hundred and eighty degrees. Now she was heading back into the tide and her speed was increased to counter the rushing tide. I called, "'eave together." Slack wire was now coming in at both ends.

In this shoal water, our fishing gear was still stuck in the wreck when the doors came to the boat's side. There were thirty fathoms of wire and chain attaching the boards to the net. I increased the engine revs further to compensate for the tidal flow and with the doors secured and disconnected, heaving recommenced. Severe load came on the after end, the weight forcing her stern round across the tide and I called out, "stop 'eavin' aft. Slack out aft an' 'eave for'ard." The weight came back on the leading wire and we stemmed the tide once more. Soon the wing end of the trawl appeared in the for'ard gallow. We could heave no more on the fore end. The net was suspended mid-water, free of the fastener but we were still stuck in the wreck by the wires and chain on the lower end of the trawling gear and I still couldn't put the engine in neutral. The tide had only recently changed, so it looked as if we'd have to wait about four hours for slack water to get out of this predicament. I gave a general announcement to the fleet saying we were caught in this wreck.

Several fishing vessels passed close, aware we were hung in the fastener, knowing we were marking the position of the wreck for them. Good fishing reports were constantly coming in over the radio and frustrated, I shouted to the lads, "try puttin' a rope strop on t' wing end an' 'eavin' it up t' liftin' pole. Slack out on t' after end if you 'ave to."

The incredulous looks suggested that this idea didn't find favour but nevertheless the men on deck followed the instructions. The wing of the net went easily up the pole and was stoppered off and the process repeated. Usually when we had a frap I'd be on deck assisting but with this tide running, I was stuck in the wheelhouse, controlling the boat. There was a chance the codend was streaming underwater unseen, alongside in the murky water close to the propeller, but this fear was allayed when the bag was spotted wrapped in the general tangle. It wasn't unusual for a trawl to turn completely inside out when coming fast before a strong tide.

Continuing to slack out cable at the after end, the lads were able to draw more net onboard for'ard. Eventually the entire trawl and ground gear was safe, though piled high in a heap on the deck. A heavy-duty rope stopper ensured this stack wouldn't fly back overboard. We were now attached to the wreck by a long bight of high-tensile chain and two thin wires but at least there was no danger of fouling the propeller. The chain and wires

*Divers returning to the Independence.*
*Photo FG Normandale*

*The Find.*
*Photo Ian Robinson*

*Dave 'Bev' Bevan on board Our Margaret.*
*Photo Dennis Dobson*

*Brian Bevan Cox'n of the Humber Lifeboat.*
*Photo Ann Bevan*

attached to the net were unshackled and the ends allowed to drop free. For the first time throughout the precarious operation, I pulled the engine control into neutral. *Independence* began drifting but only till the weight came onto the chain at the after end and she slewed round before the tide. The boat was now anchored from her starboard quarter to the wreck. As I'd hoped, the cable began jerking, gradually drawing through the submerged obstruction, until suddenly with a twang, one of the thin wires parted and we were free. The vessel was finally moving with the tide instead of riding to it. The loose ends were swiftly hauled up. We'd lost nothing but time.

It took another hour to sort out the pile of gear on deck and to replace the broken wire. There were always plenty of these spare legs stored below. We'd been very lucky. Had there been any swell in the water to add to the rush of tide, we may have lost the trawl. If we'd fouled the screw we could have been in a real pickle. I shuddered at the thought of being anchored to a wreck by the propeller. Boats have sunk in this manner. I really should have waited for slack water but time was always pressing. Other boats were catching fish.

To add to our woes, a poor weather forecast was issued in the late afternoon, though it was into the early hours of the following morning, with a couple more hauls under our belts when the weather began to change. It freshened quickly from the southeast and was soon blowing a full gale. Most of the boats had set off north for home with the wind on their quarter, making for Bridlington or Flamborough Head and would be back home in time for the morning auction. The 'Brid' boats had less distance to steam but sent their fish overland to the Hull market.

Along with Bev, Col and a couple of Whitby boats, I opted to make for Grimsby, which was much closer. It seemed logical to head for the Humber port to land our fish while the wind was in this direction, for the gale was sure to draw to the land as the low pressure weather system passed over. We'd get back to the grounds for a few more hauls before the weekend.

Initially stemming the flowing tide but steaming down wind, we followed the other vessels, spread over several miles, round the buoyage system into the river from the south. I was pleased when the lads on deck had cleared the fish from the recent haul and I could turn off the deck lights, which inhibited forward vision. We were drawing close to the can-shaped Rosse Spit buoy, flashing red, twice every five seconds, marking a long tongue of sandbank, stretching seawards on our port side. Next was the Haile Sands, a buoy of similar size and colour, indicating more offshore shoals. This also flashed red, giving three winks every ten seconds.

We entered the main channel, picking up the flowing tide and were now speeding upstream at a rate of knots, spray splashing across the decks on the port side from the gale funnelling up the river. Concentration was essential, being totally surrounded by lights from both shores, ships inbound, outbound and at anchor, plus navigation buoys and Spurn lighthouse flashing. It would be easy to get confused. It's not surprising that there'd been many accidents around here in years past. Fog was the greatest hazard in the estuary and occurred frequently. This scourge regularly brought river traffic to a standstill, prior to the advent of radar.

Even on clear nights, the radar was of tremendous assistance, operating on its six-mile range. To starboard the machine highlighted the accentuated curve of the sandy peninsular of Spurn Point, home to Britain's busiest lifeboat crew and their families. On our port side, the sweeping, low-lying, Lincolnshire coastline was well defined. Dots on the screen ahead indicated a dozen or more large ships riding at anchor beyond the Bull Light Float, awaiting a vacant berth and a pilot to escort them up the busy channel. Another blip and a single fixed light on our stem marked the 'Bull Fort', a concrete and steel edifice, constructed during the war to protect the estuary from attack by sea and air. A twin to this monster, the 'Haile Fort' stood on the south side of the river.

"Where've yer got to?" I asked of Colin, knowing he was some distance ahead and should be near the dock.

"We're just bein' penned in t' lock," Col's voice came back over the radio. "Bev's astern of us, waitin'. Both Whitbymen penned in together 'ead of us."

"'Urry up Nommy, yer'll miss t' market," came Bev's voice through the speaker. This wasn't the case. He'd just been unable to resist a comment.

Though the tide was flowing, there was insufficient water for both sets of dock gates to be opened to the sea. The dock men would open the outer gates allowing a boat into the lock then close the huge doors behind her. They'd raise the water level then open the inner doors allowing smaller craft to enter the massive dock before tide time. Of course the men on dock duty expected a fry of fish or a few quid for their trouble. *Independence,* with her large beam, would just fit in the lock diagonally with inches to spare, as I'd discovered in the past, though this wouldn't be necessary today. Equal level must have been reached, as both gates were opened as we approached. The wind was rattling through the hollow piers leading to the entrance and it was difficult to steer her through the narrow gap. Two men for'ard and aft manned fenders, protecting the wooden vessel from the uncompromising stone sides of the lock pit then we were through the passage and inside the enormous dock.

The other boats were lined up landing as we berthed tight astern of the *Cassamanda.* Our landing pole was hauled into position as the ropes went ashore. Kurt Christiansen, brother of Olaf, was our salesman in Grimsby and he was standing waiting to greet us and direct us to our pitch on the market. As always, he'd brought a case of beer to assist the discharging process. There was the usual banter on the quayside with Bev chipping in with rude comments from the next berth.

It took less than two hours to land our catch, tip the fish from our own seven-stone, wooden boxes into the bigger, ten-stone, aluminium Grimsby kits and weigh each unit. Our catch of about a hundred boxes, lined up in rows on the market looked tiptop and was comparable with the other shots on the quayside. Some of the early merchants were already admiring the combined display. This was exceptional quality fish, as our own buyers back home had previously attested. Normally, fifty percent of the purchase was lost when the fish was filleted but they'd said with fish from this region, they were able to retain fifty-five percent of flesh. "It's as fat as butter," was the description from one of the white-coated army of merchants.

At high water, with the wind still blowing strongly, we were sitting in the mess-deck having breakfast when Bev waved from the quayside, attracting our attention through the galley window. Bluey slid the glass down and we heard, "our kid's comin' t' see us."

Our gaze was drawn to the starboard window, where a superb, blue craft with orange superstructure, looked sleek and speedy as she crossed the dock in our direction. This was the *City of Bradford 1V*, the Humber lifeboat, based at Spurn Point. This was the only RNLI vessel with a full-time, retained crew, such was the demand for her services and so desolate her location. Bev's older brother, Brian, who'd previously fished from Scarborough was her coxswain and much decorated for his many, hair-raising rescues. He'd been awarded a bronze, silver and gold medal from the Lifeboat Institution in the space of six weeks, not too long ago. All had been gained in extreme weather and snowstorms. He'd added another bronze to his collection since then.

Featuring on a surprise, 'This is your Life', television programme and opening the annual 'Boat Show' in London, Bri Bev was a well-known local hero and celebrity, though quite unassuming. Small in stature, black tussled hair with short sideburns he had a healthy, weathered face, sharp, piercing eyes and wore a single, conspicuous gold earring. His modern vessel was far too large to be housed in the old boathouse, with its ramp leading down to the river, so she was usually anchored to the west of Spurn Point. This usually sheltered berth was close to home and his wife Ann, but extreme weather from a southerly direction made boarding the lifeboat from a small craft hazardous. On these occasions, her crew based themselves outside the lock gates in a small basin, which gave access to the sea at all times. Hearing his brother was in dock, Bri Bev had decided to pay a visit.

He skilfully berthed the powerful, twin-engined machine alongside the *Cassamanda,* his men lining her sides holding fenders. The appearance of this revolutionary vessel attracted the Scarborough crews in her direction. "Nar then. What ar' you lot doin' 'ere? There's nowt wrong wi' t' weather," Brian joked as we approached.

"There's nowt wrong wi t' weather when you're out playin' in that thing," Col countered, pointing to the rescue craft, "but it wouldn't be much good fo' fishin'."

Following an update of recent events relating to family, fishing and the lifeboat service, Bri invited us onboard to look round his vessel. With about a dozen interested observers onboard he called for the ropes to be thrown off. Pointing her towards the lock pits, he took his craft through the gap and into the river for a demonstration of her capabilities. The enthusiastic crew were keen to give us a conducted tour of the vessel.

This 'Arun' class lifeboat was fitted with a control point on the upper bridge for close, taxing work but we were in the cabin, where a second set of levers and dials enabled the helmsman to control the vessel in relative comfort; a far cry from the small, open 'Oakley' type boat we had at home. Opening the throttles, the Coxswain powered the craft into the gale and she leapt forward like a racehorse. Unprepared for the thrust of power, we all grabbed for handholds as the crew laughed at our ungainly stumbles. Within seconds, spray was flying high in the air as we darted from swell top to swell top at twenty knots. The craft was remarkably comfortable and stable at speed, though the seas were not large in the lee of the southern shore. Minutes later Bri put the wheel hard over and she heeled sharply to port, reversing our course in moments and again we reached for a strong point.

Unexpectedly, the helmsman pulled the controls to dead slow and the *City of Bradford* almost stopped in her tracks, such was the deceleration. This manoeuvre took us all by surprise and inertia forced us to fall forward in a heap with collective cursing. He'd certainly showed us the versatility of this boat and what a terrific tool she was for his trade.

Leaving us with our workhorses, Brian took his stallion back outside the dock to his berth in the river before the gates closed, leaving us fishermen to spend the remainder of the morning overhauling and maintaining our gear. We were stuck in port till the gates opened again at around five o'clock in the afternoon but we'd manage a few beers in the pub and a couple of hours kip before then.

Almost ten years earlier to the day, when a gale freshened quickly from the north, eleven boats from Scarborough, working in this area, had gone into Grimsby for shelter rather than punch their way home. On this occasion the weather looked to be poor for a while, so after landing their fish, the skippers organised a coach to take the crews home for a few days. Unfortunately the bus arrived late and the crews had already enjoyed a midday session in the pub. The agent had also given each boat a twenty-four pack of 'Longlife' beer for the trip home. Not satisfied with this supply, the majority had opted to stop at a country pub on the way north for more refreshments and the bus driver had experienced great difficulty in getting the men to leave again.

This turned out to be a nightmare journey for 'Dickie' Douglas, skipper of the *Progressive* and his crew. Dick was a staunch member of the Salvation Army and was thoroughly disgusted at the raucous behaviour and frequent pee stops of the other crews and vowed never to subject himself and his crew to such treatment again. There was no problem on the coach trip back to Grimsby a few days later. This was a dry affair as the crews were on their way back to sea.

The wind had gone round to the southwest by the time we sailed and the weatherman had promised some moderation. Though fresh for a few hours, the gale did fall away as forecast and we took a few more good hauls before heading home for the weekend, and in my case the end of an era. My days on this lovely, lucky vessel were over.

## Chapter 16

# Launching of *Emulator*

Dotty and I set off in the car for Scotland on a fine, February morning for the launching of my *Emulator*. Little Sarah was carefully strapped in a child seat in the rear. This in contrast to the journey a few years ago when the *Independence* was launched, when Paula and Danny travelled in the back of the car with the seats folded down to make a play area. Today the mischievous pair were travelling on the coach with their grandparents plus other family members and guests. We were due to meet up in Rosehearty.

Sadly the drive didn't agree with our youngest, who, even before we'd passed Whitby was being carsick and was distressed. It was going to be a long day for us all. Dotty was soon sat in the back with her, giving cuddles and sympathy but Sarah was having none of it and exercised her lungs to great effect, drowning any volume I could get on the radio. We discussed the option of taking Sarah to Aberdeen by train or even returning home but Dotty was certain that she would get used to the movement. We'd stop in Edinburgh or sooner if possible for something to settle her stomach and calm her down. "Meanwhile," Dotty said pointedly, "it would help if you drove a little slower."

As usual where the children were concerned, Mother was right. The second part of the journey was more relaxed and Sarah chirped up and was quite happy, sitting in her chair. Things were going well and we were knocking off the miles quickly when a bang from under the car and a loud scraping noise indicated that we had a problem. The engine noise increased dramatically suggesting an exhaust malfunction and I slowed down. Occupants in passing cars were pointing to the underside of our vehicle, where sparks were showering the road. "As if ah didn't know we 'ad a problem," I said between clenched teeth, smiling and waving to the Samaritans. It was one of those days.

We were somewhere between Perth and Aberdeen and I was sure we wouldn't be able to get this problem fixed locally with any urgency and I had no roadside insurance to call on for support.

"What are we going to do?" Dotty asked, as I pulled off the road into a gated entrance to a field.

"Ah don't know yet, I'll tell you in a minute when ah've looked at it," I replied, unsure what to expect. "Ah know a bit about boats but nowt about cars."

Lying on my back at the nearside, I looked under the vehicle and the problem was immediately obvious. The front section of the exhaust, where it should be attached to the engine had dropped off and was scraping along the road. The tube was leading forward and the exhaust pipe was already damaged beyond repair, being buckled and bent from contact with the road. "That's easily fixed," I said loudly to myself and grabbed the dangling tube. The metal was hot and I let go again quickly, this time swearing loudly. An old rag in the back proved good insulation and in a few minutes I'd levered the entire exhaust, including silencer, back and forwards enough times for the stressed metal to break off completely. I stood up and with great satisfaction hurled the offending article over the gate into the field. "I've fixed it," I declared to Dotty as I got back in the driver's seat, wiping my hands on the dirty rag.

"Oh?" she said, expressing surprise and raising her eyebrows having watched me launch the pipe-work skywards.

I turned the ignition key and the roar from the engine was loud and throaty.

"What are you going to do? Are you going to drive somewhere and get it fixed?"

"Ah bloody aren't," I replied, grinning for the first time as I indicated and pulled out into the traffic again. "We're gonna be in Rosehearty for a few days, ah'll get it fixed there." Back on the road, the slightest touch on the accelerator increased the roar of the engine, pleasingly. Travellers heading in our direction must have thought they were being stalked by a helicopter gunship.

Booming down the road, my smile grew wider and I chuckled as I spied a familiar number plate on a Vauxhall car in front of us.

Dotty questioned my inane grin. To her all cars were the same, only different colours.

Pointing ahead I said, "it's Syd" and pulling alongside the green motor, gave a wave to the four startled occupants. Syd and Col were in the front seats, travelling to the *Emulator's* launching together with a couple of other guests. With foot to the boards and sounding like a low-flying spitfire, we left them in our wake. I couldn't wait to meet up at journey's end and hear their abusive comments.

We drew close to Sandhaven and Forbes Yard, where I enthusiastically pointed out the magnificent *Emulator,* standing high on the stocks, decked out in bunting in all her glory. "Doesn't she look fantastic?" I asked Dotty, stopping to take in the view.

"Wonderful," she replied, straight-faced. "I can't compete with her."

I looked in my wife's direction and was relieved to see the twinkle in her eyes, knowing she was genuinely pleased. We pulled up behind the recently arrived coach, the passengers wanting to inspect the new vessel before moving on to their accommodation in Rosehearty. We quickly met up with family and friends, gathered around the newly painted hull, though the bolder ones had ventured up the ladder to her deck. It was there I met Dad and Danny, inspecting the deck machinery. The bubbling enthusiasm of my son was contagious and I was soon giving him, Dad and several others a guided tour, forgetting that Dotty, Paula and Sarah were waiting in the yard below.

The viewing over, everyone dispersed to the various hotels in the area to register and prepare for the evening. Most of the guests had arrived now and all were aware of their accommodation details.

We were staying in the Cliff View. I knew my family would be comfortable in the homely little guesthouse where the bar was already filling up. Our friends were taking the opportunity for some early celebrations before the official evening gathering and, though busy behind the bar, Billy was still finding time to talk to his customers. I watched him pulling pints, serving and talking with Steve, a pal from the Diving Club and heard the usual, "ya ken," frequently inserted in each sentence.

Steve was nodding sagely as he received his change but then turning from the bar clutching the bundle of glasses he looked in my direction, a confused expression on his face. "Who's this fuckin' Ken 'e keeps talkin' about?"

The evening welcome dinner was informal and of course held in the banqueting room of the Forbes Arms in Rosehearty. This was a great get-together and everyone was in high spirits in readiness for the big day. The forecast promised to be fine, with high pressure dominating the weather. There wasn't a breath of wind outside and the resulting heavy ground frost was crisp underfoot as we wandered, slightly wobbly, under a vivid mass of stars back to our cosy room.

The day of the launch dawned fine and sunny and following a hearty breakfast, several strangers to the little town could be seen promenading on the waterfront, taking the early, fresh Scottish air. All were brought to a standstill with the first of the day's bombing runs and they stood mesmerised as each plane in turn made its attack. The free entertainment had clearly caught their attention and the 'Cliff' was full of chatter and excited comment on their return.

Leaving the bairns with grandparents, Dotty and I, with several others in the party, in a variety of vehicles, headed for Pennan Cove, location of the recent film, 'Local Hero'. We'd arranged to meet some of our Scottish friends from nearby Gardenstown in the village pub. Pennan was a beautiful little place, located at the bottom of an extremely steep, curved hill, though was little more than a single street. The brightly painted houses stood on a low concrete plateau beyond the narrow, rock-strewn beach and seemed to have little defence from the sea. In the centre of the row of buildings was the Pennan Inn, a friendly little hostelry, where we discovered an enthusiastic landlord, sporting a kilt and all associated trappings. With his long hair and curled moustache, he wouldn't have looked out of place as a character in the recent movie. He must have thought it was his lucky day when our crowd descended on his establishment.

Hazel, Babs and Mary were already sitting in the little bar, nervously nursing glasses and probably feeling guilty, with their menfolk at sea. This visit to the pub to meet us was so far removed from anything they'd ever consider doing during a normal day and the ladies visibly lightened when familiar faces entered.

Armed with drinks and filling the little bar, one of our party innocently asked the host if this was the site where 'Local Hero' had been made. He immediately regretted his attempt to make conversation when from under the bar came several albums of photographs of the actors and actresses from the film set. The host enthusiastically began to run through these stills, discussing each shot at length. Amazingly, a gap appeared in the crowded room as everyone except the victim and his lecturer discussed each snap. No one was going to be involved in the discussion by proximity.

The jokes and humour were quick-fired but the clock was also fast moving and this pleasant, fun filled interlude was soon over. The serious part of the day was about to begin. Arriving back at the yard, I found Derry Forbes in a spin. Unbelievably the weather was too fine and the tide was flowing slower than expected. His cigarettes were disappearing faster than ever as his anxiety grew. It was Derry's call whether the launch took place or not. The fact that about eighty guests would soon be descending on the yard for the ceremony was not lost on him.

"Why don't you take some ballast out of her? That might help," Pete suggested.

A ray of hope came to Derry's eyes and he dashed off to find his foreman, instructing him to organise the workforce. We returned to the Cliff View to dress, ready for the launch. An hour later the crowd was assembled, waiting for Derry, who was still deliberating, despite removal of the ballast. He was looking at the height of the water on the pier at the side of the slipway and his mind must have been in turmoil. I noticed for the first time, he had a team of divers with airbags standing by. He was very worried indeed.

I looked at him, then at my watch. It was almost high water.

"She goes," he said, finally making up his mind and seemed relieved to have reached the decision.

Dotty, Paula and I, with little Sarah in my arms mounted the makeshift staircase, ready to name this beautiful, new vessel. The bottle of champagne was dangling from the whaleback, suspended by a ribbon of red, white and blue. My wife looked askance at Derry. This was a rudimentary arrangement and not what she'd experienced when launching the *Independence,* where the bottle was mounted in a cradle.

Derry pointed to the flat, iron plate, protecting the vessel's oak stem. "Jus' crack it across the corner o' the metal. It'll brrak, nay problem," he stated confidently.

"Oh no," I thought, "it's not gonna break." Never one to flout superstition, I was well aware that it was unlucky if the champagne bottle didn't break first time.

Following his instructions, Dotty picked up the heavy bottle by the neck, weighing the container in her hand, then offered the glass against the iron bar to judge the range. In a clear voice, easily heard in the hushed company, my wife declared, "I name this ship *Emulator.* God bless her and all who sail in her." Dotty swung the bottle at the corner of the iron bar as instructed but the bottle of bubbly struck with a glancing blow and bounced off the plate intact, jarring her hand. Undaunted, Dotty immediately grabbed the offending article with both hands and whacked the heavy weight against the iron with all her strength. With a pleasing 'crump' the bottle shattered into a myriad of pieces, spreading glass and froth in all directions.

Dotty turned in my direction mortified. "It didn't break first time," she said, almost in tears. "I'm sorry."

"Don't worry about it. It's no big deal," I consoled, smiling and hiding my fears. "It's only a superstition," then enclosing her with Sarah and Paula, we had a big family hug and kiss.

Derry waved to his men and the chocks, blocking the vessel's passage down the ways were quickly knocked out. Up on deck the Kelvin engineer shouted an instruction below to his mate, who pressed the starter button on the engine. Slowly at first, but soon picking up speed, *Emulator* gracefully slid down the ramps, making a huge splash as she dropped into deeper water. The 'make up' of timber supporting her gave way as designed and she was free. Sadly, she shuddered to an ungainly, premature halt. The water wasn't deep enough. Her engine was engaged in stern gear and the revolutions increased. Thick, grey smoke belched from her exhaust but it was no use, she wasn't moving. Helpless, we stood watching, wondering what would happen next. I was praying she hadn't been damaged on her keel by the impact.

A small workboat was tied to her starboard bow and the little vessel attempted to tow her head round towards the harbour entrance. For a while this ploy looked as though it would work but she only managed through ninety degrees, before all movement stopped.

Her engine was shut down and the diving team swung into action. Working quickly, within half an hour four large yellow lifting bags were attached to her hull and were being inflated but this was already a forlorn hope. *Emulator* was beginning to list to starboard and the water level against the pier had dropped substantially, leaving a wet line marking its height.

Darkness was falling and the temperature plummeting once more. The divers abandoned their attempts in the freezing waters and disappointed, we headed back to the Cliff View, Dotty still berating herself for not breaking the bottle, and me telling her not to be daft. To make matters worse, the entire proceedings had been filmed by a regional television crew and the sad episode was shown on the local news within hours of our arrival back at the hotel.

We were determined to put on brave faces throughout the evening of the official dinner, where everyone was assured that there were no problems with the boat and that she'd be floated off in the early hours, on the next high water. The usual speeches followed the excellent meal and toasts were given to all who'd been concerned with her commissioning and building. As I stood to say my few words, I saw my father-in-law, George, holding up his glass and critically inspecting his beer. George, bespectacled, thin of face with a large, dominating, hooked nose and magnificent mane of pure, silver hair, was a connoisseur of good ale and was looking at this Scottish brew with uncertainty. It struck me that today was his birthday and as he wasn't paying much attention to the proceedings I cleared my throat and began, "I'd like to thank my father-in-law, George, for this wonderful birthday party."

Dotty's Dad had just put the glass to his lips and taken a large, testing swig. He almost choked as he gulped for air at the mention of his name and the thought of the expense.

The band struck up, dancers hit the floor and the evening was going swimmingly. The small dance floor was full but I was concerned at the plight of my new baby. As it was low water I found Rory and we slipped away for a short while in his van to inspect her undersides. We must have looked a strange pair, dressed in lounge suits and wellingtons but there was no one to see us. He shone his flashlight and we walked round the huge hull, now high and dry, listing over to starboard on the hard sand. There wasn't a mark on the maroon, anti-fouled hull and quite relieved, we returned to the celebrations. Rory said a squad of volunteers were turning out before high water at two o clock in the morning to attempt to float her. At the prescribed time I was on the pier ready to assist. The launch party had ended earlier and had gone with a swing. Now family and guests were abed.

Another hard frost held sway and I was pleased to have warm working clothes to change into. The men, cursing and flapping their arms in the cold night air, laid a thick, white nylon rope along the quay from the harbour entrance, leading along the pier through snatch blocks in the direction of a truck. The outer end of the cable was passed on board the vessel via the little workboat and secured to the bits on the whaleback. Between the shore end of the rope and the lorry, a three-fold purchase was put in place. This arrangement of three pulley blocks at each end of the tackle, added an immense mechanical advantage to the truck's towing power; the equivalent of several trucks in line. The heavy-duty vehicle engaged reverse gear and backed down the long pier, taking up the slack then stretching the hawser in an attempt to drag *Emulator* into the deeper water near the entrance.

The nylon rope, now stretched to almost half its original thickness was creaking under the extreme load. No one stood anywhere near as the pressure mounted. All eyes were on the boat as torches were shone in her direction but there was little movement from her. The tide hadn't even reached the mark of the previous day and *Emulator* was still hard aground with a slight list. Suddenly, with a loud crack, the white rope parted, the ends whipping back with a twang. This was the end of another aborted attempt to float my reluctant, new baby. Amazingly, I was still able to undo the bowline I'd tied earlier to form the eye in the now parted rope. This was incredible, considering the massive tonnage that had been applied on this versatile hitch prior to the break.

Later the same morning, following a breakfast that not everyone appreciated, the guests, some looking the worse for wear, were setting off in various vehicles for the long trek south and I was there, sober, to wave them farewell. They'd witnessed the naming ceremony, watched *Emulator* take to the water for the first time and celebrated her construction but no one had yet seen her float. Dotty had opted to travel home on the coach with the bairns. The vessel's reluctance to float meant I'd have to stay behind until she co-operated.

This she did on the following tide but not without assistance. Derry engaged the services of a Fraserburgh skipper, 'Peem' Mitchell and his *Dewy Rose*. At three o'clock and high water, Peem towed *Emulator's* head round towards the entrance with no trouble at all, assisting the vessel into her natural environment for the first time.

Our vessels headed for his home port, initially alongside each other but *Dewy Rose* soon left us behind.

Peem called on the VHF, commenting that his vessel had no nozzle surrounding his propeller, which caused drag when steaming, though improved performance when towing. He also made the observation that my boat was down heavily by the stern and wasn't trimmed in the water as she should to be.

The realisation suddenly hit me. The *Emulator* was definitely sagging by the stern. The builders had removed several tons of ballast prior to launching but the cast-iron, railway fishplates had been taken from her fishroom. The hold was in the forward part of the boat and removing weight from this section of the vessel hadn't raised her draft at all. The extraction of this tonnage had sunk her down by the stern, already her deepest part. No wonder she hadn't floated when launched. When she'd been manoeuvred alongside by the yard's skipper, I stepped ashore to see that not only was her white line underwater at the stern but even a little of her blue paint. Her trim would be easily rectified when the fishplates were replaced but their removal had caused no little chaos these past twenty-four hours.

My new craft would spend the next few weeks in Fraserburgh having her finishing touches added before she was ready for the hand over, then I'd have my new command.

# Chapter 17
# Homeward Bound

Following successful trials, three weeks later, in the early evening we sailed for home. *Emulator* was fully commissioned and her fishing gear was in place, ready for shooting. I was assured by Derry that I had a superb vessel, in excellent working order and I had no reason to doubt him. With a wave to our Scottish friends, we departed from Fraserburgh for the twenty-four hour steam home. My remaining crew of Sid and Mick were joined by Gordon, known as 'Gogga', a big, balding man with a short, black beard and moustache, and young Sean, our former shore helper, who was just sixteen and recently out of school, though not officially eligible to leave till Easter.

Passing Cairnbulg Point then rounding Rattray Head, we headed south, soon passing Peterhead. All seemed to be going well and following an excellent dinner, I was contemplating going below to monitor the machine's oil level and have a general check round when the bilge alarm put an urgency in my step. I was immediately aware that something was wrong on opening the door, when the strong smell of steam hit my nostrils. Dropping down the ladder I was dismayed to discover a jet of seawater spraying from a cracked brass pipe on the starboard side of the engine. The area close to the damaged section was encrusted in salt where evaporation had left a residue and the resulting steam was rising from the hot metal. Bilge water had reached the propeller shaft and the coupling was spinning a deluge of water under the cabin floorboards.

I rushed to engage the bilge pump and fortunately, the water level began to drop, easing my immediate concerns, but for how long? We were still twenty-two hours from home and if we continued on our present course, we'd be a long way offshore during the night, while crossing the Firth of Forth. With assistance from Gogga, an end section of rubber hose was cut off from the deck pipe, split and fastened in place with jubilee clips. This slowed the flow and directed the water into the bilge, away from the engine, where it could be pumped out. We were reliant on the pumps and it wasn't uncommon in new boats to get blockages with wood shavings and other residue, from various tradesmen.

If the pipe fractured completely, we'd have to shut off the sea-cocks, situated deep below the engine-room plates, if we could reach them in time. Then, at best we'd have no main engine and no propulsion. The worst-case scenario was the possible loss of my vessel. That would be a disaster and a risk I wasn't prepared to take.

Back in the wheelhouse, I explained the problem and looked at our position on the chart. Reluctant to return to Fraserburgh or Peterhead, the only other port close was Aberdeen, which we'd passed a short while ago. It seemed logical to head for 'the Granite City' and we altered course. It was 2200 when we entered the harbour on the River Dee and following the buoyed channel upstream, we tied up near the fish market. Too late to visit the nearest pub, there was nothing to do but shut down the machinery and turn in. "How long was this jinx going to last?" I wondered again.

It was hardly daylight and a light flurry of snow was in the air when, armed with a fistful of coins, I went ashore to seek out the nearest public phone box. A call to Kelvin's initiated the despatch of an engineer, post-haste from Glasgow, though no spare pipe was available off the shelf. The next call was to home, informing Dotty we were delayed en route and asking her to put our planned welcome home party on hold for twenty-four hours and inform family and friends.

Dougie Bryden arrived within hours of the summons, saying he'd worked for the company for many years and had never experienced a failure of this nature before. Quickly removing the offending section, he took the pipe to a machine shop close to the harbour, where the crack was brazed. This was to be a temporary measure and a replacement section was promised for delivery to Scarborough as soon as possible, but this plan didn't work either. The repair didn't hold and fine jets of water, shooting through pinholes, were immediately evident in the hardened silver compound when he restarted the engine. The apologetic engineer contacted the factory and a pipe was requisitioned from a new engine, which had already been packaged and was awaiting delivery to a shipyard. Our need was more pressing. The new piece was despatched by road but we'd have to wait a few more hours yet.

The lads had gone off for a walk around the interesting port and sitting in the wheelhouse chair, scanning but not reading a daily paper, I was alone and fed up. Wondering how long this run of bad luck was going to last, I was drawn from my reverie by a small, varnished fishing vessel berthing alongside us, having discharged its cargo at the fish market. My curiosity was immediately aroused and pleased for the diversion, I went on deck to view her and have a chat with her crew. Looking at the boat's name and registration number, I was amazed to see this was the *Crimond*, KY 246. She seemed small alongside my boat, yet this was the same *Crimond* that a decade earlier had fished from Scarborough throughout the summer months, working at the North-West Dogger. Then she was owned and skippered by the tough, lowland Scot, Billy Boyter, a craggy-faced, gruff-speaking, no nonsense fisherman who wore a distinctive, black, 'cheese-cutter' cap. He'd consistently landed big trips. His new craft had dwarfed most of the local vessels and their landings. Boat building had certainly progressed unnoticed, these past few years.

There was no sign of Billy on board today. "Did you 'ave owt?" I enquired of the thin, wiry man passing me a stern line for hanging on the cleat on our starboard quarter. The size of their catches was always a talking point with any fisherman.

He was pleased to report a good landing for only a short trip to an interested party and we struck up a conversation. I told him I remembered the *Crimond* fishing from Scarborough under her former skipper, years back.

"That was mae fatha," replied Alan Boyter. "I was wi' him then, worrking oot at the 'Roughs'. He's retired noo."

I was pleased to agree to his request for a tour of my new baby and his crew joined him for the excursion. Fifteen minutes later we were back in the galley, where the impressed visitors quickly settled around the table. "D' you lads want a pot o' tea?" I enquired hospitably, pointing to the steaming kettle on the stove.

"Ha ye nae onythin' stronger?" was the reply of their spokesman.

"We've no booze aboard at all," I replied sadly, sorry to disappoint them. "It's all at 'ome, waitin' till we get there."

The group seemed astonished and one of their number declared that this was the first new boat he'd ever been on where he'd not been offered a drink. "Tae Christen herr, ye ken."

I remembered I'd been given a presentation bottle of 'Dimpled Haig' whisky by Jimmy, landlord of the Forbes Arms, as a present for my custom. Though I never touched the stuff, I was saving this special bottle for the right occasion, at a later date. Not wanting to offend the four Scotsmen I said, "I might 'ave a drop o' somethin'," and went below to retrieve the globe-shaped container from the back of my bunk.

Their eyes lit up when I produced the golden liquid and though we'd no glasses on board, they readily agreed to 'tak a wee dram' from the mugs in the rack. Four drams later and with the bottle standing empty on the table, the visitors, not the slightest bit affected by the spirit, wished me good luck in my new venture and wandered up the road to the Anchorage Bar.

Early evening found us steaming out between the piers, on our way again. We were a day late but I was feeling happier. Though we'd had a minor engine hiccup, the Kelvin after sales team had rectified the problem quickly, proving again that Scottish engineers were second to none when trouble arose. The flowing tide pushed us quickly towards home on the following afternoon and we had an incident free, pleasurable passage south. Though the temperature was cold, a warm reception greeted us from the little crowd, huddled at the pier end when we turned the corner to

*Naming of Emulator. The bottle didn't break.*
*Photo FG Normandale*

*Emulator stuck on the bottom after her launching. Her engine going full astern.*
*Photo FG Normandale*

*A trawl full of fish alongside Emulator.*
*Photo FG Normandale*

*A bag of cod coming over the side of Emulator.*
*Photo FG Normandale*

enter the harbour. There was also a cheery, "welcome home," shout from the lighthouse watch-keeper as we steamed past.

The ingredients for a party, in the form of family and friends and boxes of booze were brought onboard, the latter taken to the galley. It was far too cold to celebrate the homecoming of my *Emulator* outdoors but the heat from the engine exhaust, passing through the accommodation, ensured warmth throughout her interior. A hug and kiss from Dotty, then as expected, the ropes were quickly let go again for a trip out into the bay for a performance assessment by interested parties. Danny was already sitting in my chair, wanting to steer before we'd reached the harbour entrance. Half an hour was long enough for full approval, then a return to port.

A while later and back alongside, with everyone's curiosity and most thirsts satisfied, it was time to go home for me, Dotty and our bairns. Tomorrow there was work to be done. We'd sail on the morning tide and use the two remaining days of the week to put the *Emulator* through her paces, hoping to catch enough to cover the week's expenses.

* * * * * *

Long before daylight we were taking boxes and ice onboard. I was pleased we'd spent our time in Scotland assembling the fishing gear while waiting for the boat's completion. The many component parts of chain, wires, ground gear, net and doors took ages to put together and measure accurately.

Steaming off on a fine morning with dawn breaking and the pleasant smell of new wood in my nostrils, I was sure the jinx had now gone. We'd had no further problems and I was keen to get the trawl down and compare our performance with other vessels. Stopping ten miles east of the harbour, the net was deployed slowly, as the team, new and old, familiarised themselves with a different vessel. All went well and with the gear down, gauges reading normal, electronic equipment performing as required, I received a mug of coffee. We'd been towing about an hour and sitting comfortably in the chair, casually scanning the equipment, I had a feeling of inner contentment. A loud bang and jerk brought the boat to a shuddering halt and me from my dream state. We'd come fast on an obstruction. There was nothing untoward on the sounder or marked on the chart in this area, so I wasn't too concerned.

We heaved on the for'ard end to haul her head around into the tide as usual, then kept the engine at a reduced speed while taking in the slack wires. Clumsily, not used to handling the vessel, I let her go too far to starboard, allowing the tide to act on the port side and there was no way to get her back. In no time *Emulator* had completed a three hundred and sixty degree turn. The wires below the boat were now twisted, adding a complication, but even this problem could be addressed when the net came free from the fastener. "Wait till slack water," I told myself and knowing the boat couldn't turn to port, put another one hundred and eighty degree turn to starboard, dodging dead slow into the tide again, attempting to take the load from the new wires to avoid damaging them.

I thought the tide was never going to ease but hours and several cups of coffee later, we began heaving on each wire alternately. I was cringing, knowing the serrated cables were sawing against each other. Slowly the fore door was drawn from the water. The after warp was wrapped around the taut wire and the strands of this cable were un-laid. The central rope core was broken and half a fathom of the oiled fibre was hanging loose. The lads gamely fastened a stopper to hold the weight below the turn, then quickly slackened the after brake, passing the whole turn over the door. The for'ard door was now free to haul into place and secure. This was a minor victory.

The after door broke the surface with the for'ard cables encircled and these too, with great difficulty were stoppered and dropped over the door. The turn in the gear was now confined to the chain and wire bridles under the boat and would be more manageable, though I was perplexed why the net hadn't broken free from the fastener, now the bridles were leading straight up and down. For the first time in a while I looked at the sounder and was devastated to see an ominous red mark on the seabed, directly under the boat. This was a small wreck we were stuck in. How could this be? The location of all the wrecks and bad fasteners in the area were well known and charted. Giving the position out to other skippers in an open broadcast, I asked if anyone had a record of this object but the answering replies were negative, some even doubting there was a wreck in this position. I had no such doubts. We were stuck in the bloody thing and with a full turn in the bridles.

The winch relief valve was blowing off at 3000 pounds pressure and the air was filled with the smell of hot, hydraulic oil. The winch system was certainly getting an extensive testing but appeared to be coping so far. No matter which end we heaved on the result was the same. There was no more to be gained and *Emulator* was now laid broadside to the building tide. We'd tried slacking one end and heaving on the other but the turn in the chains nullified any advantage. Reluctant to chop either end away I shouted, "screw t' brakes down 'ard an' stand clear."

This done, I engaged the engine and with the rudder hard to port, gradually increased the revolutions. My new vessel heeled further to starboard and slowly turned in that direction, despite the opposite helm. Something must give now. It was make or break. We couldn't stay here forever. The problem was that there were no weak links in the system. The cables were new, so hadn't worn thinner with abrasion on the bottom. Usually a chain or shackle would break in extremis, partially damaging the gear but allowing release.

With the throttle at three-quarter speed, masts and stays vibrating and water splashing through the starboard scuppers, the fore-end jerked, banged then suddenly went slack. Something had parted. *Emulator* briefly stood upright, but the load on the after end arrested her and she went back to starboard. I hit neutral to assess the situation. It would have been better if the other end had given way, allowing some manoeuvrability but I wasn't that lucky. The length of chain, two broken wires and a short piece of the ground gear with a few rubber discs came up. *Emulator* was now swung with her stern into the tide, hanging on one end and I feared the worst. There was little chance of retrieving the gear now and I was resigned to losing it.

"Slack out thirty or forty fathoms," I yelled. "Gi' me some room to turn." This done and the brake screwed home, I again put down the throttle and at three-quarter speed, took a run at the snag. The sudden weight of the boat on the single end had the required effect and with a jerk we were free of the wreck but also free of our net and ground gear. The trawl was lost without us ever having the pleasure of hauling it. How unlucky was that? The days spent rigging the gear in Scotland had been futile after all. More gear was required and we had all the work to do again. When was this jinx going to end?

Tying *Emulator* alongside the pier with clear decks, was embarrassing. There were several interested onlookers wanting to see the new vessel and expecting a tour of her, yet she was devoid of fishing gear. All I wanted to do now was get re-rigged and get back to sea. To make matters worse, Bluey was in dock, landing a good catch.

Rigged up with another set of gear and ready for sea, we sailed again the next morning, hoping for a change of luck. In the bay I turned *Emulator* in a full three hundred and sixty degree circle to port, the opposite direction to the natural kick of her propeller. Curious eyes looked up to the wheelhouse.

"What's that all about?" Sid called up to the open window.

"Ah'm tryin' t' shake off our bad luck," I replied, half serious. "My old skipper, Tom Pashby used t' do that when things weren't goin' right."

"Daft bugger," he said, rolling his eyes and passing on my explanation to other interested ears.

* * * * * *

Things did seem better for a while. We had several good weeks of fishing and were now familiar with the working routine. *Emulator* proved easy to handle and was performing well. The late spring brought unseasonally fine weather and we were working further from shore than usual. Towards the end of our trip, with less than a day to fish and the sea like a sheet of glass, we began once more to heave up the trawl. The weather was so fine it was impossible to find a weather side when the net broke the surface. "Scramble it aboard as sharp as yer can lads," I encouraged, kicking the engine astern to take the way off the boat. With no wind to blow the boat away from the net, the trawl wouldn't stream clear below the surface and we could easily foul the propeller. To the lads' credit, the slack netting and long bellies were taken aboard swiftly without a problem and a good catch emptied onto the deck.

We now faced the same problem when throwing the gear back over. The telltale ribbon tied to the foremast stay, hung limp. The heavy footrope banged on the boat's side as the bottom of the trawl went overboard, dragging the lower mouth of the net downwards. The slack bellies and codend were energetically thrown over and the headline, with its thirty-plus, eight-inch, plastic floats swiftly followed. The orange netting and green bag hung lifelessly alongside the boat. A couple of quick bursts astern then ahead took the floats and codend clear of the boat and with the rudder hard to starboard, I thought we were clear to go ahead. As I engaged forward gear again I saw a slack bight of bellies being sucked towards the propeller and lunged for the throttle, just a split second too late.

The slack net was grabbed and drawn into the nozzle and though I'd stopped the screw turning before an accumulation of netting forced the engine to a halt, we still had a fouled propeller.

"Shit! Shit! Shit! When is it goin' to fuckin' end?" I bellowed out of the window at no one in particular, conveniently forgetting our fortune had been good of late. Extremely annoyed with myself for scoring an own goal, I quickly calmed down, addressing the situation. "It could be worse," I thought. "There can't be much net in t' prop' or t' engine would 'ave stopped."

"Try slacking on t' brakes," I called to the winchmen, hoping the weight of the footrope and heavy chain bridles would be enough to tear the offending part free. The mending would be negligible. The chains rattled as they ran out through the gallows, but seconds later came to a premature halt as the entire weight of the gear became suspended on the propeller. The fouled netting didn't tear away. Maybe if there had been a little swell, but not this time. "Ah'll put me divin' gear on," I called to the waiting men. "It won't be much."

Clad in black wetsuit, straddling the boat's side, rubber fins on dangling feet, I spat into the mask, rubbing the spittle on the inside of the glass with gloved hand then rinsed the piece in a bucket of salt water. This messy trick was a definite way of preventing the eyepiece from misting. Carefully putting the mask in place and with regulator in mouth I launched myself sideways. The twin aluminium cylinders on my back and twenty pounds of lead around my waist ensured I hit the water with a big splash. The first shock of cold water took my breath away but my body's heat quickly warmed the layer within the suit. The visibility was good and the red hull of the new vessel looked sleek. During winter months, I'd occasionally cleared props in the harbour when the vis' was only inches, even with a powerful torch.

I could see the small strand of netting, hanging from the nozzle and the long, stretched remainder of the trawl, leading down into the abyss. Surfacing, I encountered four curious faces, leaning over the boat's side. Taking the regulator from my mouth briefly, I requested a sharp knife and someone to push the floating codend away from the area where I intended to work. A short handled gutting knife was lowered in the bucket and the floating bag was drawn forward with the boat hook. Blade in hand, I made my way back to the nozzle.

I couldn't believe this small amount of netting, caught on the shaft and trapped between a propeller blade and the inner edge of the nozzle could create such a problem. There were only a few pieces of twine and this wouldn't take long to clear. Swimming to the front then rear of the thruster, assessing the task, I opted for the back end, nearest to the snag. With a hand on the rudder, I edged my way forward, knife leading. Without warning the propeller spun, washing me clear with the vortex and the net fell free, plummeting downwards with the codend following. Seconds later my arm would have been between the propeller blades. A broken arm would have been the best result. If I'd opted for the front of the nozzle, I wouldn't have survived being sucked into the tight space. No one on the deck would have been able to save me.

Surfacing, I spat out the regulator, cursing once more at my own stupidity. I'd forgotten to ask the lads to heave the net back up, removing the load from the prop before entering the water. I wasn't jinxed at all, I was stupid; but someone up there loved me and was watching over me.

* * * * * *

Spring had given way to summer and things were going well. Bluey's results were particularly good. He was regularly beating our catches and was now purchasing shares in the *Independence*.

The usual crowd were sitting in the Leeds Arms early on Saturday afternoon, batting the breeze when Col said, "I was walkin' up town this mornin' and was stopped by a gypsy woman. She said if ah crossed 'er palm wi' paper money, she'd grant me a wish."

"Yer didn't fall fo' that, surely?" I questioned.

"I gave 'er a tenner," he admitted.

The whole group were incredulous. "Ten quid?" Syd asked. "You gave her ten quid?"

"Ten pounds? Yer've more money than sense," Jack chipped in.

"Yer want yer 'ead lookin' at," I added.

When we'd all had our say, Colin nonchalantly carried on with his story. The woman had said to him, "I bet you're going to ask for good health for your family."

He'd replied, "no I'm not. When I go to sea tomorrow, I want to catch a 'bag of cod'."

This brought howls of laughter. "If it works, you'll be back up town lookin' for 'er again next week," Syd chuckled.

"You'll be givin' 'er a job," Jack spluttered.

At midnight when the crews were assembling on the pier, ready to sail, I related the story to Bev, who didn't believe Col could be so daft.

The fleet of vessels trickled from the harbour incognito, with only pin pricks of navigation lights marking their positions. The boats scattered far and wide, each visiting a favoured site looking for a good sample. Once at sea, Bev couldn't resist asking over the airwaves, "is it true Mr Dilt? You've paid ten quid to a woman who's promised you a bag of cod." Now every vessel within VHF radio range was aware of the skipper of the *Our Heritage's* generosity.

There was no reply to his question.

Around breakfast time, the reports of boats' first hauls began to come in. We'd taken a haul of about six kit; sixty stones of quality fish, which was a reasonable start. Bev did slightly better and other reports varied little. Col's was the last boat to haul and though he'd been promised a big bag by the mystic, no one was expecting him to achieve this goal, certainly not first haul.

"There's about sixty kit o' cod," he called out excitedly to all in earshot. "It's a big 'aul. We 'aven't got it aboard yet but there should be that alright."

"Yer jokin'," I answered. "Tell me yer kiddin'."

"'E's tekin' t' piss," commented Bev. "'E's 'avin' us on."

Again there was no response. There was no further communication from *Our Heritage* for the next two hours until Colin's distinctive deep voice came over the ether, loud and clear. "Are you on Mr Bev?"

"Gettin' yer fine," came the reply. "You were only jokin' weren't yer. Did yer bust t' net? 'Ave yer been mendin'?"

"No joke," replied the jubilant skipper. "There'll be about sixty kit o' cod. I've been on deck 'elpin' t' get it aboard."

It wasn't just Bev who was speechless now. I could think of nothing to say either. There was an air of scepticism in many voices for the remainder of the week and occasional comments, suggesting a huge spoof was being perpetrated, but the proof of Col's report was on the fish market early on Thursday morning for all to see.

Colin was seen pacing the town centre the following Saturday morning, but there was no sign of his mysterious benefactor. He never saw her again.

* * * * * *

The year was simply racing past. The herring shoals were abundant and as usual, the Dutch, Scots, and English were all pursuing the silver darlings. This year the combined fleet had been joined by a few German factory ships, named after some of that country's larger cities. These ships were clearly processing their catches onboard, evidenced by the numbers of dead herring and skeletons we were trawling up. The catching capacity of the massive vessels was far greater than the ships' factory freezing units could handle, so with an unending supply of fish, each haul's surplus was dumped back into the sea.

The dozen or more, huge, Dutch stern trawlers, ships that seemed to get bigger every year and were to be avoided, were towing colossal nets, while the half dozen Scotsmen were using purse nets. Gone forever were the days when a fleet of a hundred or more drifters from these nations lit up the offshore sky each night.

The smaller, English craft from the Yorkshire Coast ports, almost all of wooden construction, were only interested in the cod, feeding on the densely bunched fish. The pursers didn't conflict with our activities. These ships, which also seemed to be growing in size annually, improving their carrying capacity, located the herring with sonar, encircling a shoal with small mesh net, which extended from the surface to the seabed. Drawing the bag closed at the bottom, they'd haul in the wall of brown net from one end until hundreds of tons of fish were captured alongside, tightly held, to be sucked out of the trap by a high volume pump. Though extremely successful, these vessels were strictly licensed and had limited quotas that could be caught in weeks. In the winter these vessels also followed mackerel shoals off the Cornish Coast with the same ruthless efficiency.

Though the pursers weren't a problem to us, we were faced with a huge dilemma of a different nature, in the shape of an unexploded bomb. The net had been heavy when we'd hauled it up and though the codend was distorted, there was nothing obvious before the bag was lifted inboard. We regularly trawled up empty, fifty-gallon oil drums; gash bins lost or dumped from passing merchant ships. Now, surrounded by fish lay a shiny, silver, high explosive device with a black-painted rear section. This wasn't a relic, jettisoned from some wartime aircraft. The shape was more modern and the fins were an integral part of the construction, as I swiftly described to the Coastguard. The threat of being towed away by a big Dutchman now seemed insignificant.

At least we wouldn't have a problem getting the object back over the side when required. This piece was of moderate size and could be manhandled. I'd had previous experiences with much heavier, wartime ordinance, which were almost impossible to return to the sea. Even so, I wouldn't have knowingly taken this article on board.*

The recently caught fish were quickly picked up into boxes, leaving the bomb exposed. More boxes were stacked around the explosive to wedge the 'thing' into position, preventing movement as *Emulator* rolled. A couple of wet sacks were placed over the potential threat and the hosepipe positioned to play continuously on the bags. This measure should keep the temperature constant until such time as we had a plan. We headed for home and following a pot of coffee the lads gutted and cleared the catch into the fishroom below. An hour later, a mile from the Castle Headland, in ten fathoms of water, following advice from the Royal Navy Bomb Disposal Unit, we gingerly pushed the nasty looking device overboard. The silver object was gently lowered to the bottom and a marker buoy attached to the rope. We lost no time heading for home.

The Naval team of five men arrived next morning and following introductions, I drew a sketch of the offending article for the unit's Commanding Officer. "What we are looking at here sir, without doubt, is an MDW, or as we say in the trade, a 'Mine Disposal Weapon'. This must have been lost from a minesweeper and should have been reported." He went on to explain that this instrument was a tool for blowing up other mines. The weapon was guided into position alongside any rogue device and detonated remotely. The adjacent mine or bomb was either destroyed or exploded sympathetically. "We'll go and take a look at it," he said.

---

* See *First of the Flood* and *Slack Water*

*A haul of cod being gutted on board Emulator.*
*Photo FG Normandale*

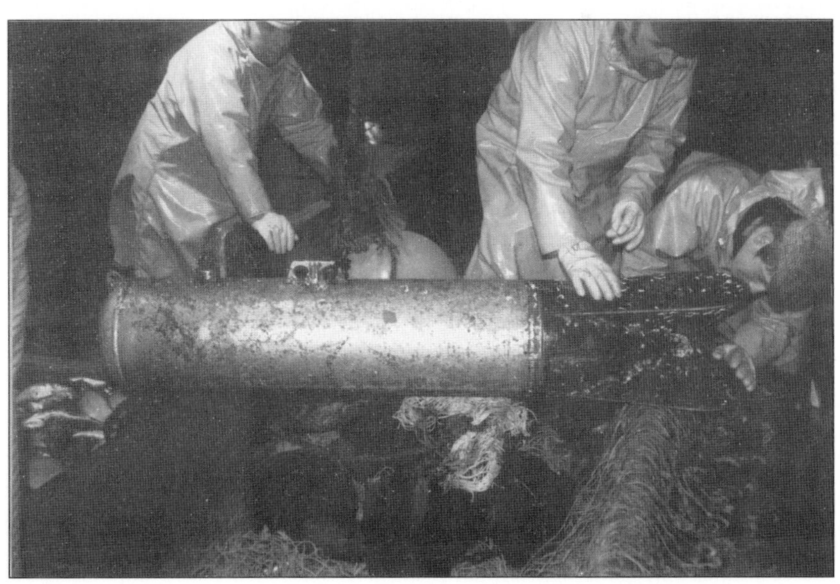

*Examining the bomb. L to R Mick Bayes, Gordon 'Gogga' Mann, Sean Crowe.*
*Photo FG Normandale*

*Boxes of fish from a good haul being gutted.*
*Photo FG Normandale*

*Imperialist on the beach at Scarborough, October 1959.*
*Photo Ken Wigg*

More confident of our safety, we sailed back to the spot and retrieved the buoy. The rope was taken to the winch and someone gently began hauling on the line to retrieve the weapon. Unfortunately the winchman caught a riding turn on the revolving drum and lost control. The explosive surged from the water, banging on the boat's side, heading towards the hanging block. Fishermen and sailors ran for cover not knowing what to expect, but the winch was stopped in the nick of time before the rope parted and the bomb dropped back overboard.

The officer, recovering quickly, confirmed his analysis of the instrument. Taking note of the various serial numbers from the attached plate he said, "we can trace the history of the device now and we'll find out which dozy bugger lost it." It was a disappointment when he said, "we'll take it away with us and return it to its owner."

We were hoping for an explosion to dispose of the menace.

There were some strange looks and exclamations from curious onlookers when the ordnance was manhandled from the boat and onto the back of the Navy truck. Excitement over, we were soon back at sea chasing herring marks.

* * * * * *

Joxy was very ill. He'd been suffering for sometime with a horrendous throat cancer and had undergone chemotherapy, though this treatment had proved unsuccessful. He had continued to mend trawls and assist in landing, despite his dreadful illness but now very weak, he decided he could go on working no longer. This man had been our mainstay for many years, keeping our trawls in tiptop condition and would be irreplaceable.

## Chapter 18

# Salvage

It was already the week before Christmas and we'd tied up for the holiday. Where had this year gone? Late afternoon found me standing at the bar in the Dolphin with Bluey and we'd already been there too long. We'd finished fishing the previous day, cleaned our vessels from top to bottom, stowed the trawls neatly and now had time on our hands. It had been a good year for us both.

*Emulator* had long since shaken off her jinx and was living up to her name. Bluey was fishing well in the *Independence* and we'd concluded the business of him buying shares in the vessel.

One of his crew entered the pub and announced to all in earshot that Larry and Bev were at sea, attempting to sweep the anchor of the *Rito.* They intended to bring the ship into the harbour and claim salvage. They were dragging a wire between their respective vessels, *Carol Anne* and *Cassamanda,* under the moored ship, in an attempt to raise her anchor. He said they'd brought the 'hook' to the surface several times but each time its own weight had caused the anchor to slip over the wire, back into the sea.

'Rito', anchored a mile from the harbour, was a small, old, grey-painted coaster of about two hundred tons, that had been abandoned by her crew. She'd sprung a leak in her engine room a few days earlier and making water, had taken a list to port. In poor weather, during the hours of darkness, she'd appeared in danger of sinking. Her crew had dropped anchor to bring the ship's head into the wind and had been taken off by the

Scarborough Lifeboat. Now, days later, the vessel was still afloat and didn't appear to have made any more water.

"We should go an' 'elp 'em," I suggested to my former deckie. "Ah'll put me wetsuit on and you can put me on board o' t' ship in t' *Independence*. Ah'll cut 'er anchor cable wi' an 'acksaw."

Bluey could see nothing wrong with this plan and leaving our beer we staggered across to where our boats were lying, side by side. While I donned my wetsuit and located the saw, the skipper started his boat's engine and took in her mooring ropes, holding his *Independence* alongside *Emulator* with a short end of line. Armed with the hacksaw and a makeshift quiver of spare blades, I let the attachment go and stepped across the gap. It was almost the shortest day of the year and the poor light was already fading.

Bluey managed to manoeuvre the *Independence* through the harbour mouth and informed the two skippers that we were on our way and that I intended to cut the cable. The weather was fresh and the vessels, standing close by waiting to pass a towrope, were rolling in the swell. Despite his intake of alcohol the skipper skilfully positioned his vessel's stem close to the rolling ship's stern, closing to within a few feet of the ship. Biding my time and waiting for an opportune moment I jumped on board the deserted vessel, grabbing the railings on the bridge deck.

The ship was in darkness and rolling, so with a thirty-degree starboard list, this was quite disorientating. I looked through the open door into the wheelhouse in passing but couldn't see much. I knew that some electrical equipment and brass fittings had been stripped from her under cover of darkness by boat-owning pirates, expecting the ship to sink. It wasn't easy getting across her decks and I staggered towards the fo'c's'le head, my eyes becoming accustomed to the dark.

Climbing the for'ard steps I located the windlass, then identified which anchor had been deployed. Kneeling, I began to saw through the chain cable. The studded links were one-inch diameter, mild steel and though initially easy, the work grew harder as the blade blunted and the cut deepened. I was soon sweating profusely in the neoprene suit and stopped for a breather. Standing, I lowered the zip to my chest and looked round. The thought, "what am I doin' 'ere?" briefly flitted through my mind as I looked at the welcoming, twinkling lights of Scarborough, to the northwest.

Addressing the job in hand, I continued to saw at the cable, finding the work easier after replacing a broken blade. Minutes later I was through the first side of the link and encouraged by this progress, attacked the other side of the steel loop with renewed vigour.

Another blade and a few more minutes labour saw the cable part prematurely due to the load it was bearing and I was pleased to hear the heavy, broken chain rattle out through the hawse-pipe into the sea. It was a weird sensation being alone on a ship, adrift at the mercy of the wind and tide, but not for long. The crews of the two waiting vessels, aware that the cable had parted, threw lines, which I secured to each bow, then the pair began pulling the old ship towards the harbour. *Independence* was fastened to the stern to act as a brake, near the entrance.

Twenty minutes later the ship was skilfully manoeuvred into the safety of the harbour, though the *Independence* was far too close to the Outer Pier than was wise and was almost dragged onto the rocks as she was hauled around the tight bend. As Captain and sole crewman of the *Rito,* I received a heaving line at the stern from the Lighthouse Officer on the Vincent Pier. Then, while the two trawlers held her in position, I dashed to the bows to secure a head rope to the shore. She was salvaged. There would be a reward.

## Chapter 19
# The *Navena*

Another New Year's Eve had been and gone, seen in with the usual crazy party celebrations at home and we were now back in the fishing routine. A message from Bev during the first week of operations said the *Rito's* insurers had decided the cost of repairing her was greater than the value of the vessel so she'd been classed as a 'constructive total loss'. Though still tied up in the harbour, the old ship was to be taken to the breakers yard. Disappointingly, there was to be no salvage money for anyone.

* * * * * *

With amazing good fortune, we'd gained the services of Eddie Temple to mend our trawls and assist with landing. Eddie, a former mate in Grimsby trawlers, had fished from Scarborough for several years before retiring from the sea. He was now a watch-keeper on the lighthouse but would address our net problems when available and was a master of his trade.

The weather had been reasonable so far this year and we'd lost hardly any fishing time, but now late in January, the shipping forecast for the next twenty-four hours was poor, with southeasterly winds, up to storm force ten, expected soon. Bev summed up my feelings over the airwaves when he said, "we aren't far from 'ome. We'll wait till it comes then bugger off in."

The gale burst swiftly and viciously about four o'clock in the morning and we weren't long scrambling our gear on board. After a two-hour steam and a hairy passage into the harbour, we were one of several vessels landing fish for the morning's market. Only a few boxes remained below to be discharged when a loud, 'boom' echoed round the 'Bottom End', followed shortly by a second, similar explosion. The lifeboat crew were being summoned and these volunteers were in for a pasting. With the heavy swell breaking on the shore, the launching operation would be hair-raising. Should the launching team mistime their operation, the boat could be washed from her carriage before she was propelled into the sea by the powerful tractor.

As the remaining three boxes of fish left *Emulator's* hold, Bev, who'd finished landing his catch, came running from his boat shouting, "ah've been talkin' t' Coastguard. T' *Navena's,* sinkin', twelve mile off. 'Er crew are abandonin' ship an' gettin' in t' liferafts. We're gonna go an' see if we can do owt."

"We'll come wi' yer," I replied.

Sid and Gogga, dragging boxes of fish from the scales, hearing the conversation, jumped back onboard as Dad and Eddie made ready to let our ropes go.

Bev yelled the same message to Col and received a similar response. Within a few minutes our three vessels were ploughing their way through the breaking seas at the pier end, joining the Scarborough Lifeboat. Her crew were crouched in the for'ard well-deck of the vessel, attempting to avoid the green lumps of sea washing over her bows.

There was a sense of urgency in the Coastguard's voice when he acknowledged our message of intent on the distress frequency. Minutes can mean the difference between life and death when men are exposed to severe, winter weather in the North Sea and this was one of those occasions.

Now clear of the pier end, our convoy headed northeast at full speed, almost broadside to the rolling swell, with the lifeboat struggling to keep up. The skipper of the *Navena* had remained on board his listing vessel and was communicating with several ships in the area, all of which were steaming at best speed in his direction but it seemed our group were the nearest and would get there first. The struggling ship soon became visible on the radar screen on the six-mile range, but at best that meant another three-quarters of an hour before we'd get to her, then we'd have to look out for the rafts, somewhere astern of her. These men were in serious danger.

Twenty minutes later we heard radio traffic from a rescue helicopter, scrambled at first light from RAF Leconfield. The chopper was almost on the scene and would hopefully get to the survivors before we could begin searching. Only minutes later the pilot reported to the Coastguard that they'd successfully picked up men from the two rafts, one of which was upturned, the survivors struggling to remain alive in the nylon, roof canopy.

"They're bloody good, them RAF lads," Col observed over the airwaves. "We might not 'ave got to 'em in time."

He was right. It was reassuring to know that when the chips were down, these helicopter crews were available to effect rescues and over the years had recorded some amazing recoveries, even refuelling on offshore gas rigs to extend their range. "D' yer remember when they took t' crew off that drilling rig in near 'urricane force winds, near 'Bay Wyke' in November '65? If on'y they could operate at night." We didn't need reminding of the occasion. Bill Sheader had been coxswain of the lifeboat, which had stood by the damaged, exploration rig *Neptune One* that night. On his return he told everyone it was the worst weather he'd ever experienced in his time with the RNLI. His crew's faces were encrusted with salt on their arrival back in port the next morning.

As we approached the listing, rust-streaked, yellow vessel, we watched the chopper lifting her skipper from the bridge top. The pilot reported once more to the Coastguard, this time saying they'd completed the rescue and some of the casualties were suffering severe exposure and were hypothermic. He was heading for Scarborough Hospital and would be landing there in ten minutes. "Such a matter of fact statement for an amazing feat," I thought.

We were now on scene, though too late to render assistance to the ship's crew but at least they were safe. The crews of the *Cassamanda* and the lifeboat each picked up an empty liferaft, the coxswain of the rescue vessel announcing he was now returning home. His soaked crew wouldn't be sorry.

What were we to do now with the stricken *Navena*? She was abandoned, her engine engaged, steering on automatic pilot, heading for shore at approximately two knots. Now less than eight miles from land, unless she could be stopped, the almost one-hundred and twenty foot, four hundred ton vessel would smash up on the rocks, somewhere near Filey Brigg within hours. The wind was falling away now but the residual, deep swell meant it was impossible to get alongside the heaving, steel ship without endangering our own weaker, wooden vessels.

"Can we foul 'er propeller wi' summat?" Col asked. "If we can stop 'er from goin' ashore, we can tek 'er in tow when t' swell falls away."

For the next two hours we moved ahead of the vessel several times, spanning her path with various permutations of vessels using ropes, wires and netting, vainly attempting to prevent her screw from turning. Some of the materials positioned in her track were sucked into her fan, but nothing we did would stop her. The big, yellow ship continued on her course relentlessly. Now she was only four miles from shore and time was against us. If we were to stop the self-destruction of the *Navena,* and the oil pollution, which would inevitably follow when she broke up, drastic action was called for.

Col came up with an idea and had a volunteer onboard his vessel willing to carry out the daring deed. Collecting *Navena's* empty liferaft from the *Cassamanda*, he intended to use the huge inflatable raft as an air cushion to protect his vulnerable craft from the rolling ship while he put his man onboard the listing trawler. The son of a tough, former Grimsby skipper, Matty Sheader, now in his mid-twenties was a wiry, bespectacled young man of fair complexion and blond, tussled hair.

We watched in amazement from ringside seats, as Colin cleverly manoeuvred *Our Heritage* alongside the wallowing ship. There was a whoosh, as some of the raft's tubes burst under the impact, but the gutsy Matty didn't stop to observe this coming together of vessels. With perfect timing, he leapt onto the empty ship, grabbing a safe hold with a sure grip. The consequences of a mistimed jump with the inevitable fall and crushing between the vessels didn't bear thinking about.

His part done, Col immediately stood off again and the three watching crews cheered the hero heartily as he collected his wits, making his way to the bridge of the rolling ship. Her wooden fishroom hatch boards were now being swilled by the swells and were in danger of washing off. This could be calamitous. If her hold filled, she would quickly fill and capsize. It was reassuring to hear Matty's breathless voice as he established radio contact with our group.

"There's an emergency stop button on t' engine panel," he gasped. "Shall ah press it?"

"Press it," I shouted into my handset. Mine was one of a trio of similar replies he received, simultaneously.

The deed done, *Navena* slowed to a stop and soon lay broadside to the swell, but now dead in the water she began to wallow and looked extremely sick. Matty gamely made his way to the bows, taking a rope from his shipmates on *Our Heritage,* making it fast to a pair of bits. He secured a similar hawser from *Cassamanda's* crew on the other bow but then a couple of bigger seas caused a series of particularly sickening rolls and the ship threatened to turn turtle under him. Matty climbed over the port bow and grabbed the rope leading to his home vessel. He deftly slid down to her after deck to be held and steadied by his shipmates.

The two improvised tugs, forming an angle of about forty-five degrees, began to tow the dead ship into the wind. Now she was making way again, the heaving vessel steadied and began conforming to her guides' directions. The weather was improving slowly as the wind fell away, though the swell and ebbing tide meant we had no chance of getting our charge into the harbour anytime soon. We'd have to be patient. The two boats, dwarfed by the inert *Navena,* spent the next few hours escorting the hulk back and forwards across the bay, with the *Emulator* in loose company. We would somehow attach a rope to a strong point on her stern, before taking the ship into the harbour and would be the brake vessel.

Delegating the watch to Mick, I happily turned in but was rudely awakened soon after by a brisk shake and a voice shouting, "there's a bloody tug 'ere an' 'e's tryin' t' tek over t' tow."

I jumped out of my bunk and was on my way up the ladder before the caller could step on the first rung.

The magnificent tug, *Yorkshireman* had arrived on the scene, probably summoned by *Navena's* insurers, her shiny, black hull and gleaming, white superstructure adding beauty to the sleek, powerful vessel. Her crew were busy flaking a heavy, platted rope along her working deck in readiness for the tow. Ignoring our presence completely, her Master began manoeuvring his vessel, intending to put a man onboard the casualty, with a view to stealing our prize. Having fought hard to save her, we were definitely not going to give up our claim now without a fight. I headed *Emulator* between the *Navena* and *Yorkshireman* to prevent the boarding. A stranger's voice, filled with authority, loudly filled the airwaves and I received a warning from the tug's master for my interference in his manoeuvre. He in turn, received several replies alluding to where he should go with his fine ship. The persistent mariner made several more, unsuccessful attempts and continued to get warning messages to stand clear of our legally acquired charge from the three musketeers. Eventually his efforts ceased and the fine ship stood away, presumably awaiting further instructions.

The next high water would be during the night and it wouldn't be sensible to attempt taking the *Navena* into the harbour in darkness so we'd have to wait till the following morning before entering the port. We considered the options of taking the ship to the deeper water of the River Tyne or a port on the Humber but these ideas were ruled out when requests by our agent, Terry, to both authorities, were met with refusals of entry. These administrative bodies didn't want to run the risk of the damaged ship sinking in their jurisdiction.

As the watery sun dropped over the back land, I placed the *Emulator* close enough to the trawler's stern for my crew to lasso a strong point. The lads paid out a reasonable length of new, nylon rope, replaced by the boat-builder following her unsuccessful launch, before making several figure of eight turns on a stern cleat.

*Emulator* was now the third vessel in the chain and was being towed, stern first. We were in position to make any manoeuvres required to keep the dead ship under control during the long night to come.

Shortly after we were attached, the Master of the *Yorkshireman* came over the airwaves, asking if he could put some of his salvage experts on board the casualty, to ascertain if she could be pumped dry while we towed her. We were in agreement with this plan and I was able to get a message ashore to some pals in the Sub Aqua Club, who proved keen to assist. The salvage team, carrying powerful flashlights were delivered to the listing ship by the wetsuited divers in their inflatable craft an hour later.

The news from the experts underlined our own thoughts. The open hatchway on her starboard quarter, which had caused the flooding, was submerged and it was impossible to close this hinged lid, due to the massive amount of fishing net swirling around the area. The ship couldn't be pumped out until the vessel was grounded and the access exposed.

Pumps were organised and would be available as soon as we made port. We resigned ourselves to spending the remainder of the night, slowly towing the casualty to and fro in a strange tug of war. There was no need for three vessels to fill this role so the *Cassamanda's* crew passed their rope to *Our Heritage* for the night and entered the harbour. They'd be back as soon as there was sufficient water to sail in the morning.

Even the simple exercise of nursing the dead ship wasn't without incident. At 0100 in the morning, I was called out again when, due to negligent watch-keeping our charge was almost ashore on rocks near the East Pier. This would have been hugely embarrassing but the situation was retrieved by Colin, who'd also been called from below and had given the *Our Heritage* a surge of power.

At daylight and almost high water, with the *Cassamanda* back in position, we began guiding our charge towards the harbour entrance. Throughout the entire proceedings we'd been in radio communication with the Coastguard and the Harbourmaster's representative in the lighthouse, so as we began our approach to the port, we were devastated to receive an instruction from the watch-keeper. He informed us that the Harbourmaster, acting on advice from the *Navena's* insurers, formally refused us permission to enter the port with the ship in tow. The perceived opinion was that, as *Navena* was dipping down by the stern and with only a small tide predicted, she may ground and block the harbour entrance. If we disobeyed this instruction then miscalculated our approach, we'd be in serious trouble, or as Bev bluntly put it, "we'd be in the shit." Furthermore, the *Navena's* insurance representative, Admiral Branson, had taken up residence in the lighthouse to watch the proceedings. Now we had no alternative but to beach her, though our own local knowledge told us we could get the ship into port. She was listing to starboard and would lean against the Lighthouse Pier, if only we could get her there.

We all remembered the Hull trawler, *Imperialist* being beached for repairs, following a collision with a cargo vessel in thick fog, in October '59. She was very deep in the water but after temporary patching, taking several days, she was eventually floated off, returning to her home port under tow, where she underwent a full refurbishment. We intended to pump the water from the flooded *Navena* as the water ebbed, then tow her off again and into the harbour on the following tide. Ours would be a much more simple operation.

A humorous thought occurred to me and even though we were busy, I felt compelled to share my wit. Reaching for the microphone I said, "if she'd got caught in t' 'arbour mouth an' fell over, your two boats would 'ave been stuck inside t' 'arbour for months. I'd 'ave been stuck outside an' would 'ave t' go fishin' on me own an' land into Whitby. I'd 'ave no one t' talk to." Elaborating, I suggested that there could be no blame attached to me for such an incident. I would have been trying to stop them taking her in, by pulling in the other direction. My thoughts weren't appreciated.

The three piers, which formed Scarborough Harbour were thronged with onlookers and television cameras were conspicuous, as we drew closer to shore. The tow ropes on the *Cassamanda* and *Our Heritage* were shortened severely, so these vessels wouldn't ground before the *Navena* touched the sand. I kept *Emulator's* engine ticking over dead slow and we were hauled backwards while preventing the towed vessel from washing broadside to the shore. The tow seemed to take forever but eventually, shortly after the

*The Rito at anchor from Scarborough lifeboat.*
*Photo Dennis Dobson*

*Navena under tow prior to being beached.*
*Photo FG Normandale*

*The giant crane Neptun raising the Navena in a successful salvage operation.*
*Photo FG Normandale*

tide had made its mark on the beach, she touched the bottom, though she'd grounded further to the west than we would have preferred.

The growling, waterproof lifeboat tractor, made available by the RNLI's Honorary Secretary, pushed out into the now calm waters. The driver of the polished, blue vehicle, together with his assistant, took the ropes via the Sub Aqua Club's rubber boat, allowing the two fishing vessels to back off into deeper water. My partners in crime entered the harbour, leaving *Emulator* holding on to the stern until the ship was firmly aground. The powerful tractor kept the tension on the front end of the severely listing vessel for the same duration.

With *Navena* hard aground, we were unable to get close enough to recover our nylon rope without touching the bottom ourselves and I could only call, "cut it," to the hovering hands. The rope's three strands spun and quickly un-laid for a fathom or more in both directions under the sharp blade. Twenty fathoms of towrope were still fastened to the ship but this could be spliced back to the main length, when recovered. I was unconcerned for the present as I steered for the entrance, keen to join Bev and Col who, with their crews and some shore staff, plus a powerful pump, were standing among the thinning crowd on the pier, overlooking the beach.

Back in the harbour, we tied our vessel alongside the *Cassamanda,* then made our way to the group, ready to assist with the pump as soon as the open hatch became exposed with the ebbing tide. At half ebb there was no sign of the list on the ship reducing. If anything, she seemed to be going further to starboard. At length Col said aloud what we were all thinking. "She's not gonna come upright. She'll finish up on 'er side before low water. We're not gonna do any good wi' that pump." He was seldom wrong and this was no exception. We simply stood, staring at the ship and at each other without speaking. It was scant pleasure to see her propeller tangled with ropes and netting. We'd evidently succeeded in our efforts to foul the screw but not enough to stop the prop from turning.

A serious young man, clad in an olive green parka jacket, toothbrush conspicuous in a pocket on the upper sleeve, introduced himself as Silas Taylor, a solicitor from the renowned, marine law firm, Andrew M. Jackson of Hull. We looked at each other fearfully, expecting to be handed some frightening legal document. The threat was lifted immediately when Silas said he was representing our insurance company, Sunderland Marine and he was here acting on our behalf.

Suddenly, this young fellow wasn't quite so scary. Silas had come to inform us that he'd been in negotiations with the *Navena's* insurers. These people had considered the situation and informed him that as we'd salvaged the vessel, if we so wished, we could keep her. "She's insured for six hundred thousand pounds," he said dramatically, "and she's yours."

Our eyes lit up.

"But don't touch it with a barge pole is my advice to you. With ownership comes liability. It's your choice."

It had certainly been a time of decision making lately, though this one didn't take much deliberating over. We already thought we were collectively in the mire now the ship was immovable. Ownership would only compound the issue. We reluctantly agreed to take Silas's advice and he went off to communicate the decision to the opposition with a gleam in his eye.

Next to arrive on the scene was Noel, our retired bank manager, also with a mischievous countenance. "What are you buggers playing at? You've made a right balls up of that," he said, pointing in the direction of the beached ship. "You should have asked me. I'd have got the bugger in for you. We could form the 'Barclay Towing Company'." His wit wasn't quite what was needed at this moment but being such a lovely man it was difficult to offend him, so three equivalents of "sod off" had to suffice.

We left the scene feeling totally helpless and went into the Lord Nelson in the company of the Godfather, to drown our sorrows. A couple of hours later someone produced a 'hot off the press' copy of the day's Scarborough Evening News. The wording under the banner headline quoted a spokesman for Scarborough Borough Council, effectively saying that the culprits of this deed would be liable for the cost of the removal of the ship from the Council's property.

We looked at each other in astonishment. Bev, with wonderful brevity, summed up our situation. "Where do we go from 'ere? We've gone from bein' 'eroes t' villains in twenty-four hours. We're well an' truly in the shit now. We could be bankrupt. Ow are we gonna get out o' this mess?"

* * * * * *

The *Navena* lay on her side on Scarborough's South Beach for three months. She was there each time we entered or left the harbour, a stark reminder of those two days in February and what might have been. The vessel changed hands several times, as various companies attempted to salvage and remove her. The regional television news reported these events with regularity and the seafront was thronged most weekends as visitors flocked to see the latest developments, creating a mini tourist boom. With Easter and the coming holiday season drawing closer, Scarborough Borough Council became concerned at the safety aspect of having the ship on the sands. They contracted a huge Dutch salvage vessel, *Neptun* to raise and remove the ship from her position at a cost of £92,000. Though extremely concerned for many months, we were not pursued for compensation from the Council, though several letters in the local press suggested we should be. Neither did we receive any salvage money, but we lived to fight another day.

# The 'Bottom End'

Bottom Enders and other characters featured in this volume, now departed this life but not forgotten.

Richard 'Dick' Sellars
Noel 'Godfather' White
Tom 'Bluey' Sheader Snr
Nancy Hines
Nick Rowley
Steve 'Stiv' Hodds
Ken Fishburn
George 'Sneady' Scales
June Colling
Alf Goacher
Ernie Eves
Margaret Normandale
George 'Sam' Colling
Lucy Alonzi
Susan Walsh
Jim Rowley
Barry 'Dobbin' Horwell
Ray Bastiman
Roger Flower
Roger Kennedy
Ken 'Punch' Eade
Les Dowkes
Kenny Hogg
Rose 'Maisie' Ward
Alice Hick

Readers will quickly identify with Fred Normandale's passionate belief in a fishing industry, which has been central to his life since being born into a prominent Scarborough fishing family. This book is written from the heart in the same true to life style as the author's widely acclaimed publications, 'First of the Flood' and 'Slack Water'. 'The Tide Turns' provides a fascinating insight into the rapidly occurring highs and lows of trawling off the Yorkshire Coast and the continuous challenge and dangers fishermen face.

The importance of managing these pressures, whilst also spending time with his family between trips is related by Fred in typical, forthright style throughout. 'The Tide Turns' covers the late 70s and 80s when UK fishermen were starting to become fully exposed to the difficulties associated with Britain's entry into the EU. True to life and an absorbing read.

David Linkie, *Fishing News*.